SET UP AND MANAGE YOUR VIRTUAL PRIVATE SERVER

MAKING SYSTEM ADMINISTRATION ACCESSIBLE TO PROFESSIONALS

Jon Westfall

Apress®

Set Up and Manage Your Virtual Private Server: Making System Administration Accessible to Professionals

Jon Westfall
Cleveland, MS, USA

ISBN-13 (pbk): 978-1-4842-6965-7   ISBN-13 (electronic): 978-1-4842-6966-4
https://doi.org/10.1007/978-1-4842-6966-4

Managing Director, Apress Media LLC: Welmoed Spahr
Acquisitions Editor: Shiva Ramachandran
Development Editor: Matthew Moodie
Coordinating Editor: Nancy Chen

Cover designed by eStudioCalamar

Distributed to the book trade worldwide by Springer Science+Business Media New York, 1 New York Plaza, New York, NY 100043. Phone 1-800-SPRINGER, fax (201) 348-4505, e-mail orders-ny@springer-sbm.com, or visit www.springeronline.com. Apress Media, LLC is a California LLC and the sole member (owner) is Springer Science + Business Media Finance Inc (SSBM Finance Inc). SSBM Finance Inc is a **Delaware** corporation.

For information on translations, please e-mail booktranslations@springernature.com; for reprint, paperback, or audio rights, please e-mail bookpermissions@springernature.com.

Apress titles may be purchased in bulk for academic, corporate, or promotional use. eBook versions and licenses are also available for most titles. For more information, reference our Print and eBook Bulk Sales web page at http://www.apress.com/bulk-sales.

Any source code or other supplementary material referenced by the author in this book is available to readers on GitHub via the book's product page, located at www.apress.com/9781484269657. For more detailed information, please visit http://www.apress.com/source-code.

Printed on acid-free paper

*Dedicated to my parents, Alan and Dianne,
who bought me my first computer.*

Contents

About the Author

Jon Westfall is an award-winning professor, author, and practicing cognitive scientist. He teaches a variety of courses in psychology, from introduction to psychology to graduate seminars. His current research focuses on the variables that influence economic and consumer finance decisions, as well as retention and persistence of college students. With applications to psychology, information technology, and marketing, his work finds an intersection between basic and applied science. His current appointments include Associate Professor of Psychology, Coordinator of the First Year Seminar program, and Coordinator of the Psychology program at Delta State University. Prior to joining the faculty at Delta State in 2014, he was a Visiting Assistant Professor at Centenary College of Louisiana and the Associate Director for Research and Technology at the Center for Decision Sciences, a center within Columbia Business School at Columbia University in New York City. He now maintains a role with Columbia Business School as a research affiliate/variable hours officer of administration and technology consultant.

In addition to his research, Dr. Westfall also has career ties in information technology, where he has worked as a consultant since 1997, founding his own firm, Bug Jr. Systems. As a consultant, he has developed custom software solutions (including native Windows 32 applications, Windows .NET applications, Windows Phone 7 and Android mobile applications, as well as ASP, ASP. NET, and PHP web applications). He has also served as a senior network and systems architect and administrator and been recognized as a Microsoft Most Valuable Professional (MVP) 2008–2012. He currently is the owner and managing partner of Secure Research Services, LLC. He has authored several fiction and nonfiction books and presented at academic as well as technology conferences and gatherings. A native of Ohio, in his spare time he enjoys knitting, crocheting, creative writing with the Delta Writers Group, and a variety of other hobbies.

For more, visit jonwestfall.com, listen to him weekly on the MobileViews podcast (mobileviews.com), or follow him on Twitter: @jonwestfall.

About the Technical Reviewer

Dr. Evan Hill is an associate professor of psychology and researcher in the field of comparative psychoacoustics. The courses he instructs at the University of Nebraska at Kearney cover various aspects of the biological basis of behavior and neural functioning. His research focuses primarily on species-level differences in hearing ability, with an emphasis on identifying structural, physiological, and ultimately functional explanations for these differences. Because his research frequently involves the use of novel species not commonly used in laboratory settings, almost everything is a DIY project. In any given study, he often must operate as a carpenter, electrical engineer, computer programmer, biologist, and veterinarian to get results.

Acknowledgments

Writing a book is never an easy task and is seldom the task of just one individual, even in a sole-author work. I am indebted to my wife, Karey, for her support throughout this process. I'm very lucky to have a soul mate who "gets" why I'm passionate about crazy topics like Virtual Private Servers (VPSs)!

I'm also thankful to my parents, Alan and Dianne, who instilled a love of reading and learning in me early in my life. Writing is only possible after spending a ton of time reading, whether it be fiction or nonfiction. I'm thankful to my friends who have listened to me talk about this project and provided feedback, including Steve Jocke, Jason Dunn, Matt Rozema, and my longtime podcasting partner Todd Ogasawara. Other friends who have supported me without knowing it (by providing inspiration for projects or stories in this book) include Christy Riddle, Tricia Killebrew, Kristen Land, Darla Poole, Kesha Pates, Jontil Coleman, Elise Mallette, Jackie Goldman, Andrés García-Penagos, Sally Zengaro, and many others in the extended Delta State family. I'd also like to acknowledge my students, for whom many of these applications originally were designed, for inspiring me to continue creating. I also am lucky to have the support of those at Apress, especially Nancy Chen, Shiva Ramachandran, and Matt Moodie.

On a personal level, I'd also like to thank the Delta Writers Group (Michael Koehler, Katy Koehler, Jason Hair, and Dick Denny) for providing a ground for sharpening my writing and critique skills regularly. I also gain so much support from friends and family, including Nate and Kristen Toney, Sarah Speelman, Maggie Ditto, Heather Hudgins, Ashley Newman, Dan, Sue, Scott, Emily, Greg, Janet, Mark, and Brenda Himmel, Margaret Lee, Christine and Carl Morris, Don Sorcinelli, Tony Rylow, Trella Williams, Eric Johnson, Elke Weber, Karen Fosheim, Carol Beard, Maria Gaglio, Hope Hanks, Tom Brady, and many others.

Introduction

"Just build it yourself" is a very ambitious statement, no matter what your art form. Another ambitious statement, "If you want it done right, do it yourself," seems to make even the most difficult task seem trivial enough that anyone could accomplish it. Is it really that easy?

When it comes to having a professional web page or software to manage your customer list and contacts or a collaborative effort like a wiki, doing it yourself can often seem daunting even to someone proficient in using a computer. People tell themselves "it's too complex" or "it's too expensive" or both. However, it is easier and more inexpensive today to turn these services into a DIY project, as long as you have a road map. That's the purpose of this book – to take you from someone who can use a computer to someone who can safely and effectively run their own virtual private server. Not only is this likely to be cheaper than commercial alternatives, it also provides a lot of peace of mind, knowing exactly who owns and stores your data.

If your initial thought was along the lines of cost and time, you are correct that there was a time when running your own server was a very expensive proposition that required a full-time IT staff. Today, thanks to virtualization, or the ability to host multiple self-contained servers on one large physical server, the only barrier to running your own server is your own knowledge. While formidable to learn everything you need to know, we're also living in a time where resources are plentiful. This book not only gives you the basic "lingo" you need in order to get your own server up and running, it also empowers you to find solutions to problems as you grow in your technical knowledge. We follow a logical approach that first tells you what a Virtual Private Server is and how it can be available at such a low price. We then take an entire chapter (Chapter 2) to discuss potential service providers out there and how to "vet" one to find if it's a good fit. Some cater more toward absolute beginners and charge a bit more for the handholding they do, while others are bargain basement dealers who require you to be at the top of your technical game. After selecting a provider, we then spend two chapters (Chapters 3 and 4) discussing the Linux operating system and how it works a bit differently than a graphical environment you may be familiar with. By the time we hit the middle of the book, we're going to ease you into topics like security and backup. Finally, we finish by showing off some of the things you can do with a Virtual Private Server, including hosting your own web pages, applications, and other fun stuff.

Along the way, you'll find a lot of examples from over 20 years of my own personal and professional explorations. I started off in IT; however, in the mid-2000s, I pivoted to a decidedly non-IT career: a research psychologist. It is my hope that the explanations that I provide will not only be easy to understand (as I'm aiming to do quite a bit of translation from "tech geek" to "normal person"!), you'll also see the clear applications for each topic – because this stuff isn't useful in the abstract, it gains its real value when you use it to speed up and simplify your life! Before we can get to the cool stuff, though, we'll need to cover the basics – namely, what is a "Virtual Private Server"?

What Is a Virtual Private Server?

Let me share a story with you that illustrates what this book can do for you in terms of personal productivity. In other words, how you can save yourself time, money, stress, and more by learning the skills this book introduces. Join me on a journey into a "psychology professor's" life for a moment.

Several months ago I had a problem, and my solution was a bit unorthodox. The problem was that people were always asking me for computer help, which was somewhat understandable since I am the Internet Editor for the Society for the Teaching of Psychology (STP). And while I like helping people, I was finding it hard to keep things organized. Who was I working with this week? What requests did they have? What about the associate editors – could I delegate this task? And what about my boss and my collaborators – were they looped in? It occurred to me that a help desk ticket system, similar to what many companies use to track customer support requests, would be useful for our group. It would let me track who I was helping and how quickly they were helped and also allow me to add collaborators easily.

So I installed one and we started using it…that day…for free (see Figure 1-1).

© Jon Westfall 2021
J. Westfall, *Set Up and Manage Your Virtual Private Server*,
https://doi.org/10.1007/978-1-4842-6966-4_1

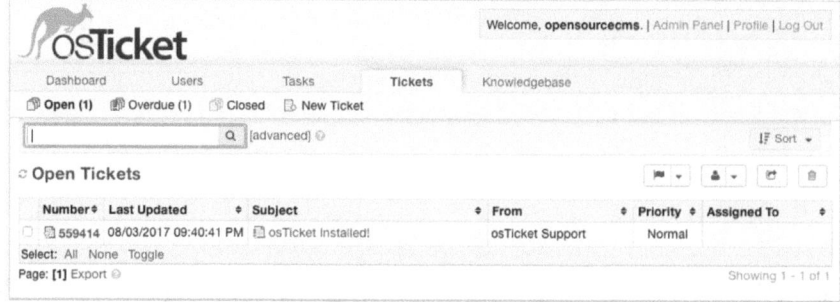

Figure I-I. A demo version of osTicket hosted on OpenSourceCMS.com, the product I installed on my own server

This sounds crazy to most people – after all, surely there must be a lot of steps involved in doing something like this. Setting up a website that can take requests and track them, making email talk to that website, setting up a way to log in and reply to the tickets, and dozens more smaller tasks. Plus you'd need a computer that was always on and connected to the Internet; otherwise, when replies to your tickets came in, how would they get to the ticket software? And to do all of this for free? It may seem like a miracle.

But it isn't – it's something that, by the end of this book, you may feel comfortable pulling off yourself. Will it take you less than a day? Probably not. But less than a weekend is certainly a possibility. You can even have time for meals and sleep. This book is about giving you the tools to pull off these tiny miracles and the flexibility to know how to use those tools in unique and novel ways. In this book, we're going to talk about Virtual Private Servers – what they are, how they work and are managed, and, most importantly, how they can change your professional and personal life for the better. Soon you'll be setting up your own Internet world!

A Brief Understanding of the Internet and Computers Connected to It

I try not to assume much in this book; however, I am about to make an assumption – you know what a computer is. If by some chance you don't, then you may be in the wrong section of the bookstore! What you may not know, though, is that the websites that you visit every day, the programs and apps that you use on your phone, and the software that runs your intranet at work all run off of computers that are actually very similar to your desktop or laptop. They aren't "special" in any way other than perhaps having more storage space or processing power connected to them and the fact that they're rarely, if ever, turned off.

And the Internet is full of them – millions of computers that all connect to each other. The majority of those computers are *clients* – they are seeking information or services from *servers*, computers that provide information or services. When you open your smartphone and launch the browser, your smartphone becomes a client, likely opening a web page that lives on a server. The lines aren't mutually exclusive though – the server that your web page lives on may need to download information from another server in order to display the page. Thus, to you it is a server, but to the other computer it is a client. Imagine the Internet as merely a series of trillions of client-server interactions happening every day. Client asks for something, and server sends it (see Figure 1-2).

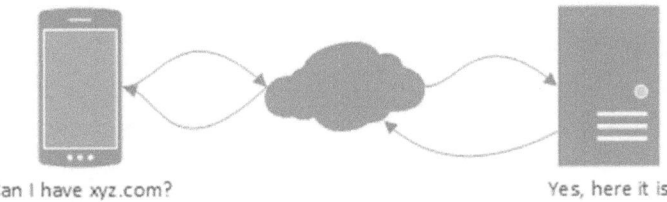

Can I have xyz.com?   Yes, here it is

Figure 1-2. A flowchart of your computer requesting a web page

Now that we've established what a server is, what is this whole "virtual" stuff that you hear thrown around in places such as the title of this book? Well, let's use another analogy – imagine a shopping mall. Inside we have 100 stores, each with their own entrances, their own staff, their own products, and their own policies for sales and returns. They all live in the same physical structure, and so all of them have to abide by the same global rules – if the mall ownership says that stores must open by 10 AM, then the smaller stores need to open by 10 AM. If the ownership says that you can stay open as late as 9 PM, then stores have permission to close early if they like, but can't go past 9 PM.

Let's call the shopping mall the "physical server" and all of the stores "virtual servers." Each store is unique and separated – the owner of one can't walk into the other without permission. Individual owners can decide to sell whatever they want, but they can't exceed the physical limitations that the mall has stipulated. In the same way, a very powerful computer server can house many less powerful virtual servers. Each virtual server runs with a subset of resources devoted to it and is isolated from the other servers running.

Translating all of this together, a virtual private server is a computer connected to the Internet that is cheaper to "rent" than a physical server, because multiple people can rent space on the same physical system. The owners of those systems, the hosting company or service, set the parameters of what each virtual server can do: how much processing power it gets, how much storage space, and how much bandwidth – think foot traffic in our mall scenario – is allowed. As long as you pay your bill and follow the rules, the owner of the physical server is happy to have you as a client (see Figure 1-3).

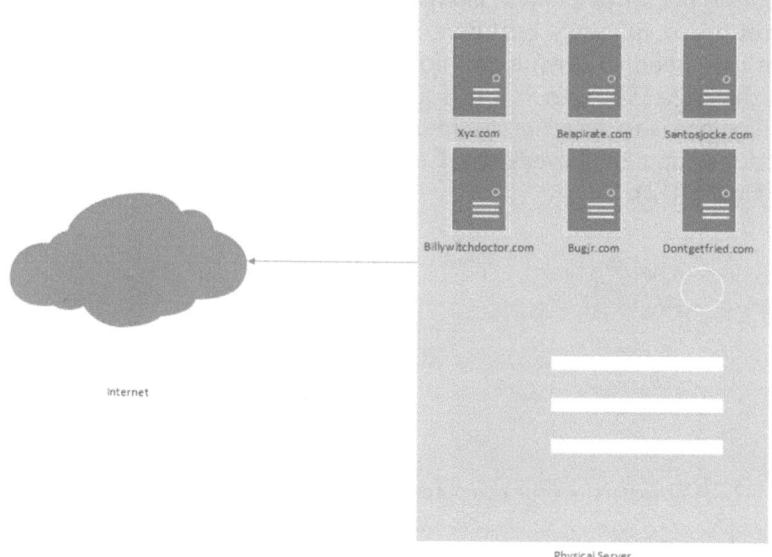

Figure 1-3. A physical server hosting multiple virtual private servers

Now that you know what a virtual private server is (smaller computer nested inside a much larger computer!), I'm going to discuss what exactly happens when you decide to open a web page, using our client-server terminology and imagining that the web page is hosted on a virtual private server.

Opening a Web Page: How the Magic Happens

If you've been using the Internet for the majority of your life, you probably don't think too much about how it works because you're used to it...well... just working! However, those of us who remember the "good old days" of the Internet (which weren't that good, but were old) may remember the lag involved in loading pages prior to broadband and wondered "Why does it take so long?" Let's dig into what happens when you try to view a web page, and then we can talk about the parts of it that you, as the owner of the web page, can control or tweak.

Imagine for a moment that you're interested in visiting a fictitious website after a vivid daydream of quitting your day job, beapirate.com (for the pirate enthusiasts of the world). You open your web browser, and you enter the address in the address bar at the top. You press Enter or click the Go button, and within a few minutes, you're being enticed to join a pirate ship and sail the open seas. But what occurred between the browser address bar and the sales pitch? Let's dig in.

First: Where Does beapirate.com Live?

The first thing that your computer did was to ask a Domain Name Service (DNS) server if it knew the numerical Internet Protocol (IP) address that beapirate.com lives at. Roughly analogous to looking up an address in a phone book, the DNS server took a look at the DNS records for beapirate. com (see Figure 1-4) that are held with various registrars around the world and found the DNS server that has authority over beapirate.com. Once it found that server, it was able to ask it directly for the address, and hopefully that server gave it that address without fail.

Assuming that the DNS settings are correctly configured, your computer got the numerical address it needed, and it moved on to the next step. However, there are ways that this can go wrong.

Records

Last updated 8/25/2020 10:03 AM

Type	Name	Value	TTL
A	@	Parked	600 seconds
CNAME	e	email.secureserver.net	1 Hour
CNAME	email	email.secureserver.net	1 Hour
CNAME	ftp	@	1 Hour
CNAME	imap	imap.secureserver.net	1 Hour
CNAME	mail	pop.secureserver.net	1 Hour
CNAME	mobilemail	mobilemail–v01.prod.mesa1.secureserver.net	1 Hour
CNAME	pda	mobilemail–v01.prod.mesa1.secureserver.net	1 Hour
CNAME	pop	pop.secureserver.net	1 Hour
CNAME	smtp	smtp.secureserver.net	1 Hour
CNAME	webmail	webmail.secureserver.net	1 Hour
CNAME	www	ghs.google.com	1 Hour
CNAME	_domainconnect	_domainconnect.gd.domaincontrol.com	1 Hour
MX	@	smtp.secureserver.net (Priority: 0)	1 Hour

Figure 1-4. The DNS records for beapirate.com

First, the domain name, beapirate.com, might not actually exist. Imagine someone typing in the wrong domain name or perhaps a domain name that used to exist but doesn't now. What should happen in this case is that your computer gets back a "no records exist" message from the DNS server and shows you an error message saying as much. However, today it's pretty fashionable for your Internet provider, whether it be cable, DSL, or through your phone, to instead send you to a page of possible search results with ads (see Figure 1-5). Not very user friendly from a technical standpoint, but perhaps it helps some people find what they were looking for. It can be confusing though – because you legitimately made an error and never find out about it.

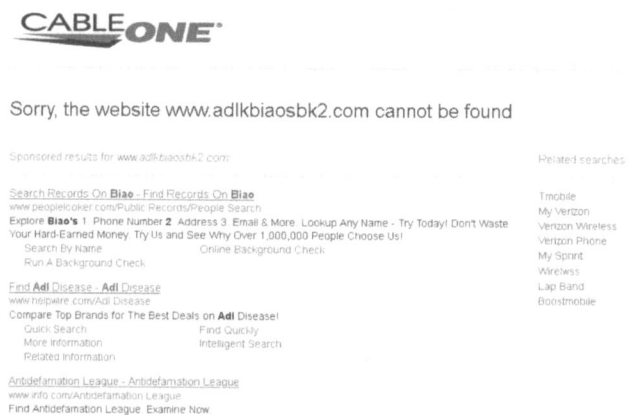

Figure 1-5. A page of search results returned when a domain name does not exist

But what if the domain name does exist but you still can't get to the page? It could be that whoever has control over beapirate.com's DNS server didn't enter the right records. In essence, they screwed up when they put the address in the address book.

And finally, it's possible that somewhere someone is messing with your DNS replies. Perhaps your ISP (Internet service provider) or work network has decided that they'd rather you not visit beapirate.com, so instead of telling you the correct answer, they "poisoned" the results – they told you it didn't exist when it really did.

We'll talk more about DNS in future chapters, but for now, let's assume that you typed in beapirate.com and got the correct address. Now what happens?

Second: Let's Knock on the (Web Server) Door

Once your computer has the address of the computer that houses beapirate. com's website, it can then connect directly to it. When it does that, it makes a connection to a specific port number on that other computer. What's a port? Well, it's a bit like a door. Imagine that the other computer is an apartment building, which just happens to have 65,535 apartments. Web pages usually always live in the same apartment – when it comes to nonsecure pages, it's apartment 80. Secure web pages live in apartment 443. When your computer goes to the "apartment building" for beapirate.com, it knows to knock on door/port 80 for nonsecure web pages and 443 for secure web pages. It's also worth noting that 65,535 is not an arbitrary number; it is 2 to the power of 16, minus 1 – the highest number that can be represented by a 16-bit binary number, which the original designers of the IP decided to use when creating port numbers.

So if your computer connects to the computer that houses beapirate.com and knocks on door 80, who answers? Well, someone listening for a knock on that door. In this case, a piece of server software that's listening for requests, which then sends the web page data to your computer. Your computer then displays it to you.

There are a few things that can go wrong here too. First, the computer that you connect to might not be running the software that listens for the knock at the door – the web server. Just like trying to read your email before opening up your inbox, it's impossible for you to view a web page if no one answers the door. Second, it's possible that the web server isn't configured properly – maybe you're knocking on the "secure" door (port 443) but the server only answers the "nonsecure" door (port 80). Finally, it's possible that the server is configured properly but there is an issue with the web page.

Perhaps that web page needs to use a database to display information, and the database isn't responding or set up.

You may be wondering why I've just gone into detail on how this happens, especially so early in this book. Well, the point to be made is twofold: First, there are a lot of "moving parts" when it comes to having your own server that does even the simplest task – displaying a web page. But second, and perhaps more importantly, there are ways to deal with the times when the moving parts break. The goal of this book is to not only introduce you to how the system works but also to talk about ways in which it can fail. Ways in which you might get frustrated and ways in which you can troubleshoot on your own before having to admit defeat. My goal by the end of this book isn't to turn you into a certifiable system administrator ready for an entry-level job in IT – because you likely already have a job that you enjoy but would just like to add these skills to your repertoire. But before we get to skill learning, we need to address some of the big questions many people have regarding purchasing, configuring, and ultimately running their own server. In this next section, we will talk about who provides services that you can purchase, how much they cost, and your responsibility for them both in time and in skill.

An Introduction to Information Technology Cloud Services

If you're like most people, you've heard the term "cloud" in referring to computers. People will say "Put that in the cloud" or "I store that in the cloud." Obviously they aren't talking about clouds in the sky, but what are they talking about?

Loosely defined, the "cloud" they speak of is a network of computers. Nothing more complex than that – leading some to say "The cloud is just someone else's computer," which is an accurate albeit slightly cynical way of putting things! Clouds exist so that you can offer services to users on the Internet without having to go the "old-fashioned" route. Let me introduce you to "the bad old days."

Physical Infrastructure

Twenty years ago, if you had wanted to run your own server, this is what you would have done. First, you would have purchased computers. Likely several of them, and as they were server-grade, they typically would cost about two to three times more than your computer at home. They'd come in special form factors, typically, to be mounted in a rack in a data center. For now, imagine that you'd just spent $10,000 on four servers (see Figure 1-6); a router that you could plug them into for network capability; operating systems for them (if you're not using an open source operating system); various wires and cables; a keyboard, a mouse, and a small monitor (as well as something called a KVM switch that would let you switch those three items between all four servers without having to unplug and replug in everything; see Figure 1-7); and mounting hardware. It's all sitting in the back of your car or, more likely, van.

Figure 1-6. Four 1U rack-mount servers. We spared no expense on labels

Figure 1-7. A monitor, keyboard, and mouse connected to a KVM

Now that you have your hardware, you can't simply plug it into your home Internet connection. In theory you could, but your Internet service provider (ISP) probably won't like you running a small business from your home Internet connection. Most home connections give you a ton of bandwidth/transfer speed to download items from the Internet, but relatively small bandwidth/ transfer speed to upload items to the Internet, so a home connection likely wouldn't work anyway because your web pages would load far too slow for people's tastes. So if you can't jack all of this into your cable modem at home, where do you put it? The answer is a data center, also known as a large room filled with a lot of computers!

Technically a data center is a bit more than that – typically these are fairly large rooms or series of rooms that have a raised floor to route cables and rows of metal racks that one can mount server hardware in. Data centers feature high-capacity cooling systems to keep the temperature safe for microprocessors (thousands of running computers can make things quite hot!), as well as redundant power systems and fire suppression systems. Given the computing power running at any given time, they also tend to be pretty loud! Large companies may run their own data centers for their servers, and several companies exist in the world that run data centers for clients to rent space in, typically called "co-location." You'll find these nestled in office buildings, industrial parks, and other random places. Given the fact that companies typically store pretty sensitive data on their servers, you'll seldom see these places highly advertised or visible from the road, and security is typically tightly controlled. Finally, there are two types of co-location: manned, where technicians from the company are present all the time in case something goes wrong, and unmanned, where you might just be given a key card to get in during off hours. Manned data centers typically cost more because as the owner of a rack, you can typically request them to perform simple procedures for you – eject a USB hard drive, unplug and replug in something, and so on. If you're at an unmanned data center and it's 11 PM at night when the server goes down and it needs you to physically hold the power button to reboot, then you're driving in to do it. Something I wish I could say I've never done before!

So assuming you have your computer equipment and a signed lease with a data center, which will run you about \$1,000–2,000 a month on the low end, you now get the joy of driving up to the data center and installing your hardware. You then set it up to connect to the network and hopefully set it up so that you can access and administer it remotely (unless you like spending time in 65-degree temperatures while millions of fans whirl around you). You now have everything you need in order to run your own server. As you may have noticed though, you've racked up a ton of costs in both money and time. Around 2005, the landscape started changing – for small business owners and individuals – it became much improved.

Web Hosting vs. Virtual Private Servers

For many years, we'd had individuals described earlier, who had just put in massive amounts of money into hardware and co-location space, offer "shared web hosting" on their servers to defray costs. A web host would typically offer you an amount of space on their server, perhaps other services such as email and database, and in turn they would manage the hardware and the software associated with it. Using a shopping mall analogy, imagine a store that has booths you can rent out to sell your own wares – in this case, the store owner rents space for the entire store, and you rent space from the store owner. The mall controls the space, then the store owner, and then finally you. In shared web hosting, you have enough control to put a basic web page together, but since you were sharing the server with hundreds of other clients, you couldn't make drastic changes or install custom software (e.g., you can't control the level of the lights in the store, since all share the same ceiling!). For many people, this model is sufficient. However, as you grow, you find yourself bumping up against the limitations of the "walled garden" you're put in. Thankfully around 2005, virtualization software became much more affordable and robust, meaning that individuals who had their own physical servers could install software to create "virtual" servers on them. You could have your own storefront, instead of living in someone else's.

A virtual server differs from web hosting in that it appears to be its own computer. You get to control what software you install on it, and the owner of the physical server can allot a portion of disk space, memory usage, and CPU usage to your virtual server. A separate computer inside a bigger computer, in essence. To you, the owner of the virtual server, it appears that you have your own system – a system you can rent for a small monthly charge instead of having to invest thousands of dollars in a physical infrastructure. The downside, however, is that you are responsible for most everything with it. While a web hosting contract might stipulate that the owner of the physical server provide support in terms of fixing software issues, backing up data, or ensuring uptime, a virtual server owner assumes these responsibilities. It really is much like the analogy I used at the start of this chapter – you're renting a store in the "mall," and it's up to you to furnish it, keep it functioning, and secure it. In return, you get a very affordable rental rate.

How Much Does It Cost?

As I mentioned before, the cost difference is what makes a Virtual Private Server attractive. To see the difference, I'm going to compare pricing at four of the top web hosting companies – HostGator, DreamHost, 1&1 IONOS, and GoDaddy – for the following three options: a shared web hosting plan, a virtual private server, and a dedicated physical server. While many options apply, I chose to look at the most comparable and realistic options for someone starting out. Shared web hosting is the cheapest, averaging around $4.63 a month. A basic Virtual Private Server runs approximately $17.49 a month, and a basic dedicated server is (somewhat intimidating) $107.25 a month! So if you're anything more than a basic user running relatively low-traffic websites, such as those for your local business or your personal blog, a VPS is 85% cheaper than a dedicated server!

Cost is relative though, because I'll freely admit to you that there are even cheaper options out there than the "big" web hosting providers. For one, there are services like Amazon Web Services (AWS) which offers a staggering amount of cloud services that you can combine to fit your needs. A basic Virtual Private Server through AWS Elastic Compute Cloud (EC2) is free for the first year and only billed by the hour after that. This means that you could spin up your VPS for just a few minutes a day if that was all you needed. Also, many of those people who did invest in $10,000 of hardware and co-location contracts run their own small cloud services and charge a fraction of what the big players do. On one site, lowendbox.com, you can regularly find deals on so-called "bargain basement" VPS providers. On the day I wrote this chapter in late 2020, the first news post was advertising a reasonably powerful VPS package for $2.50 a month, or $7.50 a quarter. Around "Black Friday" each year, it's not uncommon to find VPSs for $10–20 per year. Locking into one of these options is quite a bit cheaper and more flexible than shared hosting. However, one must remember that there is no such thing as a free lunch...

What's the Catch?

So what is the catch? Responsibility. I run several VPSs. They host my personal web page, they store collaborative data, and they run scripts and other services that I use on a daily basis. Imagine what would happen tomorrow if you woke up and the blog that you generated your income from were to disappear. What would you do?

Likely you'd be on the phone with...someone...to fix it. If it were a web hosting company, you'd call their tech support and ask them to fix the problem. If you hired a technician, you'd be calling them asking them to drop everything and get your blog back up. If you worked for a company with a robust IT department, you might be on the phone with them asking them to check why the server was down. However, if you run your own VPS, all of those roads point back to the person in the mirror: you.

Let me give you an example: The company that I rent several VPSs through, which will remain nameless, has been relatively awesome over the past 2–3 years. My websites are available nearly 99.999% of the time (an uptime referred to as the "five 9s" – a term applied to Service Level Agreements [SLAs], a contract that some providers offer their clients guaranteeing availability), and anytime I have an issue related to availability or processing power, I get an answer within 3–4 hours of submitting a help ticket. However, they weren't always this good – when they first started out, there were situations where a mismanaged physical server didn't provide reliable service for some clients or didn't enforce the rules on all clients such that some VPSs on the physical server were able to hog resources. It was growing pains, and thankfully they grew out of them. Other companies I'd worked with weren't so reliable. At least three to four times in the past 10 years, I've had to move my VPSs from one provider to another, and each time it was a process very much like packing up and moving your house – a hassle.

And even with a reliable company, there is only so much support they can give me. VPS providers tend to give you as much control and privacy as possible. If you don't break their rules on what content you can host, they don't look into your virtual private server. Thus, if I install a piece of software that breaks my VPS or my server contracts a virus, the best my VPS provider can do is "reimage" or "refresh" the VPS – basically restore it to the state it was the day I bought it. All of my data and customizations are gone and I have to rebuild. Some providers offer backup and restore capability, but not all.

What this means is that you need to be comfortable running your own server. From setup to deletion, backup and restore, security to usability, it's your responsibility. It's not particularly challenging if given the tools, but it is a risk that one must take – to trust in their own skills and resources. We'll talk about those skills and resources in the next section, and we'll also talk about who you can turn to for help in some situations. But I'll be honest with you now – if you work a job that requires 60–80 hours a week and you already have to outsource many components that individuals do themselves (e.g., you have a lawn service and a cleaning service, order delivery frequently, etc.), then you might not have the time for running your own server.

Skills and Resources

One might wonder what resources you need to be successful in running your own VPS. In this section, I'm going to go over what I assume about you already, as the reader of this book, what I plan on covering in this book, and what you'll need to continue doing for "professional development" over the next several years that you run your own VPS!

Assumptions

I've purposefully tried to assume very little in writing this book. I believe the goal of running your own VPS is attainable for many people, but there are some aspects that I cannot give you if you're already lacking them. Here's what I expect you are aware of:

1. Basic Operation of a Computer – How to turn one on, how to start a program, and how to navigate your computer's operating system and a web browser. An example command I might write would be "Open your Internet browser and navigate to www.debian.org."

2. Basic Understanding of How Computer Networks Work – The idea that computers talk to each other over the Internet and follow certain rules and guidelines while doing such. An example statement I might make would be "The server isn't responding because software isn't running on it."

3. Realization That Computers Are Usually Fixable, but That This Takes Work – Often I'll hear someone tell me "It just broke" or "They make it stop working when the new version comes out." Both of these are inaccurate. However, if you treat a computer as a magical black box that you cannot understand the inner workings of, you'll be very confused when I say "Copy the error message into Google and see if other people have had the same issue" while troubleshooting.

Skills Taught Here

Now that we have the assumptions out of the way, let's talk about what I will cover here, chapter by chapter.

Chapter	Title	Skills Taught
2	Selecting a VPS Provider	We'll go in depth on how to select a VPS provider, the different options out there, and what some of the basic terms used mean. We'll also talk about resources needed based upon what you'd like to do with your server. By the end of the chapter, you should have picked out and signed up with a VPS provider and have your own machine to "play" with!
3	Basic Linux Administration via the Command Line	We'll be using the Linux operating system in this book, and for many, this means the first time (or first time in a long time) using a command-line-based environment. Those old enough to remember DOS will likely feel at home, while others will be introduced to basic commands to work with files (e.g., mv, cp, rm), commands to start and stop services, and commands used to install new software.

(continued)

Chapter	Title	Skills Taught
4	Basic Linux Administration via GUI (Webmin)	For some, the command line is just too frustrating for everyday use. However, there is a product out there that can help – Webmin, an open source product that has been used on Linux servers for over 20 years. It allows you to configure your server through a web browser. We'll discuss pros and cons of using it and how to set it up.
5	Basics of Linux Security	Firewalls, ban lists, password hashes, and more can be daunting for first-time administrators to learn. In this chapter, we'll talk about the basics of security, from file and directory permissions to auditing what your users are doing and to making sure that only the services you want to be available actually are available to the public.
6	Basics of Backups and Version Control	Everyone needs a disaster recovery plan (DRP), and in this chapter, we'll talk about how to back up and restore your files and how to keep versions of important files so that you can always "roll back" to a previous known good version. Nothing is more frustrating than making a change to your system that you feel is small and insignificant and then finding it trashes everything!
7	Basics of Server Software Administration	I've already talked about three types of servers – DNS, web, and database. However, there are several others that I'll give a basic overview of in this chapter. You'll learn what they are, how to get started with them, and where to find more resources for each as you get yourself up and running!
8	Installing an Open Source Software Product: WordPress	WordPress is one of the most popular content management systems (CMSs) in the world and is used by millions to create web pages. While it's extremely powerful, it's also complex and can be a bit difficult to get up and running in a safe and secure manner. We'll not only cover getting started with it, we'll also talk about how to keep it running properly and out of the grasp of bad actors.
9	Administrator's Weekly Checklist	Once you have your server up and running, you'll want to take care of it regularly. I'll walk you through the tasks that you can do weekly to make sure your server stays happy and secure.
10	Open Source Application Possibilities	WordPress is one popular open source application, but there are hundreds more that are free for you to use as a Linux server administrator. I'll discuss several of these in this chapter to give you a few ideas about how you can use your server to enhance multiple areas of your work and personal life!

Professional Development

The work of a server administrator is never done, even if you're doing your weekly checklists. You also need to keep up to date on things as they change and evolve. As someone who has been working with Linux for over 20 years, there isn't a day that goes by that I don't learn of some new change or tweak that affects some part of the operating system or the operation of a server. We'll talk throughout the book about how you can stay ahead of these changes, so that you're not overwhelmed when new versions come out or new best practices are adopted.

Conclusion

Well, if you've made it this far, then I'll assume you're ready to learn about running your own virtual private server. As I mentioned, the next chapter covers finding one of them and how to get up and running with it. It's an exciting journey that we'll take one step at a time!

Selecting a VPS Provider

Often when shopping for any product, we are somewhat bound by a physical or well-delineated space. If you're purchasing a car, you go to a car lot or find a website that has the word "auto" or "car" in the name. If you're looking to hire someone to perform a service, you typically have various physical businesses you can visit (e.g., a locksmith, a temporary worker agency) or easy-to-define search terms that you can use on your search engine of choice (e.g., "unlock my car" or "house cleaning"). With selecting a VPS provider, the waters are a bit muddier as services can be offered to a variety of types of clients (e.g., individuals, small businesses, large corporations) and in many different ways (e.g., packages of services vs. a pay-as-you-go a la carte approach). Further complicating the issue are the concepts that you'll hear thrown around as you shop – the idea of a Terms of Service (TOS) or a Service Level Agreement. Without having some sort of dictionary to help you, you may find yourself confused and ultimately unable to purchase the product you want or, worse, paying for a product you don't need. In this chapter, we'll talk about the various types of providers that you can find, what the words they use in their advertisements mean, how to vet them, and ultimately how to engage with one for services.

© Jon Westfall 2021
J. Westfall, *Set Up and Manage Your Virtual Private Server*,
https://doi.org/10.1007/978-1-4842-6966-4_2

Providers: Low End, High End, and Cloud

Today in the virtual private server industry, it's an exciting time to be an entrepreneur, not just in buying a VPS to host your own business website, but in selling VPSs as well. Perhaps nowhere on earth do you find an industry where the person selling you your product could be a one-man operation (literally) or could be a giant company such as Amazon, Oracle, or Microsoft. And in some cases, while you're dealing with the one-man operation, they are actually buying services in bulk from the giant companies! It's hard to know who to trust and who can provide you with the best service. In this section, I'm going to break down providers roughly by price point/service-level grouping, discuss the pros and cons of each, and attempt to lead you toward the solution best for you given your technical ability.

Low-End Priced/Small Shop

Everybody likes a bargain, and in the VPS world, there are several people who are more than willing to give it to you. Recall my discussion in Chapter 1 recalling the "good old days" where a server owner would need to buy the hardware and contract for the connectivity? Most of those people realized early on that they could make money by reselling their own space to others, and it led to the birth of the ultra-affordable low-end priced VPS space.

You may wonder how someone would be able to offer services like this, when we typically think of technology as exceedingly complex – the type of thing that your company has an entire department dedicated to. A one-person IT department seems like an oxymoron, yet that's exactly what many of these low-end providers boil down to. Take someone who is one part technology geek and another part entrepreneur and who wants to work for themselves, and you have your typical low-end provider shop. They typically advertise on targeted websites such as lowendbox.com (see Figure 2-1) and place an emphasis on lowest possible cost.

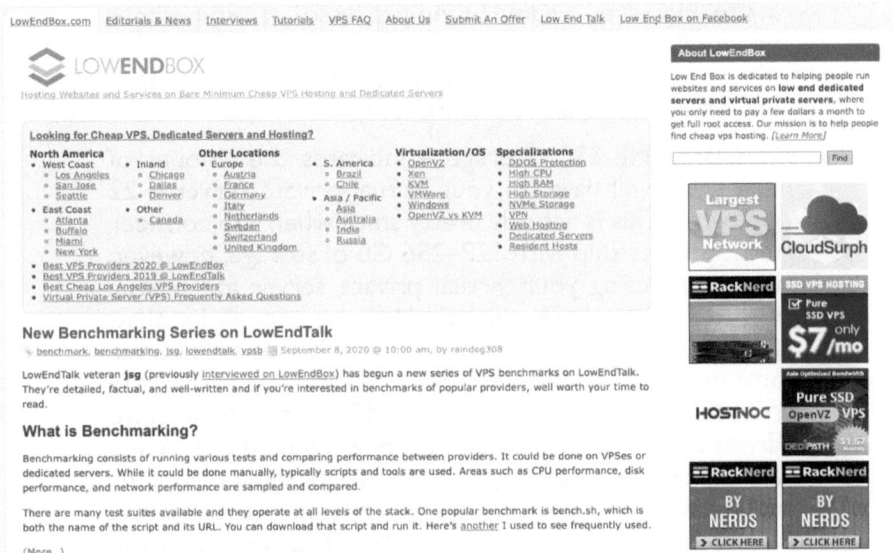

Figure 2-1. The lowendbox.com homepage

Looking at a typical advertisement for a low-end box, you're likely to see something like Figure 2-2. It might look pretty intimidating at first, but let's break down what each line is offering.

1.5 GB Ryzen VPS w/ Fast NVMe Storage

- 1x AMD Ryzen CPU Core
- 22 GB NVMe SSD Storage
- 1.5 GB DDR4 RAM
- 3000GB Monthly Premium Bandwidth
- 1Gbps Public Network Port
- Full Root Admin Access
- 1 Dedicated IPv4 Address
- KVM / SolusVM Control Panel
- LOCATION: Los Angeles
- Price: $35.59/Year

Figure 2-2. A description of a Virtual Private Server

- 1× AMD Ryzen CPU Core – Indicates that your VPS will run on a physical server that uses a multicore AMD Ryzen CPU. There are many different versions of the Ryzen processor, so at a glance this sounds impressive but it doesn't tell us which Ryzen multicore processor is in use. However, a name brand processor can sometimes be worth a bit more of a price point – but in this case, it's a clever bit of tech speak that makes it sound more impressive than just "one CPU core."

- 22 GB NVMe SSD Storage – Indicates the amount of space you will have on your virtual private server – 22 gigabytes. This is actually pretty small when you consider most phones ship with 128–256 GB of storage; however, if you are using your virtual private server for a basic website or database, this will likely be enough for that. However, you won't be turning your VPS into a file server anytime soon. The NVMe portion refers to the specification of solid state drive (SSD) used. Solid state drives are faster than traditional physical hard disk drives and are slowly becoming the standard for most computer applications and devices. If you don't see "SSD" in the advertising, it's likely that your VPS will run on traditional physical hard disk drives with moving parts.

- 1.5 GB DDR4 RAM – Indicates the amount of memory that will be available to your VPS. Again, this tends to be a bit on the small side of RAM in an age where a high-end laptop might come with 16 times that amount. However, unless you're going to be hosting a very intensive little web application or having your VPS crunching numbers 24/7, 1.5 GB is sufficient for a small to medium website with low traffic.

- 3000 GB Monthly Premium Bandwidth – This is one that will likely seem strange to you – bandwidth can refer to two different items. In one case, it can refer to speed of the connection you have to the Internet. Most VPSs are connected to the Internet through commercial-grade routing and thus typically have a fairly fast connection (it's much more likely if your VPS is running slow that you have an issue with not enough RAM or free space, not a bandwidth issue). However, in another sense, as this advertisement uses it, bandwidth can refer to the total amount of data your VPS can send or receive in a given month. More appropriately labeled "transfer," the advertisement is telling you that you can have 3,000 gigabytes of data go in or out of your VPS each month before you hit your bandwidth limit. 3,000 is a decent level for a small to medium website. If you want to calculate your exact needed bandwidth, you'll need to use a web browser tool that can determine the amount of data you download when you connect to your website (https://tools.pingdom.com/ is one such tool) and then multiply that by the number of page views you intend to have each month.

- 1 Gbps Public Network Port – This refers to the connection your VPS has to the Internet. In this case, it means that you'll have 1 gigabyte per second of connectivity with a publicly routable IP address. Since most of your connections to your server will undoubtedly be less than 1 Gbps speed (the average speed of a residential Internet connection may be one tenth of this), this is plenty fast.

- Full Root Admin Access – The administrative user on a Linux system is named "root" – this is telling you that you'll have full administrative access over your VPS. This is typically put in advertisements to remind you that you have full access, as opposed to shared hosting where most aspiring power users are graduating from.

- 1 Dedicated IPv4 Address – Each computer that is connected to the Internet needs to either have a routable Internet Protocol (IP) address or have some computer upstream act as a proxy for it. Having a dedicated IP address allows you to connect directly to this machine from your machine, which is technically not completely essential for web hosting, but is the simplest way to host a website on your server.

- KVM/SolusVM Control Panel – Here is where things can be tricky. KVM as an acronym was already discussed in Chapter 1 as the abbreviation for "Keyboard, Video, Mouse" – a special physical piece of equipment that could switch between several computers at one time. However here, KVM stands for "Kernel-Based Virtual Machine" – a piece of software called a hypervisor that allows you to run several virtual computers on one physical computer (see www.linux-kvm.org/page/Main_Page for more information). KVM is a free product, which makes it the most cost-efficient product for most VPS providers to use. SolusVM is a software package that allows VPS owners to control various aspects of their VPS. It's where you can push the virtual "power" button to turn on your VPS or the "rebuild" button that returns it to the stock configuration you had the day you bought the machine. There are other hypervisors out there that you may see advertised, with OpenVZ being the other most common.

- Location: Los Angeles – This one is pretty self-evident: the physical server that you'll be buying a VPS on is located in Los Angeles. Typically you may pick a location that is close to you (to minimize the number of systems you'll need to route through to get to your VPS, speeding up the load times), or you might pick a physical location far away from yourself for backup and redundancy (e.g., in case of natural disaster).

- Price: $35.59/Year – Lastly, another self-evident one – how much you will pay. Some providers will allow you to pay by the month; others may require a whole year to get a low rate.

Spending any amount of time around the places where low-end providers advertise, you'll see they are typically fairly "hungry" for clients. Prioritizing price above all else is great if you're on a tight budget, but you also must think about what you'll be trading off. In my experience, low-end providers tend to assume that you have a **high** level of technical knowledge and that you'll need a fairly **low** level of support from them. It's the epitome of someone renting you a storage unit and saying, "Here ya go, we'll only talk if you forget to pay your bill." You likely won't receive much in terms of support if things go wrong on your VPS, other than perhaps an offer to reset it back to the way it was when you first purchased it (requiring you to reset the entire system). You also likely won't get any amenity or perk you don't explicitly pay for. Some providers may offer backup services or security analysis, but it's not going to be included for the base cost. And lastly, with low-end providers typically being self-employed with few employees, it's always possible that you may experience service disruptions for "human" reasons. Your website might be down for a day if the owner is on vacation and isn't checking email as quickly. Or the owner may get tired of running the business and sell it or shut it down. Being on a low-end provider is incredibly cheap, but also requires a lot of investment on your part in creating, managing, securing, and safeguarding your own content. It might not be something everyone is ready for, but it might be something you move to after getting your bearings.

High-End Priced/Large Shop

A step-up from the low-end world is the high-end world, or at least higher-end, because price wise, these companies tend to still be competitive. The most common higher-end companies are listed in the following, in no particular order, and they may be names that you've heard of if you've investigated web hosting or private servers before, as they tend to have a fairly decent advertising budget:

- DreamHost
- Bluehost
- A2 Hosting
- Hostinger
- HostGator
- iPage
- InMotion
- MochaHost
- Web Hosting Hub
- 1&1 IONOS

Visiting any of these providers' websites will instantly entice you to sign up for one of three classes of products: web hosting, a virtual private server, or a dedicated physical server. I discussed all three of these products in the last chapter.

The biggest difference between these providers and the ones mentioned in the last section is the size of their operation and the robustness of their support team and infrastructure. Whereas a small operation might be a single employee or maybe two, these companies tend to have employee bases in the hundreds. They also tend to invest more in custom software solutions – a fancy client's portal, a support center, and even dedicated desktop or mobile apps instead of relying on open source software such as Solus control panel for their clients to access. And many of them include 24/7 technical support, with some going as far as to offer a Service Level Agreement, which we will talk about later in this chapter.

You do get what you pay for with these options, so paying more will enable you to have a more polished experience and allow you to contact someone if trouble starts. However again, options such as backups and security analysis will likely be extra costs, and even then, there is no guarantee that they can get you back to a working position after you've had a "crash" of some sort. While you may pay more, you still need to remain personally responsible for your content. I've seen several people burned by going with a well-established company – not in that the company didn't provide what they said they would, but in that people felt that because the company was well established, they would fix any problem that arose. Many start with a company on this list (including myself) and then branch out as their needs change. For some, they find that a low-end provider will give them the essentials and that they don't mind the lack of polish. For others, they realize that they would be better off with a provider that was more granular and allowed them to pay for just what they needed. For them, cloud infrastructures may be the way to go.

Priced by the Minute/Cloud Infrastructure

After spending some time looking at the options both in the low-end and high-end spaces, you'll likely notice that bundling services together tends to be more common than an a la carte option, both in software (e.g., your VPS has a set amount of storage space, memory utilization, processor utilization, etc.) and in price (e.g., you pay $X per month or $X per year, regardless of how much or how little you use the services). For most people, this works out really well – they aren't quite at the level where they want to completely customize their service options. However, if you find yourself in a very particular situation, you might be better off paying only for what you need and utilizing a robust cloud infrastructure. Here are a few use scenarios:

- You store a lot of data for backup purposes, but you don't often access or download that data, and you don't run any sort of public website.

- You crunch a lot of numbers every so often, say once a week, and want a server to do it for you – but the other 6 days of the week, the server would sit dormant.

- You're an accountancy firm that gets super busy around tax time, and you need your website to be much faster during those months. The rest of the year, it could be a bit slower, and no one would notice.

In these cases, once you have established your technical knowledge of how to operate a VPS and use it for your business, you might be better off to move to a cloud infrastructure. These clouds, run by large corporations, typically allow you to purchase just the resources you need and pay by the hour, minute, or data sent/received. The options are fairly robust, which also means that it can be very complicated to determine what services you need to purchase and how much you'll pay per month.

For example, one of the most popular cloud infrastructures is Amazon Web Services, or AWS. AWS, like many clouds, offers a price calculator (https://calculator.aws/#/). Adding up the same options that we saw in Figure 2-2 (or rough equivalents), we get a monthly price of around $10–15. While this is higher than the low-end price, it does come from a service that has a solid track record of reliability, redundancy, and security. In other words, you're paying somewhere between low-end and high-end prices, to be on the same platform as some of the biggest names in technology – AWS clients include Netflix, Twitch, LinkedIn, and Facebook.

In sum, a cloud infrastructure might be a great option for you once you've graduated from a beginner VPS manager to more advanced – especially if you have very specific needs. If you're curious to look more into cloud infrastructures, the following are the biggest "clouds" as of the time of this writing:

- Amazon Web Services

- Microsoft Azure

- Google Cloud Platform

- Alibaba Cloud

- IBM

- Dell Technologies/VMWare

- Hewlett Packard Enterprise

- Cisco Systems

- Salesforce

- Oracle

- SAP

- Workforce

- Adobe

Key Terms

Now that you've read a bit about your options on who to contract with, you'll likely run into a few key terms and concepts that you'll want to know more about. We've started talking about these earlier in the section explaining Figure 2-2; however, some other terms that you haven't heard are listed in the following, and we'll also dig into two very important documents – a Terms of Service and a Service Level Agreement.

For clarity, I've developed the following mini-glossary of terms that you may run across:

Term	Definition
Auto-scaling or Scaling	The ability of your VPS to dynamically change in response to what's happening. If you get a sudden spike of traffic, the software running your VPS can allocate more memory or processing power. If it's midnight and no one is visiting you, the software can limit your usage so that you pay less money.
Application Programming Interface (API)	A set of commands that software can use to control a service. Imagine building a custom smartphone app for your website that allows you to start up certain services, crunch data, or start a video conference – all of those actions would be performed by the smartphone app contacting your website's API. When it comes to cloud services, some companies allow users access to their API to help automate frequently used commands (e.g., starting or stopping their VPS).
Big Data	A phrase that has become popular over the past number of years to describe working with a large amount of data in order to understand trends, predict results, or estimate costs or sales. Big Data was coined to refer to data sets that were often too large for a single desktop computer to handle in a quick and efficient manner, thus requiring a user to use a VPS or cloud service to analyze them.
Business Intelligence or BI	A set of tools that lets you understand the data that you have. Imagine having a giant data set (e.g., "Big Data") and needing some sort of way to analyze it, summarize it, or otherwise make sense of it. A lot of cloud companies may advertise BI options as one of their add-ons.
BYOD (Bring Your Own Device)	An offering that some companies have that allows you to bring your own hardware and co-host it with them or otherwise use your own device. Typically in a VPS context, this would be an option you'd stay away from – after all, you don't want to deal with physical hardware if you can!
Cloud as a Service (CaaS) or Software as a Service (SaaS)	A relatively new set of terms that refer to making resources or services available to users over the Internet. In the past, these would have been done "on-prem" or on-premises. Again, it's not likely that you'll need to consider this if you're just building your own VPS. However, large cloud infrastructures will refer to something "aaS" to indicate that you can host things with them that you would have normally just had on your corporate network.
Cloud Backup	The concept of storing data in a cloud that can be used for disaster recovery later – it's likely you'll want some sort of cloud backup for your VPS, either to another VPS or to a cloud storage system.
Cluster	A group of computers that are all linked and can share resources or the load of requests.
Customer Relationship Management (CRM)	A special set of software that companies use to manage relationships with their customers and provide customer support. Many cloud providers may advertise how their platform is ideal to run CRM packages as a service.

(continued)

Term	Definition
Data Center	The physical location where computer servers are stored and connected to the Internet.
Data Migration or simply Migration	The act of moving content and services from one VPS to another. If you change VPS providers, you'll need to migrate your data from one company to the other.
Disaster Recovery Plan (DRP)	The plan that you have in case your data become corrupt, your VPS is hacked, or otherwise you need to restore from backup. DRPs typically discuss different options that you may have and also are useful in planning proactivity for problems.
Elasticity	Similar to scaling, this is the ability of a service to gain more resources as needed. Imagine being able to add additional RAM to your VPS before a particularly busy week of traffic.
High Availability (HA)	A term that companies use that implies they have safeguards or other plans in place to make sure your VPS stays up and running even if network issues arise.
Hypervisor	The software that runs on a physical computer that allows virtual computers to be run on top of it. There are several hypervisors on the market that can be advertised to perspective clients, with some having more commercial appeal and others being more inexpensive to operate or license.
Internet of Things (IoT)	This term refers to devices that are connected to a network or the Internet that we typically don't think of as computers. If your toaster can be controlled by your smartphone, then it's a member of the IoT. Smart speakers, smart light switches, smart home appliances, and so on are all part of IoT.
Load Balancing	Similar to scaling, the idea that a particularly heavy influx of traffic or usage could be divided over several VPSs or cloud services to prevent everything from slowing down or crashing.
Personally Identifiable Information (PII)	Information that can uniquely identify a user outside of the Internet. Storing PII can be very complex depending on regulations and thus requires you to be very careful in how you safeguard your information. If you lose or "leak" PII, it's possible that you could be held liable for identity theft.
Virtual Machine (VM)	A software computer that runs on top of a physical machine.

These are just some of the terms that you'll hear or see as you're browsing for your VPS. It can be very intimidating to someone new to the area, and so never be afraid to stop and look up terms you don't understand. Often, sadly, companies may employ some of these terms as "buzzwords" that they hope will influence you to purchase their service. But in the end, if you don't need it or aren't sure you need it, consider other alternatives. Regardless of who you work with, however, you will need to be aware of the policies that govern how they expect you to act as a customer and how you can expect them to act as a provider – hence the Terms of Service and the Service Level Agreement.

Terms of Service (TOS)

Life is all about rules, and many of those rules come in the form of complex legal documents. We see these so frequently today in situations such as installing software (in which we typically accept a license of some sort) to more traditional settings (e.g., signing an apartment lease). When it comes to your VPS, your Terms of Service document is your "lease" – it sets out the expectations of the provider on you as the end user and outlines what you are and are not allowed to do with their service.

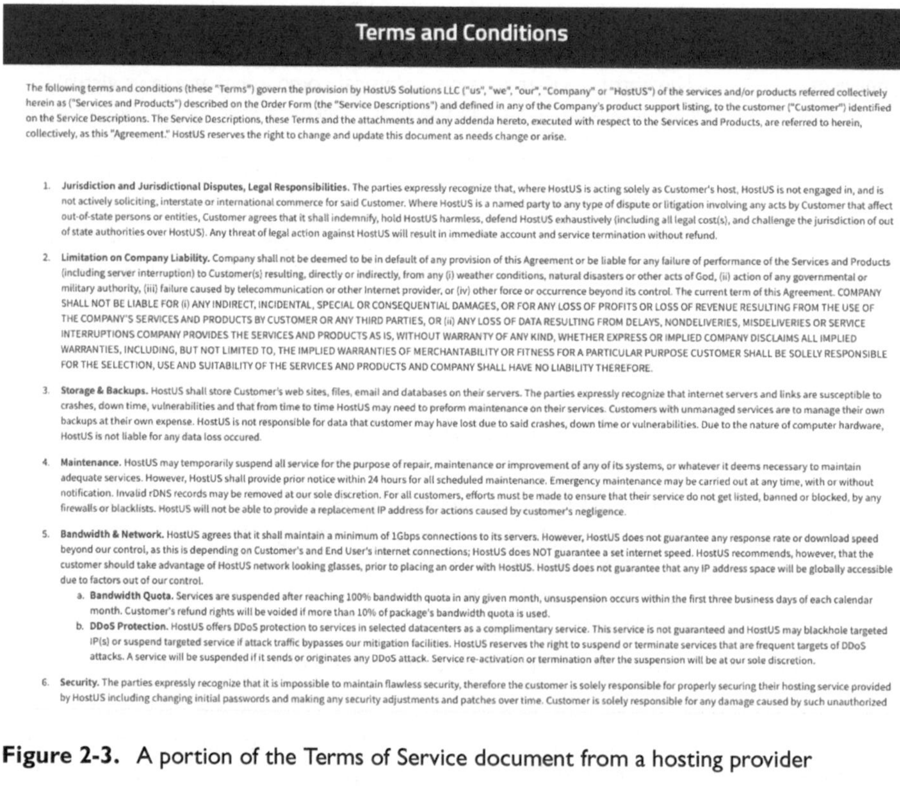

Terms and Conditions

The following terms and conditions (these "Terms") govern the provision by HostUS Solutions LLC ("us", "we", "our", "Company" or "HostUS") of the services and/or products referred collectively herein as ("Services and Products") described on the Order Form (the "Service Descriptions") and defined in any of the Company's product support listing, to the customer ("Customer") identified on the Service Descriptions. The Service Descriptions, these Terms and the attachments and any addenda hereto, executed with respect to the Services and Products, are referred to herein, collectively, as this "Agreement." HostUS reserves the right to change and update this document as needs change or arise.

1. **Jurisdiction and Jurisdictional Disputes, Legal Responsibilities.** The parties expressly recognize that, where HostUS is acting solely as Customer's host, HostUS is not engaged in, and is not actively soliciting, interstate or international commerce for said Customer. Where HostUS is a named party to any type of dispute or litigation involving any acts by Customer that affect out-of-state persons or entities, Customer agrees that it shall indemnify, hold HostUS harmless, defend HostUS exhaustively (including all legal cost(s), and challenge the jurisdiction of out of state authorities over HostUS). Any threat of legal action against HostUS will result in immediate account and service termination without refund.

2. **Limitation on Company Liability.** Company shall not be deemed to be in default of any provision of this Agreement or be liable for any failure of performance of the Services and Products (including server interruption) to Customer(s) resulting, directly or indirectly, from any (i) weather conditions, natural disasters or other acts of God, (ii) action of any governmental or military authority, (iii) failure caused by telecommunication or other Internet provider, or (iv) other force or occurrence beyond its control. The current term of this Agreement. COMPANY SHALL NOT BE LIABLE FOR (i) ANY INDIRECT, INCIDENTAL, SPECIAL OR CONSEQUENTIAL DAMAGES, OR FOR ANY LOSS OF PROFITS OR LOSS OF REVENUE RESULTING FROM THE USE OF THE COMPANY'S SERVICES AND PRODUCTS BY CUSTOMER OR ANY THIRD PARTIES, OR (ii) ANY LOSS OF DATA RESULTING FROM DELAYS, NONDELIVERIES, MISDELIVERIES OR SERVICE INTERRUPTIONS COMPANY PROVIDES THE SERVICES AND PRODUCTS AS IS, WITHOUT WARRANTY OF ANY KIND, WHETHER EXPRESS OR IMPLIED COMPANY DISCLAIMS ALL IMPLIED WARRANTIES, INCLUDING, BUT NOT LIMITED TO, THE IMPLIED WARRANTIES OF MERCHANTABILITY OR FITNESS FOR A PARTICULAR PURPOSE CUSTOMER SHALL BE SOLELY RESPONSIBLE FOR THE SELECTION, USE AND SUITABILITY OF THE SERVICES AND PRODUCTS AND COMPANY SHALL HAVE NO LIABILITY THEREFORE.

3. **Storage & Backups.** HostUS shall store Customer's web sites, files, email and databases on their servers. The parties expressly recognize that internet servers and links are susceptible to crashes, down time, vulnerabilities and that from time to time HostUS may need to preform maintenance on their services. Customers with unmanaged services are to manage their own backups at their own expense. HostUS is not responsible for data that customer may have lost due to said crashes, down time or vulnerabilities. Due to the nature of computer hardware, HostUS is not liable for any data loss occured.

4. **Maintenance.** HostUS may temporarily suspend all service for the purpose of repair, maintenance or improvement of any of its systems, or whatever it deems necessary to maintain adequate services. However, HostUS shall provide prior notice within 24 hours for all scheduled maintenance. Emergency maintenance may be carried out at any time, with or without notification. Invalid rDNS records may be removed at our sole discretion. For all customers, efforts must be made to ensure that their service do not get listed, banned or blocked, by any firewalls or blacklists. HostUS will not be able to provide a replacement IP address for actions caused by customer's negligence.

5. **Bandwidth & Network.** HostUS agrees that it shall maintain a minimum of 1Gbps connections to its servers. However, HostUS does not guarantee any response rate or download speed beyond our control, as this is depending on Customer's and End User's internet connections; HostUS does NOT guarantee a set internet speed. HostUS recommends, however, that the customer should take advantage of HostUS network looking glasses, prior to placing an order with HostUS. HostUS does not guarantee that any IP address space will be globally accessible due to factors out of our control.

   a. **Bandwidth Quota.** Services are suspended after reaching 100% bandwidth quota in any given month, unsuspension occurs within the first three business days of each calendar month. Customer's refund rights will be voided if more than 10% of package's bandwidth quota is used.

   b. **DDoS Protection.** HostUS offers DDoS protection to services in selected datacenters as a complimentary service. This service is not guaranteed and HostUS may blackhole targeted IP(s) or suspend targeted service if attack traffic bypasses our mitigation facilities. HostUS reserves the right to suspend or terminate services that are frequent targets of DDoS attacks. A service will be suspended if it sends or originates any DDoS attack. Service re-activation or termination after the suspension will be at our sole discretion.

6. **Security.** The parties expressly recognize that it is impossible to maintain flawless security, therefore the customer is solely responsible for properly securing their hosting service provided by HostUS including changing initial passwords and making any security adjustments and patches over time. Customer is solely responsible for any damage caused by such unauthorized

Figure 2-3. A portion of the Terms of Service document from a hosting provider

Terms of Service documents, or Terms and Conditions, can be very long and complex, but they are something you will want to review. In the example Terms in Figure 2-3, the following sections are discussed:

- Where legal disputes with the document can be challenged in a court of law.

- The liability of the company – which includes language in all capital letters that reminds the user that the company is not responsible for any of their data or for any lost revenue from their systems being down or corrupted. In other words, if they lose everything you hold near and dear on your VPS, there's nothing you can legally do about it.

- A reminder that unless you're paying for it, they are not backing up your data and are not responsible for any data loss.

- A notice that they may have to take down your server for maintenance purposes.

- A discussion of the amount of bandwidth and network connectivity you can expect to have, including a warning that you cannot exceed 100% of your allotted bandwidth quota or else you will be suspended or have your account terminated.

- A reminder that while the company does it's best to keep everything safe and secure, nothing is guaranteed and that if the company is "hacked," the customer cannot hold them liable.

- Policies on billing and billing disputes.

- Policies on how data migration is handled, if they offer any such migration service.

- Policies regarding copyright infringement, boiling down to "If you host copyrighted material (e.g., pirated movies) and someone tells us that you are doing it, you have to take it down within 48 hours."

- Policies on the hosting of pornographic material. Some providers have a blanket "no pornography" policy, while others are OK with legal pornography.

- Suspension and termination of service policies.

- Licenses that you can purchase for other software through the company.

- A list of services that are not allowed on their network – typically including anything with intense traffic needs or nefarious purposes (e.g., phishing websites).

- How the company communicates with the client.

- How the company safeguards the privacy of the client.

- And finally any other specific guidelines or regulations that the company would like to enforce.

It can take several minutes to read over a Terms of Service; however, it is an absolute essential – not only does it remind you of your responsibilities, it also lets you know what you can hold the company accountable to. For example, in one of the Terms of Service that I reviewed, it noted that you had a set amount of time to answer an issue that the company raised with you – if the company were to have immediately terminated your account before you had time to address the complaint, you would have legal standing to challenge them in court for not following their own guidelines.

A Terms of Service tends to be fairly one-sided; it protects the company from things clients might do. You'll want to review it carefully, enlarging the font size if necessary and looking for ways in which you might lose data or access. The best advice is to never have all of your eggs in one basket, so to speak. Store backups at a different physical site and with a different company, if possible, in case your access were to be removed during a dispute. And look for ways in which you can hold the company accountable, primarily through another document that exists – a Service Level Agreement.

Service Level Agreements (SLAs)

A Service Level Agreement is a legal contract, like a Terms of Service, that specifies the services that your VPS provider is offering to you and the level at which they assure you they will be providing them. In other words, it's a promise that they make to you that your website or service will be "up" or available.

Not all providers offer Service Level Agreements, and so if you do not see mention of one, you likely do not have this protection. Common SLAs may focus on the "five 9s," which means they ensure a 99.999% uptime. This equates to a little over 5 minutes per year of downtime. If you have an SLA guaranteeing 99.999% uptime and you have 6 minutes of downtime over a calendar year, you may be entitled to a refund, credit, or other form of compensation. If you do find an SLA that is less than 99.999%, it's not necessarily bad – but it does mean that they understand that their service might have periods of downtime that they can't account for over 5 minutes per year. A small provider who is trying to keep things agile may not offer any SLA because they know their maintenance windows would eat up 10–20 minutes per week. That's around 1,040 minutes per year, which would result in an uptime of 99.981%.

At the end of the search process for your VPS provider, if you can find a group that is willing to offer an SLA, at a reasonable price, I would argue it's appropriate to perhaps prioritize that provider over others on your list. But be warned – it might be hard to find a company willing to offer a robust SLA unless you are willing to either pay a premium or lock into a contract for a certain length of time with them. This might limit your ability to move to a better option should one become available.

Speaking of things to watch out for, what are some warning signs that one might want to be aware of when coming into the world of choosing a VPS provider?

Warning Signs

Often we think of the world as full of red flags, but if you're color-blind, you might not know which things raise alert. Over the past 20 years, I've developed a series of things that I've started watching for – here are my tips:

- While it's not necessarily bad to have a company that has just started up as your VPS provider (after all, they're likely running great deals), they are potentially inexperienced. Additionally, companies do sometimes change names in order to avoid the trail of bad PR that follows them related to their past indiscretions. If you see a company with almost too-good-to-be-true rates, either those rates are too good to be true (see the next tip) OR they're really trying to aggressively get themselves new clients. This isn't necessarily bad, but it is something to be aware of.

- The old maxim that you get what you pay for is alive and well in VPS hosting. Between 2012 and 2016, because I was comfortable moving my personal servers from place to place, I was on several different VPS providers. Some were at higher price points, and I did tend to notice that while the basic service stayed the same, their client interfaces tended to be a bit more intuitive, their support documents were more likely to be up to date, and their response times to support tickets were faster. A bargain is great when things are going well, but it can be frustrating when issues come up.

- On the other hand, larger companies can be more "bloated" than they are worth. Many accounts I have that are with companies large enough to be well known, but not large enough that everyone inside or outside of technology knows them (e.g., GoDaddy – a company that you may have heard of, unlike Microsoft, a company you definitely have heard of), can be frustrating to use because of the ever-present upselling they use. When I log in to start or stop my VPS, I do not want to have a hundred advertisements pop up trying to get me to add premium services. It's also debatable if these premium services actually add value or if they simply are a way to generate more revenue.

- Generally as you're hosting your data on someone else's computer, it is possible that if they really wanted to, they could access it (just like a mall owner could use their master key to get into an individual store after hours). However, if you find a company that forbids you from encrypting your data or setting your own passwords, that would be a big red flag. After all, the mall owner might be allowed into the bank branch after hours, but they aren't allowed into the safe!

- If a company only takes payment through methods that are untraceable or hard to trace or don't allow any protection to the payer (e.g., cryptocurrency, wire transfer), that may be a red flag unless the company builds its reputation on being "untraceable" and "anonymous." Very few companies do.

If in doubt about a company's ability to offer the services they claim to offer, always do your homework on the Internet – checking review website and asking people in web hosting or developer support forums about their experiences with a given company. Most companies also have presences on social media – if they do, engage with them before you buy. Ask the questions you have, and while the answers may help, the little details (e.g., how prompt the answer is, how well written it is) may tell you more than the content.

Assuming that you've got your potential provider picked out, let's talk briefly about the resources that you'll want to have ready at the start of your journey and then some tips on good account setup practices. Finally, you'll need to think about how to configure your first virtual machine – picking a name and a Linux distribution!

Resources and Budgeting

When it comes to getting ready to purchase a VPS, there are resources that you need to consider that are both financial and time based. These financial costs are sometimes very well determined, but they can be nebulous if you're using a cloud provider that bills by the minute or data amount used. Calculators, like the AWS one earlier, are useful in determining how much you might need. This is why it might be best to start out elsewhere – you can use your actual usage data from your first year or two on a high- or low-end provider (e.g., how much bandwidth you needed, how much disk space, etc.) to determine the values to plug into a calculator. A reasonable first year cost on a high-end provider might be around $300, after taxes and other fees. Additionally, you may want to purchase a domain name (e.g., something.com) that will allow you to connect to your server using a name and not the IP address number. This will typically cost about $10–20 per year, although most domain name providers will heavily discount your first year's price. In the following new account setup, we'll discuss how to map your name to your VPS.

Now let's address the bigger resource – time. You'll need to think about how quickly you want to get your VPS up and running and if you have the time to devote at that level. The following table outlines the basic steps that you'll take and how much time they're likely to take up for a beginner.

Step	Description	Time Estimate
Signing up for an account	Going to the provider's website, filling out a new user profile, selecting your plan, choosing a username and Linux distribution (see in the following), and completing payment information.	20 minutes.
Waiting for your account to be set up	Depending on the company's setup, this step could be nearly instantaneous, or it could take several hours. It all depends on the level of automation that the company has in the background. Plan for at least 2 hours, although 12 would not be unheard of. Generally beyond 12 hours would be excessive unless they've told you that it may take up to a day or beyond.	10 minutes to 12 hours.
Logging into your server and installing initial software	Logging into the server for the first time, installing the software you need, updating the operating system to the most recent version, and setting up access rules.	1–3 hours, with additional time if you're migrating data over.
Configuring software	Changing configuration settings, setting up firewall rules, setting up backup policies and procedures, securing the system in other ways (a.k.a. hardening).	3–6 hours.

(continued)

Step	Description	Time Estimate
Testing	Time allocated for issues that only become apparent after the server is live and people can access it. Most issues should appear within a few weeks.	Allocate 10–20 hours for problem solving; check server daily for possible issues so you can catch them early.
Weekly maintenance	Ongoing weekly maintenance step (which we'll talk about later).	Allocate 30–60 minutes per week.

As you can see, the life cycle of a server startup and testing can take some time; therefore, it's a good idea if you are migrating from another location (e.g., a shared web host or a service such as WordPress, Medium, or Wix), you may want to keep your account with those companies active for at least 1 month in case you'd need to switch back temporarily while troubleshooting.

New Account Addressing, Domains, and Access

I mentioned earlier that you may wish to purchase a domain name from a domain registrar, such as Network Solutions, Register.com, or GoDaddy, in order to have a name to point to your numeric IP address. When you sign up for a new account, most providers will send you an email or display information similar to what is in Figure 2-4.

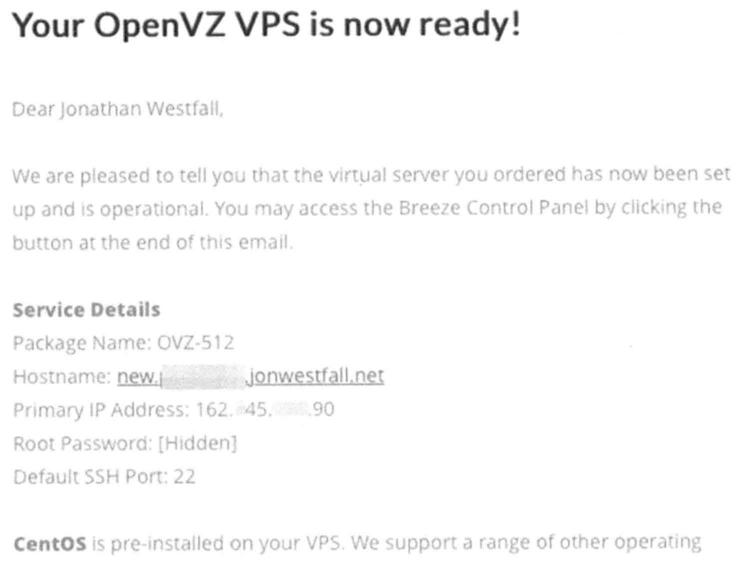

Your OpenVZ VPS is now ready!

Dear Jonathan Westfall,

We are pleased to tell you that the virtual server you ordered has now been set up and is operational. You may access the Breeze Control Panel by clicking the button at the end of this email.

Service Details
Package Name: OVZ-512
Hostname: new.| .jonwestfall.net
Primary IP Address: 162. 45.   .90
Root Password: [Hidden]
Default SSH Port: 22

CentOS is pre-installed on your VPS. We support a range of other operating

Figure 2-4. New VPS setup email

In this email, you'll notice that it lists the name that I gave the VPS when I bought it (I've partially obscured this; however, it starts with new and ends with jonwestfall.net, one of my domains), and it also lists the server's primary IP address.

It may be tempting to think that you can immediately connect to the server using the new name, but before I can do that, I actually have to connect the name to the address that was in the email. To do this, I need to create a Domain Name Service (DNS) A record. A records translate names, like new. xxx.jonwestfall.net, to IP addresses, like 162.x45.xxx.90. To add those, I need to log into the account I purchased the domain name through, in my case at GoDaddy.com, and access their DNS tools. Each provider is different – on mine, I choose a "Manage Domains" option, then find the domain I'm adding a name to (jonwestfall.net), and choose the Manage DNS option (see Figure 2-5).

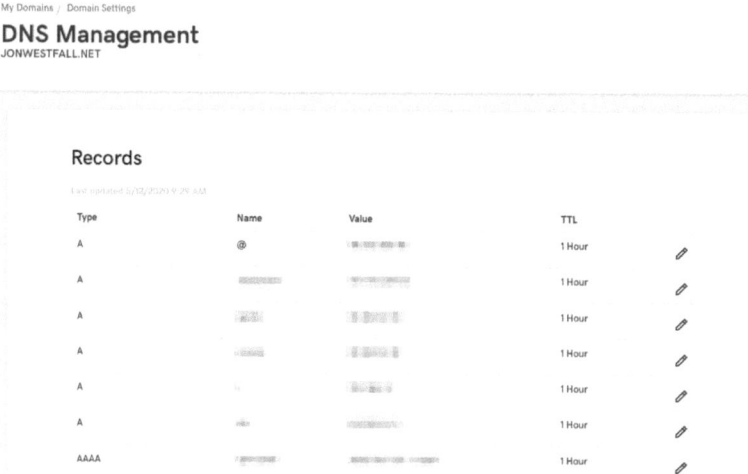

Figure 2-5. DNS settings for jonwestfall.net

From this screen, I can choose an "Add New" option and add in the DNS record I need to connect my domain name with my new VPS. See Figure 2-6.

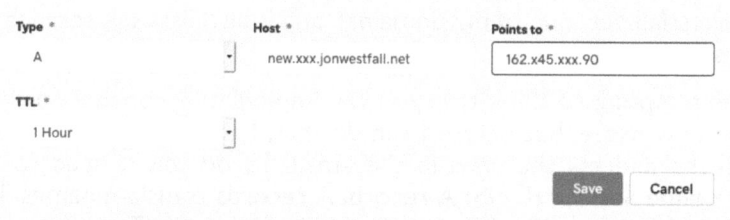

Figure 2-6. The Add New DNS option

You'll notice an option for "TTL." This stands for "Time To Live." It's a marker for computers (and humans alike) to determine how long you should trust this value before checking again to see if it's changed. DNS records propagate around the Internet, with each server that grabs them usually caching (or keeping) them for a certain period of time to speed up future queries. The TTL lets those servers know how often they should check with the authoritative name server to see if the value has changed. This is why it can sometimes take 2–4 hours for a DNS change to fully propagate around the Internet, as servers typically respect the TTL but some may not be fully compliant. This means that for you, the first time you access your VPS, you may need to use the IP address to direct to it, since the name might not be fully set up. Let's talk about accessing your server!

Access and Security

So you've just bought a shiny new VPS and you want to "play" with it. Sadly, there isn't much to see. But before you can even see the little there is, you need to know how to access it.

Typically servers are set up to be accessed through the Secure Shell (SSH) protocol. SSH allows you to authenticate with the VPS and then will drop you to a command prompt that allows you to start working with it.

The simplest way to use SSH is through a username and password, and the default username of the administrative user on a Linux machine is root. But it's not likely that your VPS will be fine with you logging in directly as root in some cases. This is because it's very easy for those with ill intentions to just randomly sweep servers across the Internet and try to log in as root. In fact, as I was writing this, I accessed one of my servers, named alexandria, and used a command to scan the last 50 entries in the authentication log. Figure 2-7 shows that in the last minute, at least eight bots had tried to log in as the root user.

```
root@alexandria:/var/log# tail –n 50 auth.log | grep "Failed password for root"
Sep 10 14:40:01 alexandria sshd[2295]: Failed password for root from 198.245.49.37 port 35044 ssh2
Sep 10 14:40:02 alexandria sshd[2297]: Failed password for root from 134.209.7.179 port 50310 ssh2
Sep 10 14:40:10 alexandria sshd[2302]: Failed password for root from 218.92.0.190 port 19691 ssh2
Sep 10 14:40:11 alexandria sshd[2300]: Failed password for root from 217.182.70.150 port 47712 ssh2
Sep 10 14:40:12 alexandria sshd[2302]: Failed password for root from 218.92.0.190 port 19691 ssh2
Sep 10 14:40:14 alexandria sshd[2302]: Failed password for root from 218.92.0.190 port 19691 ssh2
Sep 10 14:40:33 alexandria sshd[2311]: Failed password for root from 200.69.234.168 port 56940 ssh2
Sep 10 14:40:34 alexandria_sshd[2309]: Failed password for root from 149.56.100.237 port 50980 ssh2
```

Figure 2-7. Authentication log results from the last minute

Unfortunately for the bots, but fortunate for me, not only is my root password ungodly long for this server (thus not likely to be guessed), it's also not possible to log in via SSH as root – one must log in as another user first.

When you first set up your VPS, your VPS provider will let you know how to connect via SSH. Some of them will give you a root password and have your VPS configured to allow root to log in directly. This isn't very secure, so you'll want to change that later – something we can talk about in Chapter 5. Some will set up another user for you, give you that information in order to log in, and then have you switch to the Linux root user for administrative commands using either the su or sudo command (again, we'll cover those in Chapters 3–5). Finally, some of them may provide you with a private keyfile. These keyfiles are long cryptographic strings that rely on something called public/private key cryptography. On the server, a matching "public" key is preloaded, and when you connect with your "private" key, it is matched to the unique signature of both files. It then knows that you are who you claim to be and lets you in.

It is *very* important to note that most providers that use a private key as the initial way to get into your server *only allow you to download it one time* – typically on the page that you set up the server on. Therefore, if you are prompted to download a file with a .ppk or .key extension, download it and keep it safe. It's your key into the server!

Now that we've talked about how to get in, let's talk about the software needed. If you're running macOS or Linux, you already have the software you need – the SSH client. You can open a terminal window and connect using a string such as this, replacing "IPAddress" with the IP address provided to you:

```
ssh root@IPAddress
```

If you are required to use a different username, you'd replace `root` with that username. And if you're required to use a private keyfile, you'd add the `-i` switch to the command (see the following example) and point it toward the private keyfile on your computer. Assuming I store my private key as /Users/jon/Downloads (not a great place, but probably where it went when I downloaded it from the website), my command might look like this:

```
ssh -i /Users/jon/Downloads/privatekey.ppk root@IPAddress
```

If you are on a Windows machine, you will need to download an SSH client. The most popular client is the freely available PuTTY, which you can download at `www.putty.org`. You'll enter the same information as you did earlier, in the PuTTY client window (see Figure 2-8).

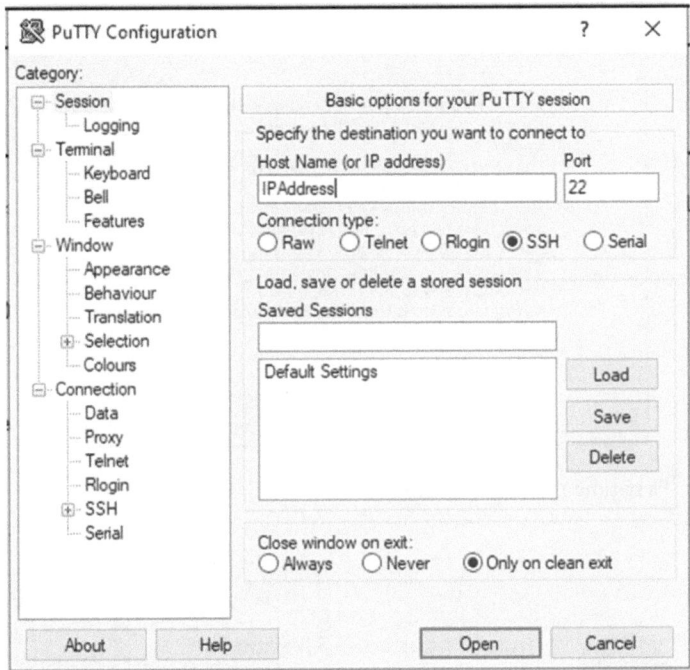

Figure 2-8. PuTTY configuration window

Regardless of your operating system, the first time you connect to a new server over SSH, you will receive a message similar to the one in Figure 2-9. Part of the SSH protocol is a built-in check to make sure that you are not connecting to a server that is masquerading as the server you intend to connect to. Imagine that I'm a bad guy – I know you're connecting to goodguy. jonwestfall.net. If I wanted to, I could trick your computer into thinking that goodguy.jonwestfall.net lived somewhere else. (Remember those DNS records? I could mess with them on just your computer.) Then when you tried to connect to goodguy.jonwestfall.net, you'd actually be connecting to my computer, and that computer could steal your authentication information. To help prevent this, your computer stores a cryptographic hash of every SSH server you connect to, the first time you connect, in a file named known_ hosts. Once you say "Yes, this is the server I want," your computer writes the hash to that file. Then every time after that you go to connect, it compares the hash it gets to the one in known_hosts, and if you try to connect to one that has changed, you get an error message saying that the host isn't known yet (see Figure 2-10). This is a way to let you know that someone might be interfering with your regular work.

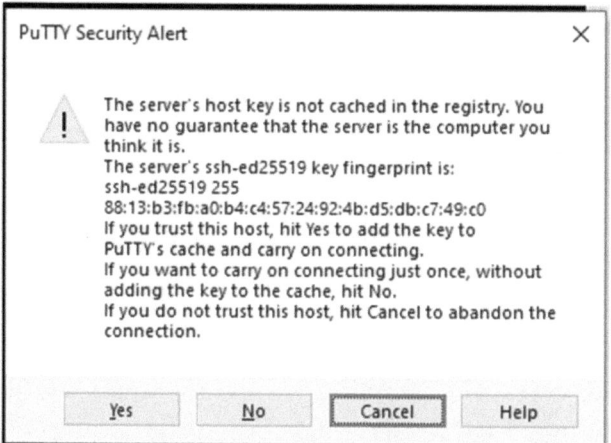

Figure 2-9. First-time connection dialog

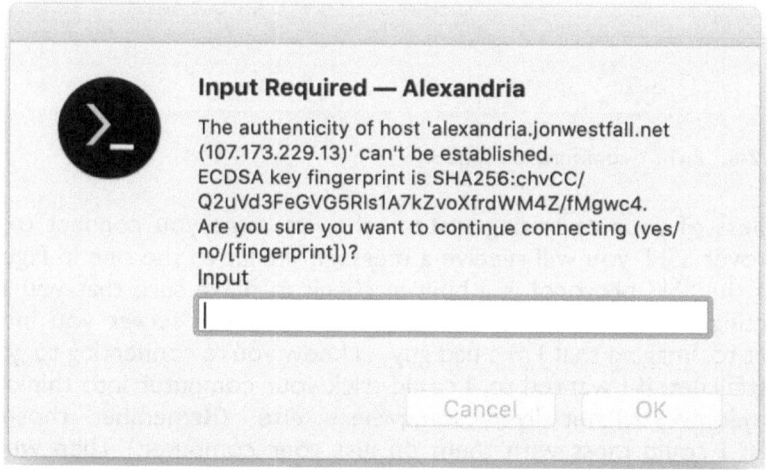

Figure 2-10. Cannot Verify Identity dialog

Now that you've got your authentication information squared away, you'll connect to your server and see something like Figure 2-11, a basic command-line interface (CLI). Congratulations – you've successfully connected!

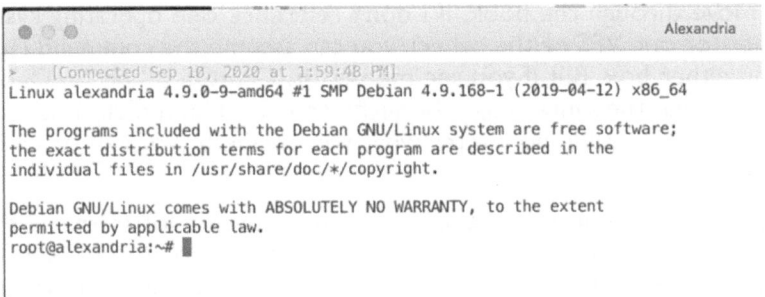

Figure 2-11. Successfully connected to a VPS

Choosing Your Linux Distribution: CentOS or Debian

One last thing we need to discuss in this chapter – and that is the "flavor" of Linux that you would like to run on your VPS.

Linux, while likely the most common operating system on the planet, is actually not just one operating system. The heart of Linux, the kernel, was developed in 1991 by Linus Torvalds, and the software we call Linux today is an open source collaboration. This means that anyone can take the Linux kernel and build up their own distribution of Linux around it. Two of the oldest and most well-known Linux distributions are Debian and Red Hat (both established in 1993), although one that you might know very well could be running on your own smartphone: Android!

Anyway, today in the VPS world, most companies offer you the choice of Linux distribution, and the two most common are the latest versions of Debian (as of this writing, 10.6) and CentOS (which is the free version of Red Hat Enterprise Linux; its name stands for Community Enterprise Operating System, and it's current version is 8.2.2004; you can always find the most up-to-date versions by visiting http://debian.org or http://centos.org and looking at the recent news items). While fundamentally the same operating system, with many of the exact same commands when working with files, there are subtle differences in Debian and CentOS that make people flock to one over the other. In this book, I'll be using two separate virtual machines to take screenshots of and discuss – **Lilo** (powered by Debian) and **Stitch** (powered by CentOS). (As a Disney fan, it was either Lilo and Stitch or Elsa and Anna. I assume if your children are young, you may not have quite as many PTSD flashbacks when I use the former vs. the latter; sometimes it can be hard to let it go!)

As we move through the book, if I don't reference one operating system or the other (or one VPS or the other), you can assume the command I give will work on either box. But if you see me say "In CentOS..." or "In Debian...," you'll know that the syntax might be slightly different. Hopefully this will make the book equally usable no matter what you decide to go with or what your provider offers you.

It's been a long trek in this chapter – we've covered a lot of things to think about as you contract and build out your VPS. In many ways, subsequent chapters will be much more technical and less "big thought" – but in order to be able to be technical in the future, we need to start with a good foundation! In the next chapter, we'll get comfortable with the command line and start customizing our server!

Basic Linux Administration via the Command Line

The Linux operating system was built to be an open source clone of a series of older operating systems, but primarily of Unix, a multiuser computer operating system that was built by AT&T during the 1970s. At that point in computer history, the desktop powerhouse that we have today was unknown – all computing took place on a central computer system that you would connect to using a "dumb" terminal, a keyboard and monitor that was connected to the central computer, either directly or through some form of early networking. You'd log in and issue commands, and they would be executed off in the distance – very similar to how you'll be using your VPS today!

© Jon Westfall 2021
J. Westfall, *Set Up and Manage Your Virtual Private Server*,
https://doi.org/10.1007/978-1-4842-6966-4_3

In this chapter, I'm going to walk through the very basics of Linux system administration through a command-line interface (CLI). In the next chapter, I'll address graphical interfaces that you might be able to use; however, it's much more advantageous to learn the CLI as the most efficient way to configure, troubleshoot, and administer your system will be through CLI commands. This is one area where computer veterans might have an advantage over younger users in that they may have grown up typing terminal commands. If you remember using DOS (Disk Operating System) in any form, then the mechanics of a CLI are familiar. The commands, however, likely are not. Whereas DOS uses commands that typically are the entire name of the function you'd like to use (e.g., copy), Linux tends to abbreviate these (cp), sometimes excessively so (e.g., du is the command for disk usage).

We'll start by reviewing the basics – getting into your VPS through SSH was mentioned in the last chapter, and we'll start assuming that you can see a command prompt (see Figures 3-1 and 3-2). I'll then talk about how you can move files onto or off of your server through SFTP. We'll then talk about setting up your own user account, the basic commands you'll use frequently, and how Linux uses different directories. Once we're comfortable talking about finding, opening, editing, and moving files around, we'll talk about how your VPS starts up and shuts down, important files you might want to be aware of, and finally how to install and update software. Let's jump in!

```
Debian GNU/Linux 10 lilo tty1

lilo login: jon
Password:
Last login: Wed Sep 23 11:18:35 EDT 2020 on tty1
Linux lilo 4.19.0-5-amd64 #1 SMP Debian 4.19.37-5 (2019-06-19) x86_64

The programs included with the Debian GNU/Linux system are free software;
the exact distribution terms for each program are described in the
individual files in /usr/share/doc/*/copyright.

Debian GNU/Linux comes with ABSOLUTELY NO WARRANTY, to the extent
permitted by applicable law.
jon@lilo:~$ _
```

Figure 3-1. *The command prompt, after logging into a Debian Linux machine as the jon user*

```
CentOS Linux 8 (Core)
Kernel 4.18.0-193.14.2.el8_2.x86_64 on an x86_64

Activate the web console with: systemctl enable --now cockpit.socket

stitch login: root
Password:
Last login: Tue Sep 22 17:46:37 on tty1
[root@stitch ~]# _
```

Figure 3-2. *The command prompt, after logging into a CentOS Linux machine as the root user*

Logging In and Uploading Files

At the end of the last chapter, we talked about how to log into your account via PuTTY (Windows) or on the built-in terminal in macOS. This has likely left you with a blinking command prompt, with the name of the administrative user (root) and the name of your VPS (either something you set or perhaps something that the hosting company provided – in my example, the computer's name is "lilo"). The command prompt, likely something like root@lilo:~$, may look intimidating. Before we can really explore though, I want to talk about moving files back and forth on and off your server, through a protocol called SFTP (secure file transfer protocol).

Originally most file transfers were done using FTP, or file transfer protocol. You ran a special piece of FTP server software and connected using an FTP client. Today, the preferred method is to use SFTP, which is built off of the same building blocks as the Secure Shell (SSH) protocol that you've just used to connect to your account, either via PuTTY or the command prompt.

To use SFTP, you need an SFTP client. In the Windows world, one of the most popular clients is WinSCP (https://winscp.net) which is free. On the macOS side, Cyberduck (https://cyberduck.io) is a good free option that also includes a Windows version.

To use the software, once you download and install, you'll need to start it and create a new connection using the same login information you have for your SSH connection, including the password or keyfile. Upon logging in, you're placed in your home directory or, if you're the root user, /root typically. From there you can upload files. SFTP clients usually are set up in two windows, one showing the files on your local computer and one showing the files on the remote computer. Dragging and dropping files from one to the other initiates the transfer. In Figure 3-3, which shows WinSCP running on a Windows 10 machine, I can easily move files by double-clicking them, and they will copy to the other location, from my computer to the VPS or from the VPS to my computer. Less frequently you may see a single window that shows the remote computer's files (Cyberduck uses this approach), and it's up to you to drag files either from that window to your computer (e.g., into Windows Explorer or Finder) or drag files from Finder or Windows Explorer into the Cyberduck window (see Figure 3-4).

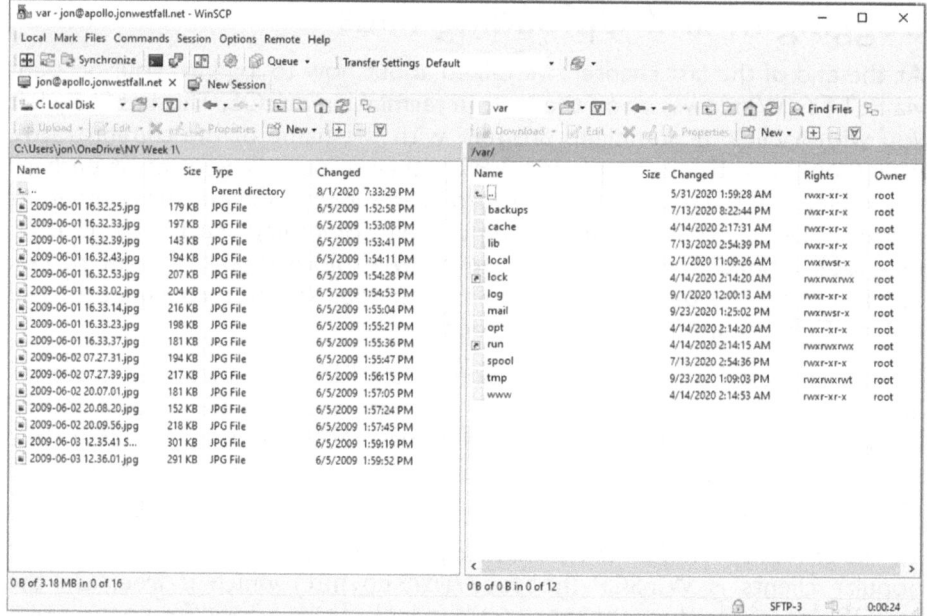

Figure 3-3. WinSCP, in the Commander interface, where I can move files by double-clicking them

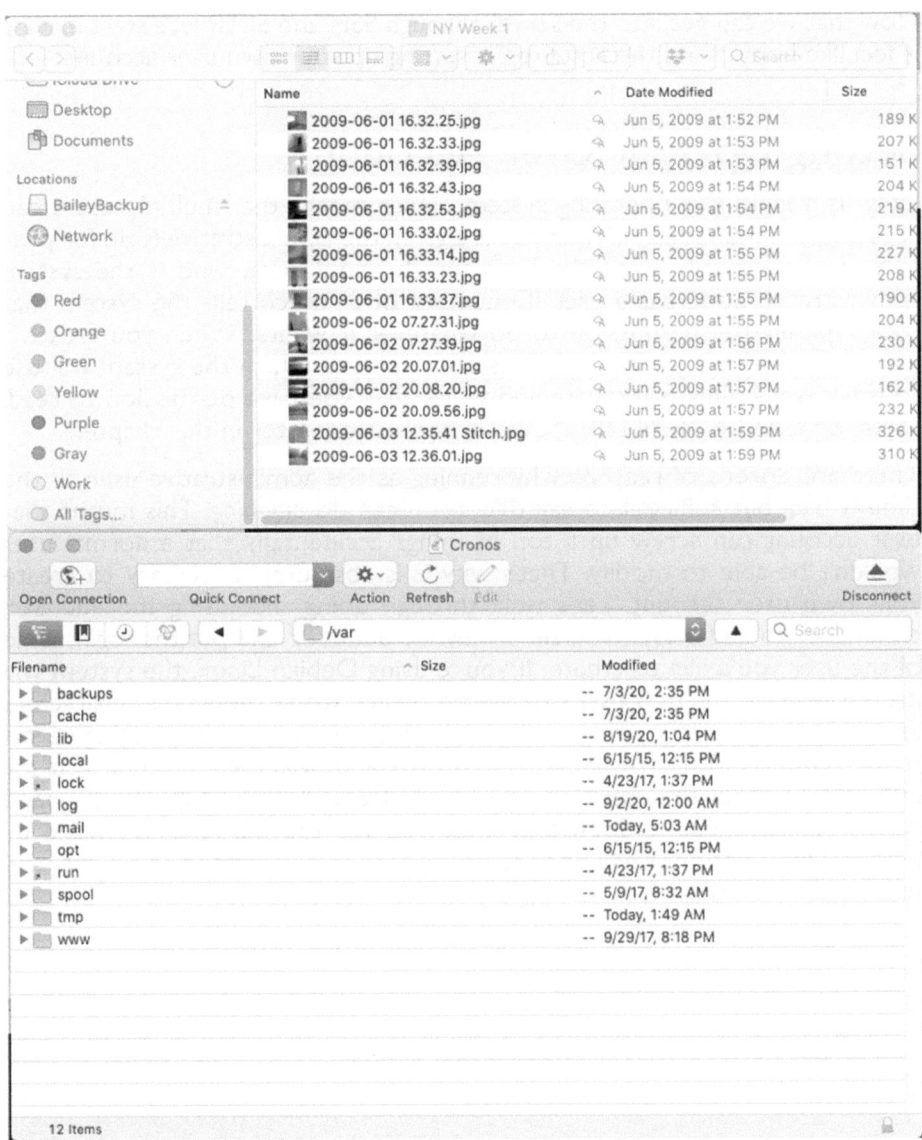

Figure 3-4. Cyberduck, where I can drag files from the Finder window at the top to the VPS at the bottom

When you're first starting out, it's likely you won't have any files you need to transfer to your VPS. However, if you're migrating files from one VPS to another, you'll likely compress all of your files on your old machine to an archive file and then copy it to your new machine, where you can decompress the files and move them to their new home. We'll talk more about file transfers throughout the book.

Now that we can get into the server through SSH and SFTP, let's start making it feel like home. And the first step is setting up your own user account.

Setting Up Your User Account

Linux is a multiuser operating system, which means that multiple users can access it, simultaneously. When you are given the administrative login for your VPS, you're typically given the login for the root user, who is the system administrator. root has a user ID number of 0, which tells the system that root typically has permission to do whatever it wants. When you create a new user, you'll be given a higher user ID number, which the system will use to track which files you create and which files you have permission to read, write, or execute. We'll talk about file permissions later in this chapter.

There are dozens of reasons why running as the administrative user all the time is bad, but suffice it to say that root can do *anything*. This means that user account can screw up a ton of things accidentally that a normal user wouldn't be able to modify. That's why it is absolutely necessary to create your own user account. Let's walk through doing that using the adduser command. To add a user, you simply invoke adduser and put the login name of the user you'd like to create. If you're using Debian Linux, the system will prompt you for the new user's password (which won't show up as characters as you type, as a security measure, so don't be alarmed when nothing seems to be input as you type in the password) and will then prompt you for information about the user (Figure 3-5). On CentOS, the adduser command works similarly, but it doesn't prompt you for the person's password or personal information. You'll need to use the passwd command to set the new user's password (Figure 3-6).

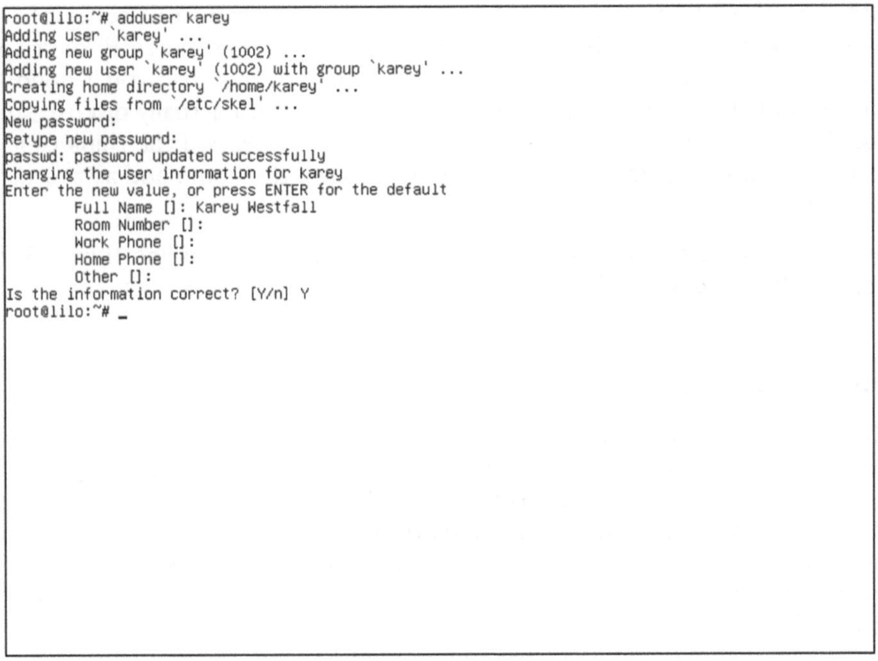

```
root@lilo:~# adduser karey
Adding user `karey' ...
Adding new group `karey' (1002) ...
Adding new user `karey' (1002) with group `karey' ...
Creating home directory `/home/karey' ...
Copying files from `/etc/skel' ...
New password:
Retype new password:
passwd: password updated successfully
Changing the user information for karey
Enter the new value, or press ENTER for the default
        Full Name []: Karey Westfall
        Room Number []:
        Work Phone []:
        Home Phone []:
        Other []:
Is the information correct? [Y/n] Y
root@lilo:~# _
```

Figure 3-5. adduser command on Debian Linux

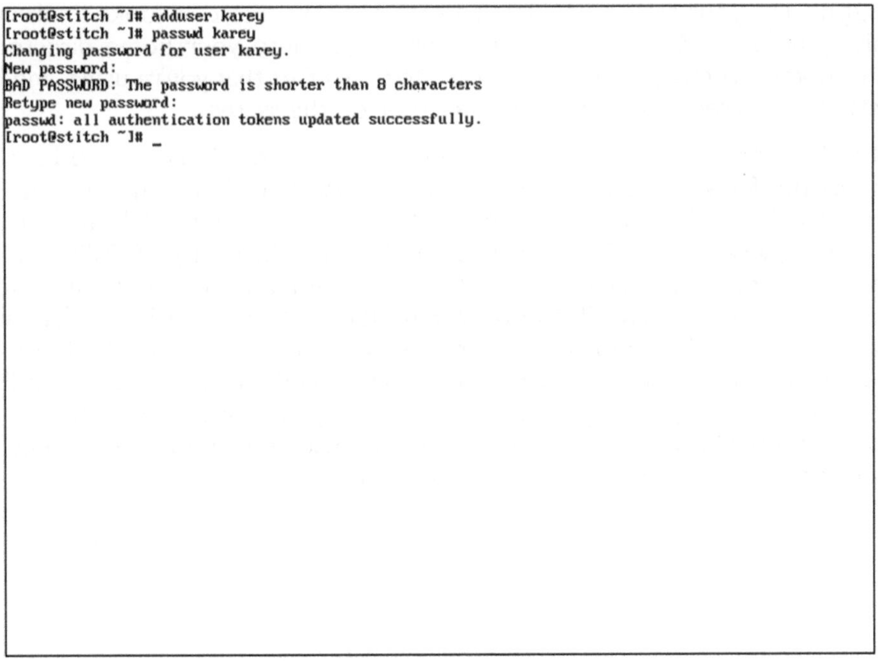

```
[root@stitch ~]# adduser karey
[root@stitch ~]# passwd karey
Changing password for user karey.
New password:
BAD PASSWORD: The password is shorter than 8 characters
Retype new password:
passwd: all authentication tokens updated successfully.
[root@stitch ~]# _
```

Figure 3-6. adduser command on CentOS Linux

Also, you should be aware that if you have decided to try out some of this material on a Linux machine that isn't a VPS (e.g., a Raspberry Pi or a Live Linux distribution), it may be configured in such a way that you'll need to append sudo before most of the commands I use. We'll actually discuss sudo later in this chapter and again in Chapter 5, but for now you can think of it as a special prefix that tells the computer to execute the command as the root user, instead of your usual user account.

Now that you're set up, let's get into this whole command-line thing. Don't worry. We'll take it slow!

Basic Commands

The Linux command line can seem intimidating at first; however, once you become familiar with it, you'll appreciate the speed with which you can easily navigate, configure, and perform maintenance on your VPS. In order to prevent that prompt from appearing quite so scary, in this section, I will walk through the directory structure of Linux; how to navigate around it; how files are found, secured, and edited; and finally how to check the overall health of your VPS.

The Directory Structure

Logging into your server, you'll find a command prompt that looks similar to this: jon@lilo:~$. By default, Linux drops you into your home directory. Your home directory is where you can store any files that you're using, and by default, they aren't visible to any other user on the system.

The Linux directory structure starts with / – the root directory. Notice the use of the forward slash (/) instead of the backslash (\) which you may be more familiar with if you're used to the Windows/DOS world. (Unsure which is which? Recall the advice of Phill Conrad at the University of California at Santa Barbara, who reminds us that if a stick person is leaning backward, their back is a backslash, and if they're leaning forward, their back is a forward slash!) The root directory contains several directories that we'll talk about, as well as the kernel image (usually named vmlinuz) and the initialization ramdisk image used during bootup (initrd.img). You may also find backup copies of both of these files with .old appended to their names. Generally you wouldn't store anything in /, preferring to keep it clean.

The following is a table of the directories that you'll find on a Linux system and what each holds:

Directory	Contents
/bin	The essential *binary* files that your computer needs in order to run and in order for you to navigate it. Most of the commands we'll talk about in this chapter, such as mv, ls, and others, are stored in this directory.
/boot	The files that your VPS uses when it boots up. Typically you won't need to modify these for any reason, unless you want to specify a certain bootup parameter or configuration.
/dev	In Unix-type operating systems, everything is represented by a file – even if it isn't really a file! In this case, the /dev directory has files that represent physical *devices* on your computer. For example, /dev/hda might be your hard drive. Additionally, there are special devices here such as /dev/random which can generate random numbers and /dev/null which discards whatever you send to it.
/etc	System-wide configuration files are stored here. Apparently in the early days of Bell Labs' Unix, configuration files didn't really have a home, so developers placed them in the *etcetera* folder, meant for miscellaneous files that didn't belong anywhere else. Today we use /etc exclusively for configuration.
/home	The *home* directories for each user are stored here in the format of /home/username. This is the only place, by default, that a regular user has permission to write files. All of the other directories we've discussed or will discuss can only be written to by the administrative user, root.
/lib	Libraries of code that can be used by multiple applications on the system live in this directory. This allows multiple files to use the same code, reducing file size.
/lost+found	If the worst things happen to your file system (e.g., power is removed at a crucial time before all of the files have been written), any corrupted or recovered file can be placed in lost+found on the next bootup. Hopefully, you won't have to go spelunking through here looking for something valuable!
/media	Removable media devices, such as CD-ROM drives or USB drives, are accessible under media. However, you can't usually directly access them; they'll need to be mounted first.
/mnt	This is the directory where both physical and removable file devices (hard disks, CD-ROMs, USB drives) are mounted. You might wonder why you can't just access these directly under /media. It's because the process of mounting a device allows the operating system to specify the type of files that it's accessing and also establish parameters to access them securely and reliably. You may decide that you only want to access a USB drive as read-only, for example, to avoid accidentally overwriting an important file on it. Typing mount at the CLI will show you all of the current devices mounted on your computer and their mount points.

(continued)

Directory	Contents
/opt·	Optional software packages are stored in this directory. Pretty much used when a software package doesn't follow the same directory rules as the rest of the operating system – here's a place where it can be self-contained and different!
/proc	Kernel and process files. Just like /dev, this directory doesn't actually contain files – it contains information about the system. You may occasionally read files from this directory to learn about your system, for example, cat /proc/uptime will print the amount of time the system has been up, in seconds.
/root	The home directory for the root user. Originally some distributions didn't have a dedicated home for the administrative user; however, over time, /root has been developed as a place for administrators to store files, especially perhaps source files of manually installed libraries and applications.
/run	A special directory that includes state and status files for running applications. It's a place that applications can use similar to temporary storage, but they don't have to worry about the system periodically deleting the files there.
/sbin	System administrative *binary* files are stored here – binary files that really are only useful to the administrative users of the server. The systemctl command that we'll talk about later in this chapter lives here, as well as the shutdown command.
/srv	A directory that stores information for the various services that the system runs – basically the information that you plan on using this server to share out to others. Sometimes people will store their website data under a directory such as /srv/www, or they may prefer to store it under /var.
/sys	A directory introduced by the Linux 2.4 kernel and above that is used by the kernel to store information, similar to the way /proc is used.
/tmp	The system temporary directory – files here can be wiped at any time by the system to free up space. However, if you're an application that needs to do a bunch of file operations (or a user who needs somewhere to store things that you're working on for a few seconds), this is the place to do it.
/usr	User binary files and software – a place that stores files and applications that are used by users of the system, rather than by the system itself. It's a very nebulous distinction, to the point that today many distributions simply link /bin to /usr/bin and /sbin to /usr/sbin to avoid confusion. We'll talk about linking files later in this chapter.
/var	Variable data files – /var is to /usr what /srv is to /bin in essence, a place for those software packages to store their data. However, as stated before, this is becoming less and less of a distinction over time. Today the most common uses for /var are for log files (under /var/log) and for web server files (under /var/www).

Now that you know where files are, let's talk about navigating around the file system.

cd, pwd, ls, cat, and less

Upon logging into your VPS, you'll notice a command prompt that includes your login name, the computer name, and the ~ character (similar to jon@lilo:~$). The ~ is a shorthand character by your shell (the software component that shows you the command prompt) to tell you that you are in your home directory, which by default is under the /home directory. If you change directories, you will see the prompt change to tell you the new directory that you're in. And how do you change directories? With the cd command. Here are a couple of cd examples:

- cd by itself will move you back to your home directory.

- cd Documents moves you into a directory below the current directory named Documents, assuming you have one. If you don't have a Documents directory, you can easily make one by using the command mkdir Documents.

- cd ~/Documents does the same thing; however, in this case, you included ~/ which uses the ~ symbol to tell the shell to insert your home directory, and /Documents gets tacked on. If your home directory is /home/jon like mine, your VPS takes this command and expands it automatically to cd /home/jon/Documents.

- cd /var/log would change you to the directory /var/log.

- cd .. moves you up one level in your directory, by using what's called a relative path. So if you are in /var/log and you type cd .., you are now in /var.

You may sometimes wonder "Where am I?" when navigating around the system. Thankfully there is a command that can help you – pwd, which stands for Print Working Directory. Issuing pwd will tell you the full path to the directory you're currently working in, from the root / directory (see Figure 3-7). We call these paths absolute paths, since they start from /, vs. relative paths, which start from ./ (the current directory you are in).

```
jon@lilo:~$ cd /var
jon@lilo:/var$ cd log
jon@lilo:/var/log$ pwd
/var/log
jon@lilo:/var/log$ _
```

Figure 3-7. The pwd command showing my current working directory

We'll talk a lot about relative and absolute paths when we get to the discussion of the rm command in the following. For now, be aware that you want to make sure you use the absolute path if you're doing something potentially dangerous, like deleting a lot of files.

Once you are in a directory, you might want to know what files are inside of it – thankfully the ls command is useful for that. Here are some examples:

- ls will show you a listing of all of the files in the directory. In this view, directories and files all look the same, although some distributions will color-code them based on the type of file or directory they are.

- ls -la will give you the long version of the listing and show all files. In Linux, files that start with a period (.) are normally hidden from view. This is typically done so that they don't get accidentally modified (see Figure 3-8).

- ls -lh gives you file sizes in "human-readable" format, which simply means it tells you the size in units you might be more comfortable with – kilobytes, megabytes, gigabytes, and terabytes, instead of just bytes!

```
jon@lilo:~$ ls -la /
total 72
drwxr-xr-x  19 root root  4096 Jul  9  2019 .
drwxr-xr-x  19 root root  4096 Jul  9  2019 ..
lrwxrwxrwx   1 root root     7 Jul  9  2019 bin -> usr/bin
drwxr-xr-x   4 root root  4096 Jul  9  2019 boot
drwx------   2 root root  4096 Jul  9  2019 .cache
drwxr-xr-x  17 root root  3180 Sep 23 11:39 dev
drwxr-xr-x 119 root root  4096 Sep 22 17:34 etc
drwxr-xr-x   6 root root  4096 Sep 22 17:34 home
lrwxrwxrwx   1 root root    30 Jul  9  2019 initrd.img -> boot/initrd.img-4.19.0-5-amd64
lrwxrwxrwx   1 root root    30 Jul  9  2019 initrd.img.old -> boot/initrd.img-4.19.0-5-amd64
lrwxrwxrwx   1 root root     7 Jul  9  2019 lib -> usr/lib
lrwxrwxrwx   1 root root     9 Jul  9  2019 lib32 -> usr/lib32
lrwxrwxrwx   1 root root     9 Jul  9  2019 lib64 -> usr/lib64
lrwxrwxrwx   1 root root    10 Jul  9  2019 libx32 -> usr/libx32
drwx------   2 root root 16384 Jul  9  2019 lost+found
drwxr-xr-x   3 root root  4096 Jul  9  2019 media
drwxr-xr-x   2 root root  4096 Jul  9  2019 mnt
drwxr-xr-x   2 root root  4096 Jul  9  2019 opt
dr-xr-xr-x  87 root root     0 Sep 22 11:14 proc
drwx------   4 root root  4096 Sep 17 10:41 root
drwxr-xr-x  22 root root   620 Sep 23 11:39 run
lrwxrwxrwx   1 root root     8 Jul  9  2019 sbin -> usr/sbin
drwxr-xr-x   2 root root  4096 Jul  9  2019 srv
dr-xr-xr-x  13 root root     0 Sep 23 10:18 sys
drwxrwxrwt  10 root root  4096 Sep 23 11:38 tmp
drwxr-xr-x  14 root root  4096 Jul  9  2019 usr
drwxr-xr-x  11 root root  4096 Jul  9  2019 var
lrwxrwxrwx   1 root root    27 Jul  9  2019 vmlinuz -> boot/vmlinuz-4.19.0-5-amd64
lrwxrwxrwx   1 root root    27 Jul  9  2019 vmlinuz.old -> boot/vmlinuz-4.19.0-5-amd64
jon@lilo:~$ _
```

Figure 3-8. The ls -la command on the root directory of a Debian Linux installation

This brings up an interesting feature of Linux – the ability to pipe information from one command straight to another, using the | character. You'll notice I didn't give you an example to sort your directory any way other than alphabetical (the default). By using the pipe, you can do this using the sort command, asking it to reverse sort the order. The command looks like this: ls | sort -r. As you can imagine, you can craft very elaborate commands by piping input from one to another to another. For example, under /var, there are four directories that start with the letter l – log, lock, local, and lib. What if I want to show only those four in reverse alphabetical order? I simply use a wildcard (*) character which Linux interprets as "anything else," with the command ls -rd l*.

Wildcards and pipes can be combined in hundreds of ways to produce powerful commands. We'll see some of those as we work through this chapter and others. Many Linux administrators compile a list of their "favorite" go-to commands for common procedures, which enable them to do complex operations without a lot of pointing and clicking that one might do on a Windows or macOS machine.

Finally, our last goal in this section is to actually read a file. Let's use the list of users on our machine, stored in /etc/passwd, as an example. Who else has a user account other than me on my machine? I can find out by using the cat command, which stands for concatenate. Using the command cat/etc/passwd, my screen quickly fills up with many lines – each one identifying a separate user account. Most of these accounts are used for different services or software running or installed on my VPS. My user account is listed at the very bottom.

You might have so many user accounts on your computer that they don't all fit on one screen. By default, Linux will display the entire contents of a file, even if they fill up multiple pages. However, thanks to the less command and the pipe feature we saw earlier, we can break it up into just the amount that fits on one screen at a time. cat /etc/passwd | less will show you one screen full of the user list, and you can then use the space bar to advance to the next screen or the arrow keys to go up or down in the list. Press q when you're ready to get back to the command line (if you're curious why the command is named less, it's because it's an upgraded version of a program called more which had fewer features – less is more plus more is, in this case, a true statement!).

Now that we've moved around a bit, let's talk about basic file operations using the move and copy commands.

touch, mv, and cp

Before we can get into moving and copying files, we first need a few files to work with. I'm going to create three new files using the touch command. touch technically is used to change file timestamps; however, if the file doesn't exist, it will create it for us. The command I'll issue is touch file1 file2 file3. It creates three new files, named file1, file2, and file3, respectively.

Now that I have my files, I can demonstrate the mv and cp commands. Here are a few exercises:

- mv file1 ./Documents moves file1 from the current directory to a directory below this one (using the relative path) called Documents.

- mv file1 ~/Documents moves file1 from the current directory to the Documents directory below my home directory, since I used the tilde (~). (Note, if you execute this command after the first, it will fail because you already moved the file! You can either recreate the file using touch again and then move it again (in which case it will overwrite the first file) or simply skip executing these sequentially!)

- mv file2 file4 will move file2 to file4 – although we typically think of this as renaming!

- cp file3 file3.copy will make a copy of file3 called file3.copy.

This brings up an interesting difference between Windows and DOS and Linux, namely, file extensions and file naming. You may be familiar with common file extensions on a Windows computer, such as .exe for an executable file or .txt for a text file. On Linux, files can be named however you like, with the extension not affecting how the operating system treats them. It's not uncommon for people to use periods in file names, especially if they're variants of an original file. For example, if you have a configuration file named mysettings, you may want to create a backup before editing it, by using the command cp mysettings mysettings.bak. You can then edit mysettings and know if you screw something up, you can always just delete it and rename the backup using the move command: mv mysettings.bak mysettings.

Speaking of deleting things, how does one do that? Well, you do it with what is likely the most dangerous command on the system: rm.

rm, the Most Dangerous Command

Strictly speaking, there is nothing inherently bad about the remove command (rm), but it gets a negative reputation for what it is capable of doing. Technically, all rm does is unlink files from the file listing, leaving the data "abandoned" on the storage medium until something needs that space and overwrites it. Here are a few examples of how to use rm responsibly:

- rm /home/jon/file1 would delete the file1 that I created in the preceding section.

- rm ~/file1 does the same thing, using the shorthand notation for my home directory.

- rm ./file4 deletes file4 from the current working directory, which I can find out the path of if I do a pwd command.

- rm -r mydirectory deletes the directory named mydirectory.

Now let's talk about some of the more...risky...options that rm offers. The first is one you saw in the last example, the -r switch or command argument. This stands for recursive, and it tells rm to descend down into the path below the directory. This is useful if you are deleting a directory with a lot of subdirectories under it. However, if you aren't quite sure what's below a directory, you might be better off substituting rm for ls — it simply lists all of the files. That way you can see what you're going to delete, before you nuke it all.

Another danger of the rm command is the -f switch, which stands for force. It removes all safety prompts on a remove operation. So imagine what happens if you issue this command: rm -rf /.

Absolutely nothing good! It will happily, assuming you have the permissions, go through and delete your entire system. If this sounds like a hypothetical horror, know that it happens more than you think. After all, say I have a whole directory of files that I need to remove. If I'm in that directory, the command to clean out the entire directory would be rm -rf ./ — notice the only difference is the period (.) indicating a relative and not absolute path. For this reason, and many others, it's never a good idea to run as the root user, as a screwup of a relative vs. absolute path as root could mean an unusable system.

find, or How to Find a File, and How to Consult a Manual Page

One of the common issues new system administrators have with Linux is finding files that they need to modify. You might remember part of the name, but perhaps not where the file was located. Using wildcard characters (*) can be useful in combination with the ls command (e.g., "I know the file started with r and was in this directory... I'll run ls r* and see what comes up"), but isn't always enough. Adding in the fact that Linux is case-sensitive (e.g., readme is a different file than Readme and README), you could have a rough time remembering the exact name and location of a given file.

Thankfully, Linux has a variety of commands that can help you, with the most basic being find. find asks you to specify where to look and then what to look for. For example, if I want to search the current directory for files that have "file" in the name, I can issue the following command, showing the output in Figure 3-9:

```
find ./ -name "*file*"
```

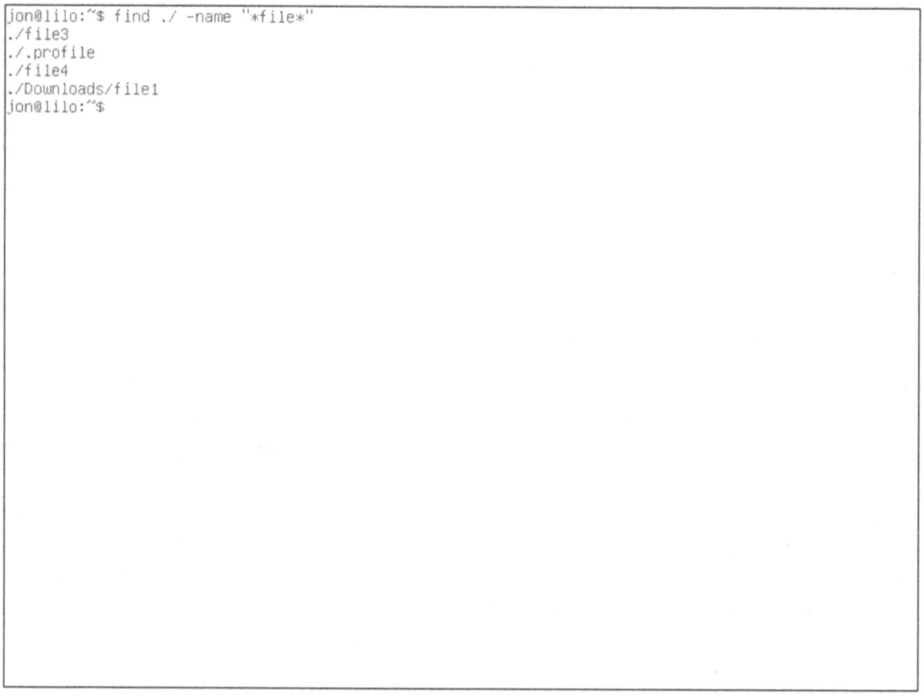

```
jon@lilo:~$ find ./ -name "*file*"
./file3
./.profile
./file4
./Downloads/file1
jon@lilo:~$
```

Figure 3-9. The output of the find command

As you can see in Figure 3-9, this not only finds files in the current directory, it also searches directories below and finds hidden files, such as .profile. The -name switch is not the only switch available to you. You can also search for just files or directories (using -type f or -type d, respectively), and you can look for files that were changed or created within a certain period of time (using -mtime or -ctime, respectively). With all of the options available to you, you may wonder how you can know all of the possible ways to use the find command. Well, thankfully Linux includes a user manual! Typing man find will launch the manual page for the find command (you can man any command to get the manual page for it). As seen in Figure 3-10, the manual page tells you what find does and what options you can use with it. Manual pages tend to be very long and detailed, and the entry for find is no exception. I'd encourage you to skip down to the Examples section (see Figure 3-11) when reading a manual page for the first time – it generally shows a number of examples that you might actually use, and you can easily see how you might modify them for your needs. For example, in the Examples section, you are given the command find $HOME -mtime 0 to find files in your home directory that have been modified in the last 24 hours (1 day). It's easy to think about how looking for a file modified within the last week would just require changing the argument for -mtime from 0 to 7.

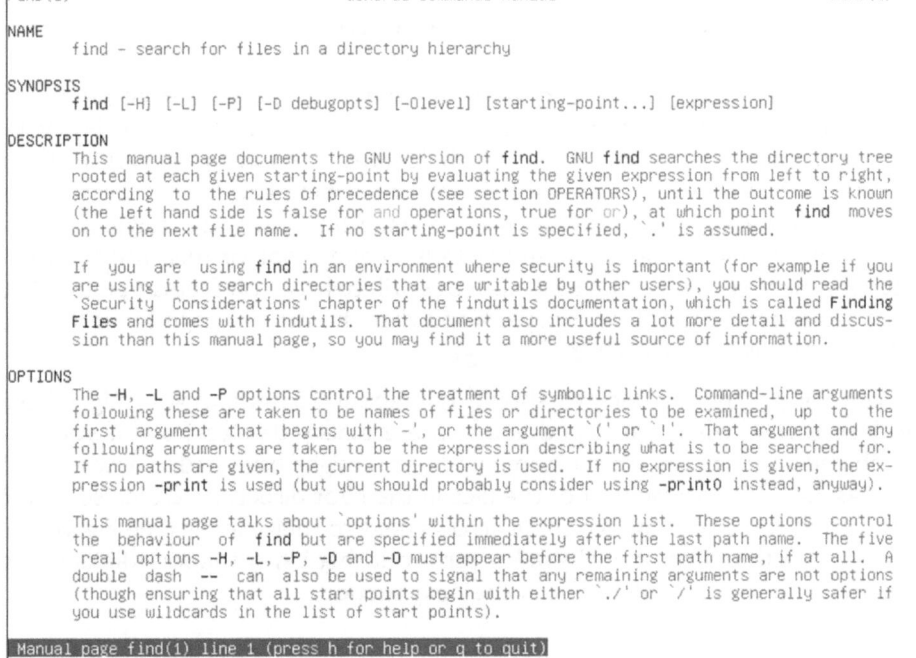

```
FIND(1)                        General Commands Manual                        FIND(1)

NAME
       find - search for files in a directory hierarchy

SYNOPSIS
       find [-H] [-L] [-P] [-D debugopts] [-Olevel] [starting-point...] [expression]

DESCRIPTION
       This  manual page documents the GNU version of find.  GNU find searches the directory tree
       rooted at each given starting-point by evaluating the given expression from left to right,
       according  to  the rules of precedence (see section OPERATORS), until the outcome is known
       (the left hand side is false for and operations, true for or), at which point  find  moves
       on to the next file name.  If no starting-point is specified, `.' is assumed.

       If  you  are  using find in an environment where security is important (for example if you
       are using it to search directories that are writable by other users), you should read  the
       `Security  Considerations' chapter of the findutils documentation, which is called Finding
       Files and comes with findutils.  That document also includes a lot more detail and discus-
       sion than this manual page, so you may find it a more useful source of information.

OPTIONS
       The -H, -L and -P options control the treatment of symbolic links.  Command-line arguments
       following these are taken to be names of files or directories to be examined,  up  to  the
       first  argument  that  begins with `-', or the argument `(' or `!'.  That argument and any
       following arguments are taken to be the expression describing what is to be searched  for.
       If  no paths are given, the current directory is used.  If no expression is given, the ex-
       pression -print is used (but you should probably consider using -print0 instead, anyway).

       This manual page talks about `options' within the expression list.  These options  control
       the  behaviour  of  find but are specified immediately after the last path name.  The five
       `real' options -H, -L, -P, -D and -O must appear before the first path name, if at all.  A
       double  dash  --  can  also be used to signal that any remaining arguments are not options
       (though ensuring that all start points begin with either `./' or `/' is generally safer if
       you use wildcards in the list of start points).

Manual page find(1) line 1 (press h for help or q to quit)
```

Figure 3-10. The beginning of the manual page for the find command

```
EXAMPLES
       find /tmp -name core -type f -print | xargs /bin/rm -f

       Find files named core in or below the directory /tmp and delete them.  Note that this will
       work incorrectly if there are any filenames containing newlines, single or double  quotes,
       or spaces.

       find /tmp -name core -type f -print0 | xargs -0 /bin/rm -f

       Find files named core in or below the directory /tmp and delete them, processing filenames
       in such a way that file or directory names containing single or double quotes,  spaces  or
       newlines  are  correctly  handled.  The -name test comes before the -type test in order to
       avoid having to call stat(2) on every file.

       find . -type f -exec file '{}' \;

       Runs `file' on every file in or below the current directory.  Notice that the  braces  are
       enclosed in single quote marks to protect them from interpretation as shell script punctu-
       ation.  The semicolon is similarly protected by the use  of  a  backslash,  though  single
       quotes could have been used in that case also.

       find / \( -perm -4000 -fprintf /root/suid.txt '%#m %u %p\n' \) , \
       \( -size +100M -fprintf /root/big.txt '%-10s %p\n' \)

       Traverse  the  filesystem  just  once,  listing  setuid  files  and  directories  into
       /root/suid.txt and large files into /root/big.txt.

       find $HOME -mtime 0

       Search for files in your home directory which have been modified in the  last  twenty-four
       hours.   This command works this way because the time since each file was last modified is
       divided by 24 hours and any remainder is discarded.  That means that to match -mtime 0,  a
       file will have to have a modification in the past which is less than 24 hours ago.

       find /sbin /usr/sbin -executable \! -readable -print
 Manual page find(1) line 1142 (press h for help or q to quit)
```

Figure 3-11. *The Examples section of the find manual page*

Returning to locating files, while the find command is the most common file searching command on a Linux machine, it isn't the only one. Another very common command is whereis, which locates the binary file for a given command. Recall that programs on a Linux machine can live in a variety of places – /usr/bin, /bin, /sbin, and so on. Sometimes you might need to know where a binary file is, and whereis is a handy tool for this. You can even get very meta with it – whereis whereis will tell you, on Debian Linux, that whereis lives at /usr/bin/whereis and that the manual page for it lives at /usr/share/man/man1/whereis.1.gz.

Before we go any further, we should talk about something you might have noticed earlier when we talked about these binary directories – if you had combined some of my earlier commands, you might have issued a command such as ls -la / to view all of the files in the root directory. Doing so, you'll notice that some of those files have arrows next to their names (See Figure 3-8 above). What's that all about? Well, it turns out that Linux supports linking files together, which we'll talk about in the next section.

Linked Files

If you've used a Windows computer, you may be familiar with the idea of a shortcut — an icon that you can place on your desktop or Start menu that, when clicked, launches a file that actually lives elsewhere. This way you can organize your files anyway you like and still have fast and easy access to them. In Linux, this is referred to as a link. For example, in Figure 3-8, the file vmlinuz is linked to /boot/vmlinuz-4.19.0-5-amd64. This is because this file will be updated every time a new kernel image is downloaded, and it makes it easier for the system to always know that the kernel is at /vmlinuz instead of having to keep track of the version number of the kernel that's stored under /boot.

There are two kinds of links on a Linux system, hard and soft. A hard link is a direct link to the underlying file that you are referencing. In technical speak, imagine having a house with two mailboxes out front, each with its own address. A soft or symbolic link is a special sort of file that has the address of the original file stored in it. Imagine having a house with one mailbox out front and then another mailbox across town that simply has the address of the house inside it, telling people who want to drop something off, "Go over to this other place." Symbolic or soft links are what we think of mostly when we're talking about shortcuts or links. Hard links aren't used very often and can also be a bit dangerous when it comes to file permissions, a topic we'll discuss in the following.

To create a link, you use the ln command, typically with the -s option to create a symbolic/soft link. You then specify the original file name and then the link's name. In my example, I've issued ln -s file3 thefile which links the physical file named file3 to my link, thefile (see Figure 3-12). Importantly, if I delete thefile using rm thefile, it just deletes the link — file3 remains.

```
jon@lilo:~$ ln -s file3 thefile
jon@lilo:~$ ls -la
total 80
drwxr-xr-x 15 jon   jon  4096 Sep 23 10:27 .
drwxr-xr-x  6 root  root 4096 Sep 22 17:34 ..
-rw-------  1 jon   jon    52 Sep 22 11:04 .bash_history
-rw-r--r--  1 jon   jon   220 Sep 17 10:42 .bash_logout
-rw-r--r--  1 jon   jon  3526 Sep 17 10:42 .bashrc
drwx------ 11 jon   jon  4096 Sep 17 15:40 .cache
drwx------ 10 jon   jon  4096 Sep 17 15:38 .config
drwxr-xr-x  2 jon   jon  4096 Sep 17 15:33 Desktop
drwxr-xr-x  2 jon   jon  4096 Sep 17 15:33 Documents
drwxr-xr-x  2 jon   jon  4096 Sep 22 17:45 Downloads
-rw-r--r--  1 jon   jon     0 Sep 22 11:36 file3
-rw-r--r--  1 jon   jon     0 Sep 22 11:36 file4
drwx------  3 jon   jon  4096 Sep 17 15:33 .gnupg
-rw-------  1 jon   jon   306 Sep 17 15:32 .ICEauthority
drwx------  3 jon   jon  4096 Sep 17 15:32 .local
drwxr-xr-x  2 jon   jon  4096 Sep 17 15:33 Music
drwxr-xr-x  2 jon   jon  4096 Sep 17 15:33 Pictures
-rw-r--r--  1 jon   jon   807 Sep 17 10:42 .profile
drwxr-xr-x  2 jon   jon  4096 Sep 17 15:33 Public
drwx------  2 jon   jon  4096 Sep 17 15:33 .ssh
drwxr-xr-x  2 jon   jon  4096 Sep 17 15:33 Templates
lrwxrwxrwx  1 jon   jon     5 Sep 23 10:27 thefile -> file3
drwxr-xr-x  2 jon   jon  4096 Sep 17 15:33 Videos
jon@lilo:~$
```

Figure 3-12. Linking file3 to thefile

Before we talk a bit more about Linux commands, we need to address an important aspect of how the Linux operating system works – file permissions. Not everyone can read, write, or execute any given command – they need to have permission to do so. Let's dig in.

File Permissions, su, and sudo

To explain file permissions, let's imagine your own home. You own it, and thus you should be able to go inside, change whatever you want, and run the appliances. Your family consists of yourself and your child, and while you like the idea of your child being able to go inside the house and perhaps run the appliances, you really don't want them changing things. And your next-door neighbor is kind of clumsy with appliances, so you'd rather prefer they just be able to come in the house, but not start the dishwasher or turn on the oven.

The Linux operating system would have you covered in this example. In Linux, files and directories have three permissions: read, write, and execute. They are also applied across three groups: the owner, the owner's group, and everybody else (other). Looking at Figure 3-12, when I issued the command ls -la file3, I was given permission information about file3, although it may take a moment to figure out how to read it. The string -rw-r--r-- can be broken down into three sets of permissions: owner, group, and other. It tells me that the owner has read and write access, the group members have read, and everyone else has read as well. I can change these permissions, as the owner, by using the chmod command, which can work in two different ways. chmod og+w file3 will give the write permission (+w) to the group (g) and the other (o). chmod +x file3 would give the execute permission to everyone, and chmod u-w file3 would take the write permission away from the owner (here abbreviated as u for user).

You'll also see chmod used with numbers, something similar to chmod 777 file3 which would give read, write, and execute to the owner, group, and everyone else. These numbers correspond to different values added together: read access is 4, write access is 2, and execute access is 1, and each number represents the user, group, and other in order. Here are the same examples I just gave earlier in this notation:

- chmod 666 file3 gives read and write permissions to the group and other (and makes sure the user still has them).

- chmod 111 file3 gives execute permissions to everyone and nothing else.

- chmod 467 file3 would give read-only to the user, write to the group, and everything to everyone else (which would be a very strange permission to use!).

By default, when you create a file, the system applies your umask, typically set to 0022, to subtract privileges from your other group members and everyone else. This lets everyone read your files, but not modify them. Additionally, when the execute privilege is given to a directory, it allows users to list the file contents of that directory. If it's removed, you'll get a permission denied error when you issue ls to see a list of files.

The next portion of the file permissions, as seen in Figure 3-12, is the listing of the user and group, in this case both named jon. By default, when you create a new user, a new group is also created with that user as the only group member. This is a security precaution and is not mandatory – you can create as many groups as you like on a Linux machine, and a user can be a member of multiple groups (which you can find out by issuing the groups command – e.g., groups root will show you what groups root is a member of). If you want to change the owner or the group, you'll use the chown or chgrp command.

You may wonder what would happen if you accidentally set your permissions wrong or how to change permissions on files you don't own. That's where you'd need to use the root user. root doesn't have to obey any file permissions and can read, write, and execute whatever it wants (by default, root does have to manually add the execute permission first though, for security reasons). How do you become root? You have three options:

1. Log out of your current account using the logout command and log in as root with the root password. (Remember that this also will likely disconnect you, meaning you'll have to reopen your terminal program (such as PuTTY) or reconnect using the ssh command.)

2. Use the switch user command (su). By default, issuing su will prompt you for the root password and will then let you act as root. However, you can also use the command to switch to another user by providing their username and password (e.g., su karey).

3. Use the sudo command, once installed. Sudo is a special piece of software that lets you give access to the power of the root user to regular users and is highly configurable. For example, you could set it up to allow certain user accounts to reboot or shut down the server, but not to be able to do anything else. You could also set it up to allow all members of a given group to execute root commands. The wheel group was traditionally used for this.

Out of these, #2 is the simplest and quickest. In the following example, I've navigated to the /var/log directory and tried to read the last few lines of the auth.log using the tail command. However, my user account (jon) doesn't have permission to do so, so I've switched to root, provided root's password, and then read the file and finally exited back to my normal user account. The commands I used are as follows, and you can see their output in Figure 3-13:

cd /var/log tail auth.log su tail auth.log exit

```
jon@lilo:~$ cd /var/log
jon@lilo:/var/log$ tail auth.log
tail: cannot open 'auth.log' for reading: Permission denied
jon@lilo:/var/log$ su
Password:
root@lilo:/var/log# tail auth.log
Sep 23 10:57:50 lilo su: (to root) jon on tty1
Sep 23 10:57:50 lilo su: pam_unix(su-1:session): session opened for user root by jon(uid=1001)
Sep 23 11:00:13 lilo su: pam_unix(su-1:session): session closed for user root
Sep 23 11:00:18 lilo su: pam_unix(su:auth): authentication failure; logname=jon uid=1001 euid=0 tty=
tty1 ruser=jon rhost=  user=root
Sep 23 11:00:21 lilo su: FAILED SU (to root) jon on tty1
Sep 23 11:00:25 lilo su: (to root) jon on tty1
Sep 23 11:00:25 lilo su: pam_unix(su:session): session opened for user root by jon(uid=1001)
Sep 23 11:00:58 lilo su: pam_unix(su:session): session closed for user root
Sep 23 11:02:15 lilo su: (to root) jon on tty1
Sep 23 11:02:15 lilo su: pam_unix(su:session): session opened for user root by jon(uid=1001)
root@lilo:/var/log# exit
exit
jon@lilo:/var/log$
```

Figure 3-13. Output of the commands that show the end of the auth.log

Always be sure to use the exit command to get back to your own user account immediately after you execute any command as root – this way you won't accidentally cause damage to your system. Finally, before we finish up this section on basic commands, let's talk about another common task: editing files!

Editing Files

Many files on a Linux system are compiled, which means they're in a binary format that you cannot modify. However, simple text files do exist, and many are used to control how the system operates. Nearly all versions of Linux support the vim editor, descended from the classic editor vi, and most now have nano installed by default. There are also many other editors that we can talk about. Let's first start by creating a file by directing the output of the echo command (which echoes whatever you write, typically to the screen) into a file named echoed. I'll do this with the command echo This is sample text in a file named echoed > echoed, with the > directing the output into a new file. Issuing the command cat echoed will show me the output – "This is sample text in a file named echoed." Now let's edit it.

Vim

Vim has a bit of a difficult editing process to get used to. To start, we issue vi echoed. This gives us a screen as seen in Figure 3-14, which at a glance doesn't seem to be working. Your arrow keys work, but you can't enter text. This is because by default Vim enters in as read-only. To get it into insert mode, you need to either press the insert key on your keyboard or in some cases the letter i. To exit Vim, you need to get into the command interface (by pressing Escape) and then issue the quit command (q) (perhaps adding a ! if you intend to exit without saving your file). To save changes before you quit, use the w command. You can chain these together as well; pressing :wq will write the file and quit.

Figure 3-14. Opening the echoed file in Vim

Vim is very basic and not very friendly, which is why most administrators prefer something with a few more features, such as nano.

Nano

Launching Nano is as easy as Vim – the command is simply nano echoed to open our echoed file. You'll notice from the start (see Figure 3-15) that it works a bit more like a modern editor. You can move around easily and enter text. The bottom rows give you commands that you can access using the Command key. Command+O will write the changes to the file, Command+X will exit, and you can even use rudimentary copy-and-paste features, as well as undo and redo using Option+U or Alt+U.

Figure 3-15. Opening the echoed file in Nano

This wraps up our section on basic commands. It's been a long one, but hopefully you've now gotten the hang of how to navigate the Linux command line. Remember that pretty much every command has a man page associated with it, and consulting these manual pages can give you reference quickly right on the VPS. A quick Internet search that ends with "linux command line" usually also can give you some quick pointers! Now we'll turn our attention to how our VPS boots up and how we install software onto it.

How Your Server Starts Up and Shuts Down

Virtual Private Servers are computers, and computers have a set series of steps they use when they start or stop, so that the user can have everything they need ready to go when they start using the system, the system can respond to events without the user's intervention, and data can be safely stored when the work is done. Both Debian and CentOS have a startup process, which varies slightly.

Bootup with Systemd

In both Debian and CentOS, the computer starts with some form of BIOS (Basic Input/Output System). This software is built into the computer's hardware, typically, and in a virtual machine it's emulated. The purpose of it is to make sure the hardware is functioning properly and then to load a piece of software called the boot loader. The boot loader starts the process of loading the kernel – or the base of the operating system. The kernel is responsible for governing how everything is processed and handled – in essence, it's the operating system's brain power. Various boot loaders exist, with GRUB being the most common, but there is typically just one kernel, the latest stable release for Linux.

The kernel is loaded over two different stages, an initial "mini-Debian" stage and then a final "normal" stage. The purpose of this is to provide some form of basic operating system if the "normal" stage doesn't fully load. Hopefully you'll never need to use it, but it's there just in case you need something to fall back to. Starting with Debian Jessie (version 9) and CentOS 7, the standard initialization program uses a service manager named systemd – systemd is responsible for starting all of the programs that need to run on startup on top of the kernel. Without systemd, you'd be left with a system that was technically running, but not running any of the software we use to communicate with the computer or ask it to perform work.

Systemd is responsible for starting

- Services, or software processes that are started and stopped automatically.

- Devices, typically used to communicate with hardware on a computer.

- Mounts, a file system that the kernel will read or write data to.

- Swap, a special device or file that the kernel will use to temporarily store data – think of this as the computer's scratch pad.

- Sockets, a special mechanism for the computer or network devices to connect to specific software on this computer.

- Timers, slices, and scopes, which are for specific purposes of device and computer management.

- Finally, Targets – which you can think of as a series of guidelines or rules for which preceding items need to be started, stopped, or managed depending on how the person is using the computer.

Think of "targets" as a usage scenario – for example, two of the targets available are graphical.target and multi-user.target. If your system is set to start with graphical.target, you'll get a nice full-color login screen with mouse support, similar to what you'd find on a Windows system. However, if you switch it to multi-user.target, you'll get a CLI with a simple login prompt. Most server computers are set to multi- user.target to reduce the memory usage that graphical.target requires and because the CLI will typically be faster. The command that allows you to modify startup or shutdown of the system is systemctl. Running the command systemctl get-default as root will tell you the default startup target. Using systemctl set-default multi-user would change a graphical system to a multiuser system, upon the next boot. It's also good to note that systemd is backward compatible with the older Linux System Process Initialization (SysV), which used runlevels.

Services

Now that we've talked about how your computer starts up, let's talk about the software that runs on it in the background, which we call services. Listing the currently loaded services, which are either running or have recently run, can be done with the systemctl list-units --type=service command. If you want to see services that are installed but not activated, you can use systemctl list-unit-files to show everything, activated or inactive.

As you can see, Lilo, my Debian box, has 40 services loaded after a normal bootup (see Figures 3-16 and 3-17). Some of these have very helpful descriptions, such as the NetworkManager.service which tells us that it is the network manager. Others are not as useful – cups.service, for example, just tells us that it's the "CUPS scheduler." Does my computer need to drink something? No, CUPS is an acronym for Common Unix Printing System, which was developed by Apple for macOS and Unix-compatible systems to communicate with physical printers. This begs the question – why does my

VPS that isn't anywhere near a physical printer need CUPS running? It doesn't, so we'll turn it off using the following commands (see Figure 3-18): `systemctl stop cups.service` and `systemctl disable cups.service`. Rebooting the system and running `systemctl list-units --type=service` once more, I can see that the cups.service apparently didn't listen to me – it's still running! What's going on here?

```
UNIT                                                          LOAD    ACTIVE SUB      DESCRIPTION
alsa-restore.service                                          loaded  active exited   Save/Restore Sound Card S
alsa-state.service                                            loaded  active running  Manage Sound Card State (
anacron.service                                               loaded  active running  Run anacron jobs
apparmor.service                                              loaded  active exited   Load AppArmor profiles
avahi-daemon.service                                          loaded  active running  Avahi mDNS/DNS-SD Stack
console-setup.service                                         loaded  active exited   Set console font and keym
cron.service                                                  loaded  active running  Regular background progra
cups-browsed.service                                          loaded  active running  Make remote CUPS printers
cups.service                                                  loaded  active running  CUPS Scheduler
dbus.service                                                  loaded  active running  D-Bus System Message Bus
getty@tty1.service                                            loaded  active running  Getty on tty1
ifupdown-pre.service                                          loaded  active exited   Helper to synchronize boo
keyboard-setup.service                                        loaded  active exited   Set the console keyboard
kmod-static-nodes.service                                     loaded  active exited   Create list of required s
ModemManager.service                                          loaded  active running  Modem Manager
networking.service                                            loaded  active exited   Raise network interfaces
NetworkManager.service                                        loaded  active running  Network Manager
polkit.service                                                loaded  active running  Authorization Manager
rsyslog.service                                               loaded  active running  System Logging Service
systemd-fsck@dev-disk-by\x2duuid-09f87b61\x2d8658\x2d487b\x2d8012\x2de5d0682ed814.service loaded act
systemd-fsck@dev-disk-by\x2duuid-abd6b7a5\x2dcdde\x2d4ba4\x2dbc7a\x2d301e8330c3be.service loaded act
systemd-journal-flush.service                                 loaded  active exited   Flush Journal to Persiste
systemd-journald.service                                      loaded  active running  Journal Service
systemd-logind.service                                        loaded  active running  Login Service
systemd-modules-load.service                                  loaded  active exited   Load Kernel Modules
systemd-random-seed.service                                   loaded  active exited   Load/Save Random Seed
systemd-remount-fs.service                                    loaded  active exited   Remount Root and Kernel F
systemd-sysctl.service                                        loaded  active exited   Apply Kernel Variables
systemd-sysusers.service                                      loaded  active exited   Create System Users
systemd-timesyncd.service                                     loaded  active running  Network Time Synchronizat
systemd-tmpfiles-setup-dev.service                            loaded  active exited   Create Static Device Node
systemd-tmpfiles-setup.service                                loaded  active exited   Create Volatile Files and
systemd-udev-trigger.service                                  loaded  active exited   udev Coldplug all Devices
systemd-udevd.service                                         loaded  active running  udev Kernel Device Manage
systemd-update-utmp.service                                   loaded  active exited   Update UTMP about System
lines 1-36
```

Figure 3-16. The first page of running services on my Debian Linux machine

```
ifupdown-pre.service                              loaded active exited  Helper to synchronize boo
keyboard-setup.service                            loaded active exited  Set the console keyboard
kmod-static-nodes.service                         loaded active exited  Create list of required s
ModemManager.service                              loaded active running Modem Manager
networking.service                                loaded active exited  Raise network interfaces
NetworkManager.service                            loaded active running Network Manager
polkit.service                                    loaded active running Authorization Manager
rsyslog.service                                   loaded active running System Logging Service
systemd-fsck@dev-disk-by\x2duuid-09f87b61\x2d8658\x2d487b\x2d8012\x2de5d0682ed814.service loaded act
systemd-fsck@dev-disk-by\x2duuid-abd6b7a5\x2dcdde\x2d4ba4\x2dbc7a\x2d301e8330c3be.service loaded act
systemd-journal-flush.service                     loaded active exited  Flush Journal to Persiste
systemd-journald.service                          loaded active running Journal Service
systemd-logind.service                            loaded active running Login Service
systemd-modules-load.service                      loaded active exited  Load Kernel Modules
systemd-random-seed.service                       loaded active exited  Load/Save Random Seed
systemd-remount-fs.service                        loaded active exited  Remount Root and Kernel F
systemd-sysctl.service                            loaded active exited  Apply Kernel Variables
systemd-sysusers.service                          loaded active exited  Create System Users
systemd-timesyncd.service                         loaded active running Network Time Synchronizat
systemd-tmpfiles-setup-dev.service                loaded active exited  Create Static Device Node
systemd-tmpfiles-setup.service                    loaded active exited  Create Volatile Files and
systemd-udev-trigger.service                      loaded active exited  udev Coldplug all Devices
systemd-udevd.service                             loaded active running udev Kernel Device Manage
systemd-update-utmp.service                       loaded active exited  Update UTMP about System
systemd-user-sessions.service                     loaded active exited  Permit User Sessions
unattended-upgrades.service                       loaded active running Unattended Upgrades Shutd
user-runtime-dir@1001.service                     loaded active exited  User Runtime Directory /r
user@1001.service                                 loaded active running User Manager for UID 1001
wpa_supplicant.service                            loaded active running WPA supplicant

LOAD   = Reflects whether the unit definition was properly loaded.
ACTIVE = The high-level unit activation state, i.e. generalization of SUB.
SUB    = The low-level unit activation state, values depend on unit type.

40 loaded units listed. Pass --all to see loaded but inactive units, too.
To show all installed unit files use 'systemctl list-unit-files'.
lines 13-48/48 (END)
```

Figure 3-17. The second page of running services

```
root@lilo:/home/jon# systemctl stop cups.service
root@lilo:/home/jon# systemctl disable cups.service
Synchronizing state of cups.service with SysV service script with /lib/systemd/systemd-sysv-install.
Executing: /lib/systemd/systemd-sysv-install disable cups
Removed /etc/systemd/system/multi-user.target.wants/cups.path.
Removed /etc/systemd/system/printer.target.wants/cups.service.
Removed /etc/systemd/system/sockets.target.wants/cups.socket.
root@lilo:/home/jon#
```

Figure 3-18. The commands used to disable the CUPS service

In this case, we're dealing with a stubborn service. Because services can depend on each other, it turns out that another service that is enabled is starting up CUPS, despite CUPS not automatically starting. We can figure out which system this is by using the command systemctl --reverse list-dependencies cups.service. It reveals that the cups- browsed.service is using CUPS, so when it starts, it starts up CUPS along with it. A simple systemctl disable cups-browsed.service will now stop that service from starting up, and in turn, CUPS won't be started. After a reboot, the CUPS services are no longer listed.

Technically, best practice would be for you to regularly audit your services to determine if you need everything that is starting each time the system loads. This means you'll likely need to search on the Internet for what certain services do, if it's not immediately apparent, and you'll also want to be very careful — because disabling the wrong service could lead to the system not booting. If you're really concerned about services, your best bet would be to download a Linux virtual machine onto your own PC, play around with services there, and make sure the system can still reboot properly, before you deploy your changes to your VPS.

Before we leave this section to discuss the merits of the graphical target vs. the multiuser CLI target, let's look at some quick `systemctl` commands that might be useful to you.

Command	What Does It Do?	Example
systemctl start	Start a service	systemctl start cups.service
systemctl stop	Stop a service	systemctl stop cups.service
systemctl status	See the status of any given unit, process, or device	systemctl status cups.service
systemctl list-dependencies --all	Provide a comprehensive map of dependencies for each unit	Same as column I
systemctl enable and systemctl disable	Enable or disable service	systemctl enable cups.service
systemctl poweroff	Power off the server	Same as column I
systemctl reboot	Reboot the server	Same as column I
systemctl reload	Reload a service – useful if you've changed a configuration file	systemctl reload apache2.service

Finally, there is the `systemctl mask` command that will completely prevent a service from starting. This should be used with extreme caution – it disregards information about the service dependencies!

Graphical vs. CLI

For most VPSs, you'll have a default "server" operating system setup, which means that you won't have any sort of graphical environment. If you want to, you could install one of the desktop environments that Linux offers, such as GNOME. In general though, this probably won't be very useful to you. Instead, you may want to look into an administrative tool that runs through a web browser, which we'll talk about in the next chapter.

However, there are times when graphical environments make sense. If you want to use your VPS as a remote desktop, for example, you could install GNOME and a suite of tools that you can connect to at any time and use. For example, you may want to work on a project and have it continue processing or computing while you're moving between offices. Having it run on your VPS means that you can turn on and off your laptop without interrupting anything. You may also use your VPS as a secure location to browse the Web from that can be connected to from any of your other devices and doesn't leave any evidence behind on a device as to what you were browsing. Installing a graphical interface is beyond the scope of this book; however, we do need to talk about installing software, which we'll do in the next section!

Installing and Updating Software

If you're familiar with Windows, you may know about installer files (e.g., setup.exe that you would run to set up new software). If you've used a smartphone, you know about the Apple App Store or the Google Play store, where you pick which application you would like to install and press a download button to get it installed directly. Linux is a little less graphical, but can be just as easy to install most software on.

In the early days of Linux, software had to be compiled for each new machine from the original source files. You'd download the source files or copy them over on disk and then use a series of commands, which we'll discuss later, to compile the binary files. You'd then copy those files to the appropriate place on your system (e.g., binary files in /bin, library files in /lib, etc.). Today, however, most distributions use some form of package management tool – a tool that helps keep track of what software is installed on the system, ensures that software dependencies aren't broken by accidentally removing a file that another file needs, and helps maintain different versions of software for specific needs. In Debian, this package manager format is known as dpkg, which can install and modify files that end in .deb, or Debian packages. Typically we use a package management system like APT (Advanced Package Tool) to easily download, install, update, and remove Debian packages. In CentOS, this package manager format is known as RPM (Redhat Package Manager), and we use YUM (Yellowdog Updater, Modified) as the package management system. Both APT and YUM do fundamentally the same tasks, which we'll go through in the following.

Installing New Software

On a Debian system, installing new software is done using the apt command, which must be run by root in order to install software. Also note that you'll commonly see the command apt-get as it provides much of the same functionality. The first step to installing new software is to update your package information – the command apt update will download all of the repository information to your machine, making sure you have the most up-to-date information on software available to install.

The next step is to specify the package you wish to install. You'll need to know the exact name, so using the command apt search can be helpful in this case. For example, if I wanted to install the Apache 2 Web Server, I could issue apt search apache 2, and it will give me a list of packages that I can install. Looking through them, the very first one is named apache2, and the description reads "Apache HTTP Server" – that's the key.

Next, I issue the installation command: apt install apache2. This will kick off the installation, and at the end, you should have the software installed and configured with its default options. For Apache 2, this means it will be set to start up automatically and have a default "landing" page installed if you go to your server's address in a web browser.

On a CentOS system, the yum command defaults to dnf, which is the next major version of YUM; however, the yum command will still remain working to ensure backward compatibility. Installing software works similarly. To find the name of the Apache 2 package, you can run yum search apache which will tell you that the package on CentOS you're looking for is httpd.x86_64. You can then use yum install http.x86_64 to install it.

Updating Existing Software

System administration requires that you have your tools up to date. Thankfully, both APT and YUM provide commands to automatically update all of the existing software on the system that they have installed.

On Debian, use apt upgrade and apt dist-upgrade to get a list of all packages to update, and then begin the updating process. On CentOS, use yum update to list the packages to update, and begin the updating process.

Both operating systems will show you the list of packages to be updated, give you the option to cancel the update (perhaps because of the time it will take or the amount of software that will need to be installed), and also show you updates on the installation process throughout. I typically recommend that one updates software on their system about once per week, to make sure that you have the latest software for security purposes. However, you're free to do it as frequently as you like.

Removing Software

Finally, when software isn't needed any longer, you may wish to remove it in order to save space.

On Debian, use apt remove to remove a specific package and apt autoremove to remove all unused packages that were installed in the past that aren't required for the software currently running on the system.

On CentOS, the commands are similar – yum remove and yum autoremove.

Note that any files that you've modified will likely not be removed, including data files and configuration files. The configuration files aren't likely to take up considerable space; however, the data files probably will. You'll want to remove them manually.

Installing from Source

Recall that originally all software on Linux had to be installed from source. Today, this is likely not something you'll have to do often. But there is a chance that you'll want to use software that hasn't been compiled and packaged for your version of Debian or CentOS. This typically requires you to download the source and use the following three commands:

- ./configure – Most software will come with a script that will check many items on your VPS to make sure that the software can be compiled and run. If anything is missing, you will likely get errors that list packages you'll need to install.

- make – The make command compiles the software into binary form that your VPS can execute. This typically takes the longest in terms of the installation.

- make install – A special script that can be run to install the software to the proper locations on your machine.

Of these three steps, the first two should be run as your normal user account, although you'll probably need root to run make install since it modifies files in directories only root has access to, such as /bin.

Installing from source is a topic that an entire chapter could cover, but as mentioned, is done infrequently. If you want to practice your skills installing from source, I'd suggest downloading a virtual Linux machine onto your own computer first, testing out the installation there, and then deploying it to your VPS. You can download prebuilt virtual machines from OSBoxes (http:// osboxes.org, Figure 3-19), in either Debian or CentOS flavor (Figure 3-20). They can be run with the free virtualization software, VirtualBox (http:// virtualbox.org). In general, this can also provide you with a playground to test out anything else we do in this book, from the safety of your own computer, before you try it on your VPS.

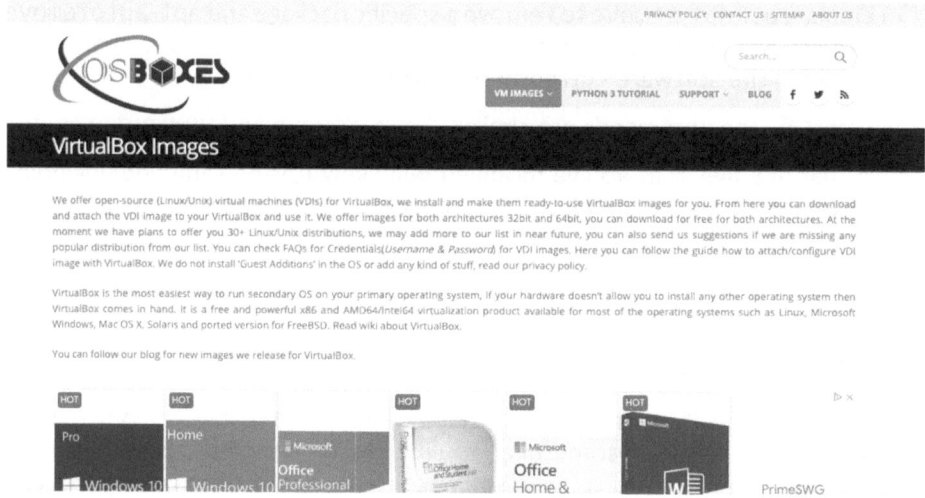

Figure 3-19. The osboxes.org homepage

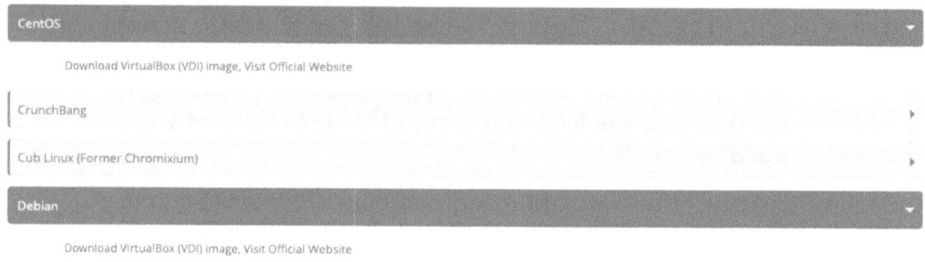

Figure 3-20. The entries for Debian and CentOS

Conclusion

This chapter has been a long haul, but hopefully its goal - to make you a bit more familiar with the interface of your VPS, give you the basic commands that you'll be using again and again, and also show you "under the hood" of how your VPS starts up and gets things ready for work. In the next chapter, we'll discuss administration through a graphical interface, Webmin, that may help you speed up your administrative tasks!

Basic Linux Administration via GUI (Webmin)

Sometimes the command-line environment can be a bit frustrating, and in those cases, you might really wish you had a prettier option that held your hand a bit more. Thankfully, one exists in the well-established Webmin project. Founded by Jamie Cameron and first released in October 1997, Webmin is an open source project that can be used for both commercial and noncommercial purposes, making it very useful to us. It also provides the same administrative interface on both Debian and CentOS, which means that using it on either machine is nearly the same experience. And finally, it can be extensively customized, as I'll talk about in this chapter. So let's dig into Webmin, first by talking about if you need it (and what you might need it for) and then by discussing the installation, securing, and customizing of the tool.

© Jon Westfall 2021
J. Westfall, *Set Up and Manage Your Virtual Private Server*,
https://doi.org/10.1007/978-1-4842-6966-4_4

Do You Need a GUI?

For many of us, using a computer is a visual affair. We're used to pointing and clicking, tapping and drawing, and interacting with our machines through a ton of different ways – except, ironically, the command line that we talked about in the last chapter. This means that for many, the option to have a graphical user interface (GUI) is very tempting. However, before we get this up and running, it's worth discussing if you need it and why you might not want to run it if you don't.

When I found Webmin (Figure 4-1) as a young Linux system administrator near the turn of the century (a statement which makes me sound way older than I am), I felt it was a godsend. I knew my way around the DOS command prompt, but Linux was a new beast to me. I relied on Webmin a lot in those early years, to do very basic tasks. Along the way, I picked up some knowledge of the command line, mostly by watching Webmin's output as it told me what commands it was executing. Then, around 10 years after starting to use Linux, I started to wonder if Webmin was worth it in every situation.

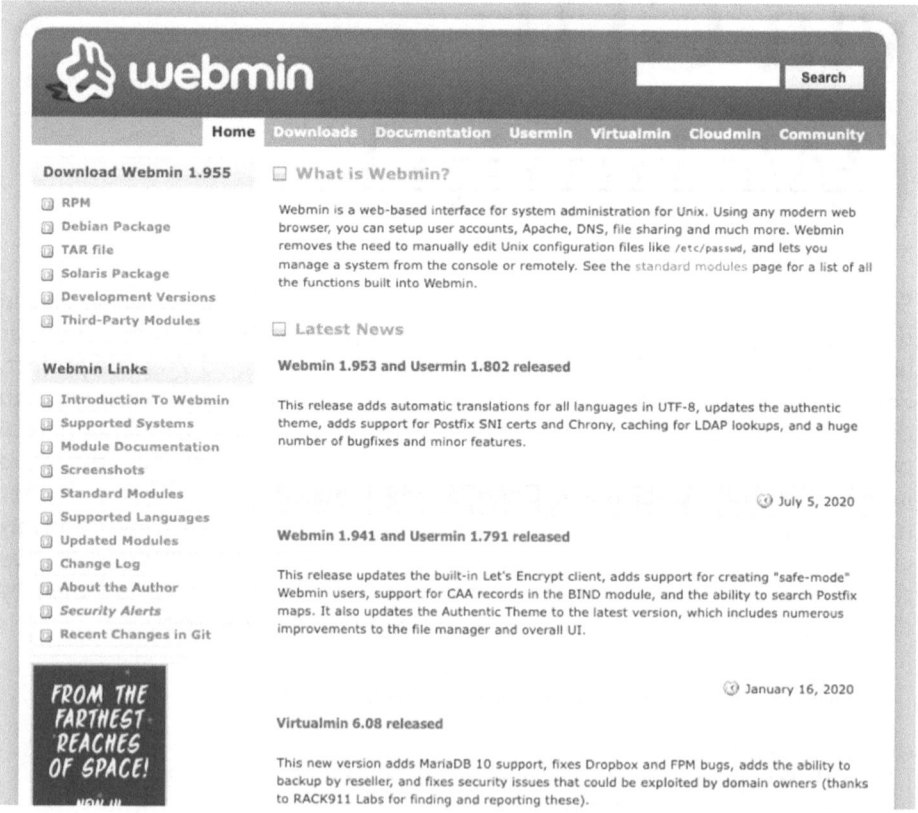

Figure 4-1. Webmin homepage, webmin.com

First, one must consider the fact that anytime you install software on your VPS, you're opening up potential security concerns. More code installed, more opportunities for vulnerabilities to be found and exploited. In the case of Webmin, a piece of software designed to manage the entire VPS, if it were to be compromised by a hacker, it could be very dangerous. Thankfully, the software is updated regularly and has a good security track record, but there is always a slight bit more security risk by running it than by not.

Second, more software running on your VPS also means more usage of resources – RAM, processing power, and storage space. Admittedly, Webmin is pretty minor in these regards – it's not a resource hog. But still, less to run also means less to go wrong or have to troubleshoot when things are broken.

Finally, by relying on Webmin, I had become pretty complacent with my Linux system administration skills. I knew some of the basic commands, but there were elements that I discussed in Chapter 3 that I'd never used, even after relying on the operating system to run my web server for over a decade. In a way, Webmin (or any GUI) can rob you of learning more about what you're doing when it comes to running your VPS.

On the flip side, however, there are some very good arguments for Webmin. First, it does simplify the administration process. It provides a bit of safety and security by preventing most typos in configuration files or the confusion of figuring out which configuration file to edit. It also easily allows you to divide up management duties of your VPS in that it allows you to create multiple users and tailor their access easily (something that the sudo command also does on the command line). For those other users, it also provides an environment that allows for simple explanation of what they must do to accomplish their goals – you could write an easy series of steps to follow without requiring them to type a command exactly as written to get the achieved effect. It also eliminates the possibility that they'll insert a typo in a command and cause destruction (imagine telling them to issue rm -r ./ and having them forget the period!). Webmin also includes the Usermin module, which can be used to set up a very basic web environment for users of your VPS, including allowing them to check email hosted on the machine as well as any databases or websites they manage. We'll discuss this later in the chapter.

So in sum, you may have very good reasons to use a GUI, related to both learning and ease of management. However, I would avoid becoming overly dependent on it. Not only does it rob you of a learning experience, it also is worth noting that the command line will still be faster and easier to use on a small screen device (such as a smartphone). Assuming you've decided to install and use Webmin, let's continue through that process!

Downloading and Installing Webmin

At one time, Webmin was included in the base Debian and Ubuntu distributions (Ubuntu is built on Debian). However, there were issues related to how the distributions store their default configuration files that caused Webmin to periodically fail to find the proper configuration file, and thus we need to install it manually today. However, just because it's not a package in the distribution doesn't mean we'll need to install from source – thankfully, the maintainers of Webmin provide both a Debian package file and a Red Hat/CentOS package file that's built for the appropriate operating system already. In the next section, I've chunked up the downloading and installing of Webmin relative to the system in question – Debian or CentOS. While very similar, the commands will change slightly.

Debian

To install Webmin on a Debian Linux system, follow these steps:

1. Visit `www.webmin.com`.

2. Right-click the "Debian Package" link in the left-hand-side menu (see Figure 4-1). Choose the option for your browser that lets you copy the link. As of the writing of this chapter, the direct link to the Debian package is `http://prdownloads.sourceforge.net/webadmin/webmin_1.955_all.deb`, although it's likely that the version number will change before you read this.

3. In your VPS, type the following command, pasting in the proper link that you copied in step 2: wget `http://prdownloads.sourceforge.net/webadmin/webmin_1.955_all.deb`. This will use the wget application to download the file straight to your VPS. See Figure 4-2.

```
root@lilo:~# wget http://prdownloads.sourceforge.net/webadmin/webmin_1.955_all.deb
—2020-09-28 16:04:00—  http://prdownloads.sourceforge.net/webadmin/webmin_1.955_all.deb
Resolving prdownloads.sourceforge.net (prdownloads.sourceforge.net)... 216.105.38.13
Connecting to prdownloads.sourceforge.net (prdownloads.sourceforge.net)|216.105.38.13|:80... connected.
HTTP request sent, awaiting response... 301 Moved Permanently
Location: http://downloads.sourceforge.net/project/webadmin/webmin/1.955/webmin_1.955_all.deb [following]
—2020-09-28 16:04:01—  http://downloads.sourceforge.net/project/webadmin/webmin/1.955/webmin_1.955_all.deb
Resolving downloads.sourceforge.net (downloads.sourceforge.net)... 216.105.38.13
Reusing existing connection to prdownloads.sourceforge.net:80.
HTTP request sent, awaiting response... 302 Found
Location: https://newcontinuum.dl.sourceforge.net/project/webadmin/webmin/1.955/webmin_1.955_all.deb [following]
—2020-09-28 16:04:01—  https://newcontinuum.dl.sourceforge.net/project/webadmin/webmin/1.955/webmin_1.955_all.deb
Resolving newcontinuum.dl.sourceforge.net (newcontinuum.dl.sourceforge.net)... 2607:ff50:0:11::32, 64.79.96.4
Connecting to newcontinuum.dl.sourceforge.net (newcontinuum.dl.sourceforge.net)|2607:ff50:0:11::32|:443... connected.
HTTP request sent, awaiting response... 200 OK
Length: 29280954 (28M) [application/octet-stream]
Saving to: 'webmin_1.955_all.deb'

webmin_1.955_all.deb          100%[===================================================================>]  27.92M  34.3MB/s    in 0.8s

2020-09-28 16:04:02 (34.3 MB/s) - 'webmin_1.955_all.deb' saved [29280954/29280954]

root@lilo:~#
```

Figure 4-2. Downloading the Debian package using wget

4. Update and upgrade your system to the most current versions of all available packages by running `apt-get update && apt-get dist-upgrade`.

5. You can now use the dpkg application to try to install Webmin. Issue the command `dpkg -i webmin_1.955_ all.deb`, replacing the version number with the version you've downloaded in step 3.

6. It's likely you'll get errors, similar to the ones in Figure 4-3. This is because your system does not have the necessary packages installed. Thankfully, we can fix that using the apt-get command. Type `apt-get -f install`.

```
root@lilo:~# dpkg -i webmin_1.955_all.deb
Selecting previously unselected package webmin.
(Reading database ... 23037 files and directories currently installed.)
Preparing to unpack webmin_1.955_all.deb ...
Unpacking webmin (1.955) ...
dpkg: dependency problems prevent configuration of webmin:
 webmin depends on libnet-ssleay-perl; however:
  Package libnet-ssleay-perl is not installed.
 webmin depends on libauthen-pam-perl; however:
  Package libauthen-pam-perl is not installed.
 webmin depends on libio-pty-perl; however:
  Package libio-pty-perl is not installed.
 webmin depends on apt-show-versions; however:
  Package apt-show-versions is not installed.
 webmin depends on shared-mime-info; however:
  Package shared-mime-info is not installed.

dpkg: error processing package webmin (--install):
 dependency problems - leaving unconfigured
Processing triggers for systemd (241-7~deb10u4) ...
Errors were encountered while processing:
 webmin
root@lilo:~# █
```

Figure 4-3. Errors installing Webmin using the dpkg command

7. Apt will download the needed packages after you confirm (see Figure 4-4) and then install them. Since it knows Webmin is pending install, it will also install it as well. You should get a message toward the end of the output saying that Webmin install is complete.

```
root@lilo:~# apt-get -f install
Reading package lists... Done
Building dependency tree
Reading state information... Done
Correcting dependencies... Done
The following additional packages will be installed:
    apt-show-versions libapt-pkg-perl libauthen-pam-perl libio-pty-perl libnet-ssleay-perl perl-openssl-defaults shared-mime-info
The following NEW packages will be installed:
    apt-show-versions libapt-pkg-perl libauthen-pam-perl libio-pty-perl libnet-ssleay-perl perl-openssl-defaults shared-mime-info
0 upgraded, 7 newly installed, 0 to remove and 0 not upgraded.
1 not fully installed or removed.
Need to get 1245 kB of archives.
After this operation, 6743 kB of additional disk space will be used.
Do you want to continue? [Y/n] y
Get:1 http://ftp.debian.org/debian buster/main amd64 perl-openssl-defaults amd64 3 [6782 B]
Get:2 http://ftp.debian.org/debian buster/main amd64 libnet-ssleay-perl amd64 1.85-2+b1 [308 kB]
Get:3 http://ftp.debian.org/debian buster/main amd64 libauthen-pam-perl amd64 0.16-3+b6 [27.6 kB]
Get:4 http://ftp.debian.org/debian buster/main amd64 libio-pty-perl amd64 1:1.08-1.1+b5 [33.7 kB]
Get:5 http://ftp.debian.org/debian buster/main amd64 libapt-pkg-perl amd64 0.1.34+b1 [71.2 kB]
Get:6 http://ftp.debian.org/debian buster/main amd64 apt-show-versions all 0.22.11 [32.6 kB]
Get:7 http://ftp.debian.org/debian buster/main amd64 shared-mime-info amd64 1.10-1 [766 kB]
Fetched 1245 kB in 1s (1376 kB/s)
Selecting previously unselected package perl-openssl-defaults:amd64.
(Reading database ... 81063 files and directories currently installed.)
Preparing to unpack .../0-perl-openssl-defaults_3_amd64.deb ...
Unpacking perl-openssl-defaults:amd64 (3) ...
Selecting previously unselected package libnet-ssleay-perl.
Preparing to unpack .../1-libnet-ssleay-perl_1.85-2+b1_amd64.deb ...
Unpacking libnet-ssleay-perl (1.85-2+b1) ...
Selecting previously unselected package libauthen-pam-perl.
Preparing to unpack .../2-libauthen-pam-perl_0.16-3+b6_amd64.deb ...
Unpacking libauthen-pam-perl (0.16-3+b6) ...
Selecting previously unselected package libio-pty-perl.
Preparing to unpack .../3-libio-pty-perl_1%3a1.08-1.1+b5_amd64.deb ...
Unpacking libio-pty-perl (1:1.08-1.1+b5) ...
Selecting previously unselected package libapt-pkg-perl.
Preparing to unpack .../4-libapt-pkg-perl_0.1.34+b1_amd64.deb ...
Unpacking libapt-pkg-perl (0.1.34+b1) ...
Selecting previously unselected package apt-show-versions.
Preparing to unpack .../5-apt-show-versions_0.22.11_all.deb ...
Unpacking apt-show-versions (0.22.11) ...
Selecting previously unselected package shared-mime-info.
Preparing to unpack .../6-shared-mime-info_1.10-1_amd64.deb ...
Unpacking shared-mime-info (1.10-1) ...
Setting up libapt-pkg-perl (0.1.34+b1) ...
Setting up libio-pty-perl (1:1.08-1.1+b5) ...
Setting up apt-show-versions (0.22.11) ...
** initializing cache. This may take a while **
Setting up perl-openssl-defaults:amd64 (3) ...
Setting up shared-mime-info (1.10-1) ...
Setting up libauthen-pam-perl (0.16-3+b6) ...
Setting up libnet-ssleay-perl (1.85-2+b1) ...
Setting up webmin (1.955) ...
/var/lib/dpkg/info/webmin.postinst: 4: /var/lib/dpkg/info/webmin.postinst: cannot create /etc/webmin/stop: Directory nonexistent
Webmin install complete. You can now login to https://lilo.jonwestfall.net:10000/
as root with your root password, or as any user who can use sudo
to run commands as root.
Processing triggers for man-db (2.8.5-2) ...
Processing triggers for systemd (241-7~deb10u4) ...
```

Figure 4-4. *Apt downloading and installing all of the necessary files*

8. You should now be able to navigate to the login address listed at the end of the installation. For me, this was https://lilo.jonwestfall.net:10000. It's possible that you'll get an error such as the one in Figure 4-5. This is because, while the connection is cryptographically secure, the cryptographic certificate was generated by your VPS. Your browser is warning you that the only computer telling you that it's your VPS is your VPS itself. Basically no other computer has verified it actually is the computer it claims to be. We'll fix that later. For now, you'll need to make an exception on your computer to visit the Webmin's login page (see Figure 4-6).

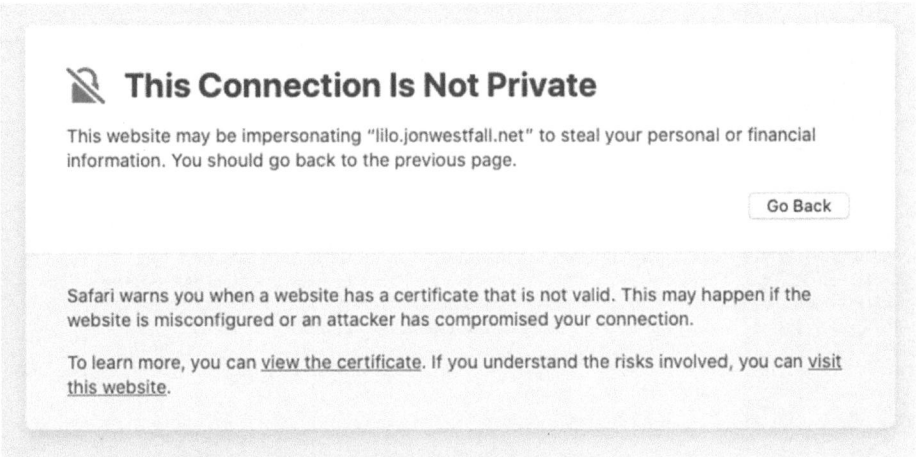

Figure 4-5. The security error in the Safari browser

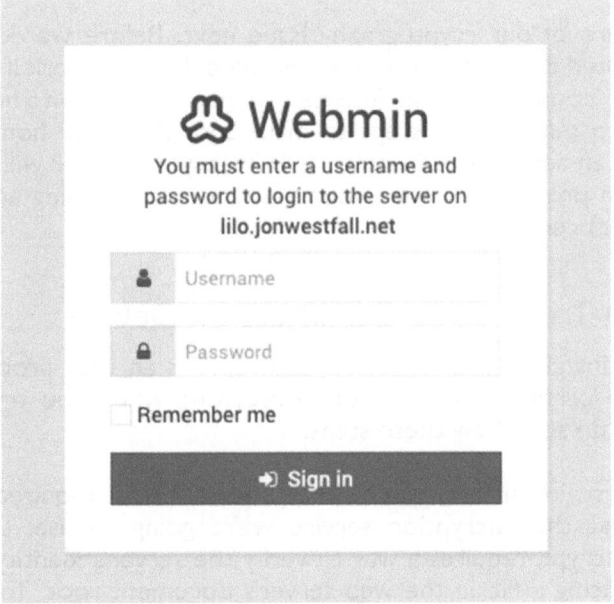

Figure 4-6. The Webmin login page

9. Once you've logged in with your `root` username and password, you will see the Webmin Dashboard (Figure 4-7).

Figure 4-7. The Webmin Dashboard

Let's take care of our cryptography issue next. Before we do, however, it should be noted that the following steps will only easily work if you are using a VPS directly connected to the Internet. If you are testing on a home machine, you'll need to take certain steps to make sure that your home machine is reachable by an actual domain name. It is likely your router will prevent Let's Encrypt from properly verifying your machine and installing an SSL (Secure Sockets Layer) certificate.

Installing a Trusted SSL Certificate on Debian

On Debian, installing a trusted SSL certificate is an easy process. This will clear up the certificate errors you're receiving when you try to log into Webmin. To do so, follow these steps:

I.   First, install the Apache Web Server. This is required so that the encryption service we're going to use, Let's Encrypt, requires a way to verify the server's identity by placing a file in the web server's document root. To do this, click "Un-used Modules" in Webmin and then "Apache Webserver" (see Figure 4-8).

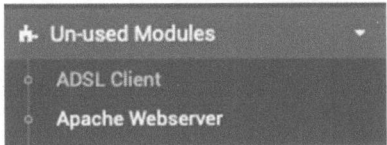

Figure 4-8. Apache Webserver under the Un-used Modules menu

2. Click "Install Now" to install the Apache Web Server (see Figure 4-9).

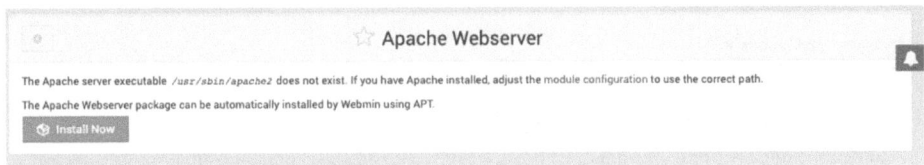

Figure 4-9. Install Now option

3. Webmin will then tell you which packages it will download and install. Click "Install Now" again to confirm that you'd like to install those packages (Figure 4-10). Once it's done, you should get a notification that the install was successful (Figure 4-11). You can verify this by going to your server in a new browser window. In my case, the appropriate link is http://lilo.jonwestfall.net (Figure 4-12). It should also be noted that if you are running Webmin on a local network, perhaps for testing, you may need to use the IP address assigned to your test machine. You can typically find this by looking in your router's information screen under "DHCP Leases."

Install Packages

Building complete list of packages ..

Are you sure you wish to install the 11 packages listed below? This may include dependencies of packages that you selected.

⟳ Install Now

Package	Current version	New version	Description
libapr1	None	1.6.5-1+b1	
libaprutil1	None	1.6.1-4	
libaprutil1-dbd-sqlite3	None	1.6.1-4	
libaprutil1-ldap	None	1.6.1-4	
libbrotli1	None	1.0.7-2	
libjansson4	None	2.12-1	
liblua5.2-0	None	5.2.4-1.1+b2	
apache2-bin	None	2.4.38-3+deb10u4	
apache2-data	None	2.4.38-3+deb10u4	
apache2-utils	None	2.4.38-3+deb10u4	
apache2	None	2.4.38-3+deb10u4	

← Return to Apache Webserver

Figure 4-10. The packages to be installed

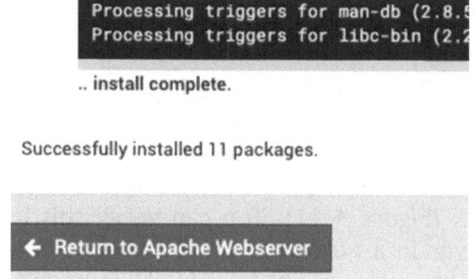

```
Processing triggers for man-db (2.8.5
Processing triggers for libc-bin (2.2
```

.. install complete.

Successfully installed 11 packages.

← Return to Apache Webserver

Figure 4-11. Confirmation that installation was successful

Apache2 Debian Default Page

debian

It works!

This is the default welcome page used to test the correct operation of the Apache2 server after installation on Debian systems. If you can read this page, it means that the Apache HTTP server installed at this site is working properly. You should **replace this file** (located at /var/www/html/index.html) before continuing to operate your HTTP server.

If you are a normal user of this web site and don't know what this page is about, this probably means that the site is currently unavailable due to maintenance. If the problem persists, please contact the site's administrator.

Configuration Overview

Debian's Apache2 default configuration is different from the upstream default configuration, and split into several files optimized for interaction with Debian tools. The configuration system is **fully documented in /usr/share/doc/apache2/README.Debian.gz**. Refer to this for the full documentation. Documentation for the web server itself can be found by accessing the **manual** if the apache2-doc package was installed on this server.

The configuration layout for an Apache2 web server installation on Debian systems is as follows:

```
/etc/apache2/
|-- apache2.conf
|       `--  ports.conf
|-- mods-enabled
|       |-- *.load
|       `-- *.conf
|-- conf-enabled
|       `-- *.conf
|-- sites-enabled
|       `-- *.conf
```

- apache2.conf is the main configuration file. It puts the pieces together by including all remaining configuration files when starting up the web server.

Figure 4-12. The default Apache homepage

4. In Webmin, go to the Webmin menu and then choose "Webmin Configuration" (Figure 4-13).

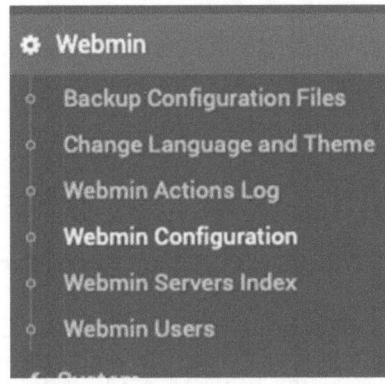

Figure 4-13. The Webmin Configuration option

5. Choose "SSL Encryption" (Figure 4-14).

Figure 4-14. The SSL Encryption option

6. Choose the "Let's Encrypt" tab. Let's Encrypt is a free service that will install an industry-recognized SSL certificate onto your machine. I recommend selecting the "Months between automatic renewal" option and setting it to 1 and the second Website root directory for validation file option, listing "Default," as seen in Figure 4-15.

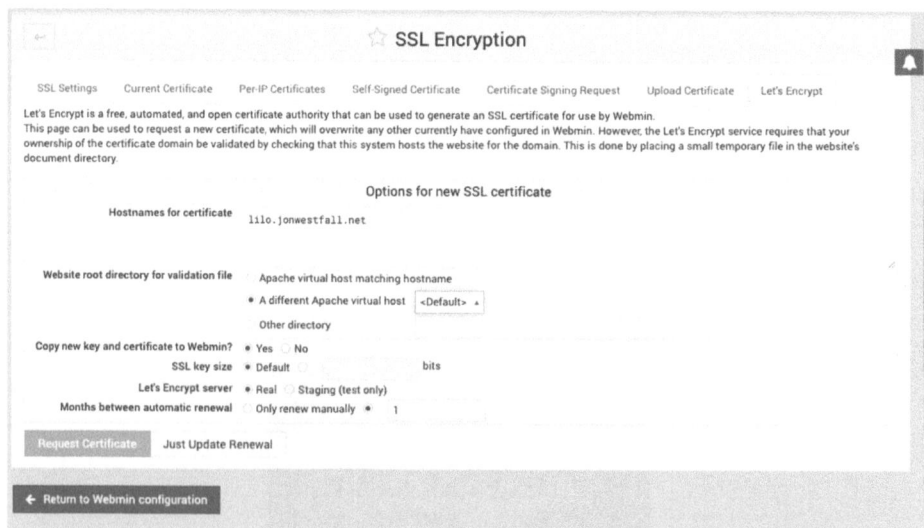

Figure 4-15. The Let's Encrypt settings used to download and create a new SSL certificate

7. Restart Webmin by going into the Webmin Configuration and choosing the restart button, and refresh your web browser. Your certificate information should change from something similar to Figure 4-16 to a new certificate from Let's Encrypt, similar to Figure 4-17.

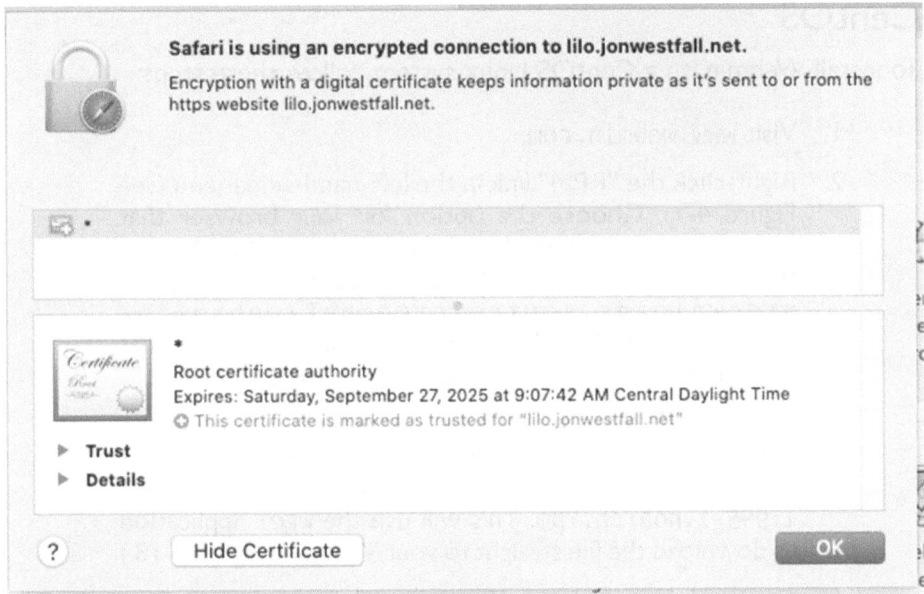

Figure 4-16. Self-signed certificate that causes errors

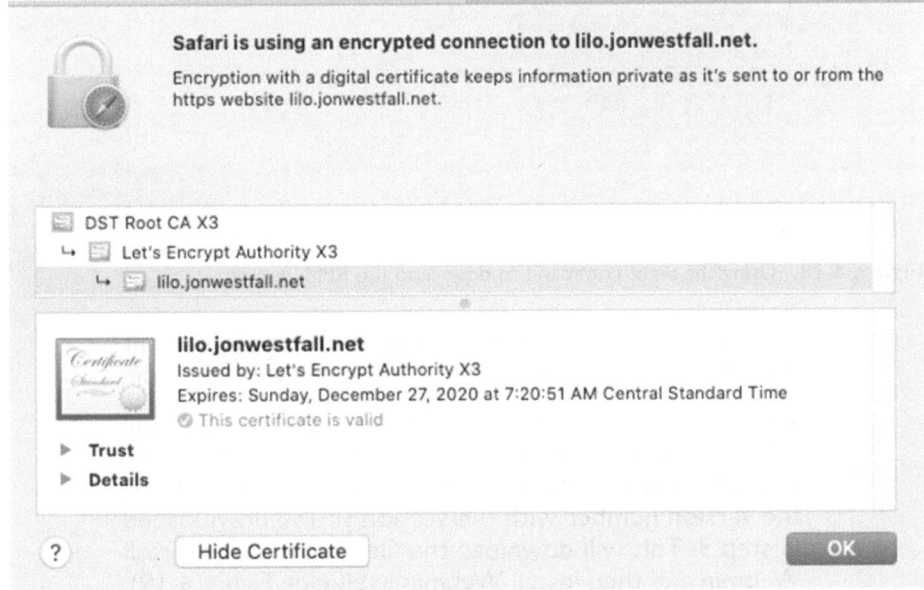

Figure 4-17. An industry-recognized SSL certificate from Let's Encrypt

CentOS

To install Webmin on a CentOS Linux system, follow these steps:

1. Visit www.webmin.com.

2. Right-click the "RPM" link in the left-hand-side menu (see Figure 4-1). Choose the option for your browser that lets you copy the link. As of the writing of this chapter, the direct link to the Red Hat/CentOS package is http://prdownloads.sourceforge.net/webadmin/webmin-1.955-1.noarch.rpm, although it's likely that the version number will change before you read this.

3. In your VPS, type the following command, pasting in the proper link that you copied in step 2: wget http://prdownloads.sourceforge.net/webadmin/webmin-1.955-1.noarch.rpm. This will use the wget application to download the file straight to your VPS. (See Figure 4-18.)

```
[root@stitch ~]# wget http://prdownloads.sourceforge.net/webadmin/webmin-1.955-1.noarch.rpm
--2020-09-28 16:24:57--  http://prdownloads.sourceforge.net/webadmin/webmin-1.955-1.noarch.rpm
Resolving prdownloads.sourceforge.net (prdownloads.sourceforge.net)... 216.105.38.13
Connecting to prdownloads.sourceforge.net (prdownloads.sourceforge.net)|216.105.38.13|:80... connected.
HTTP request sent, awaiting response... 301 Moved Permanently
Location: http://downloads.sourceforge.net/project/webadmin/webmin/1.955/webmin-1.955-1.noarch.rpm [following]
--2020-09-28 16:24:57--  http://downloads.sourceforge.net/project/webadmin/webmin/1.955/webmin-1.955-1.noarch.rpm
Resolving downloads.sourceforge.net (downloads.sourceforge.net)... 216.105.38.13
Reusing existing connection to prdownloads.sourceforge.net:80.
HTTP request sent, awaiting response... 302 Found
Location: https://cfhcable.dl.sourceforge.net/project/webadmin/webmin/1.955/webmin-1.955-1.noarch.rpm [following]
--2020-09-28 16:24:57--  https://cfhcable.dl.sourceforge.net/project/webadmin/webmin/1.955/webmin-1.955-1.noarch.rpm
Resolving cfhcable.dl.sourceforge.net (cfhcable.dl.sourceforge.net)... 146.71.73.6
Connecting to cfhcable.dl.sourceforge.net (cfhcable.dl.sourceforge.net)|146.71.73.6|:443... connected.
HTTP request sent, awaiting response... 200 OK
Length: 40407256 (39M) [application/octet-stream]
Saving to: 'webmin-1.955-1.noarch.rpm'

webmin-1.955-1.noarch.rpm       100%[===================================================================>]  38.54M  73.2MB/s    in 0.5s

2020-09-28 16:24:58 (73.2 MB/s) - 'webmin-1.955-1.noarch.rpm' saved [40407256/40407256]

[root@stitch ~]#
```

Figure 4-18. Using the wget command to download the RPM version

4. Update and upgrade your system to the most current versions of all available packages by running yum upgrade.

5. You can now use the yum application to try to install Webmin. Issue the command yum --nogpgcheck localinstall webmin-1.955-1.noarch.rpm, replacing the version number with the version you've downloaded in step 3. This will download the files you need to install Webmin and then install Webmin itself (see Figure 4-19).

```
[root@stitch ~]# yum --nogpgcheck localinstall webmin-1.955-1.noarch.rpm
Last metadata expiration check: 0:24:17 ago on Mon Sep 28 16:05:46 2020.
Dependencies resolved.
=================================================================================================
 Package                    Architecture      Version              Repository            Size
=================================================================================================
Installing:
 webmin                     noarch            1.955-1              @commandline          39 M
Installing dependencies:
 perl-Encode-Detect         x86_64            1.01-28.el8          AppStream             90 k
 perl-Net-SSLeay            x86_64            1.88-1.el8           AppStream            379 k

Transaction Summary
=================================================================================================
Install  3 Packages

Total size: 39 M
Total download size: 469 k
Installed size: 123 M
Is this ok [y/N]: y
Downloading Packages:
(1/2): perl-Encode-Detect-1.01-28.el8.x86_64.rpm                     321 kB/s |  90 kB    00:00
(2/2): perl-Net-SSLeay-1.88-1.el8.x86_64.rpm                         1.0 MB/s | 379 kB    00:00
-------------------------------------------------------------------------------------------------
Total                                                                1.0 MB/s | 469 kB    00:00
Running transaction check
Transaction check succeeded.
Running transaction test
Transaction test succeeded.
Running transaction
  Preparing        :                                                                        1/1
  Installing       : perl-Net-SSLeay-1.88-1.el8.x86_64                                       1/3
  Installing       : perl-Encode-Detect-1.01-28.el8.x86_64                                   2/3
  Running scriptlet: webmin-1.955-1.noarch                                                   3/3
Operating system is CentOS Linux

  Installing       : webmin-1.955-1.noarch                                                   3/3
  Running scriptlet: webmin-1.955-1.noarch                                                   3/3
Webmin install complete. You can now login to https://stitch.jonwestfall.net:10000/
as root with your root password.

  Verifying        : perl-Encode-Detect-1.01-28.el8.x86_64                                   1/3
  Verifying        : perl-Net-SSLeay-1.88-1.el8.x86_64                                       2/3
  Verifying        : webmin-1.955-1.noarch                                                   3/3

Installed:
  perl-Encode-Detect-1.01-28.el8.x86_64      perl-Net-SSLeay-1.88-1.el8.x86_64      webmin-1.955-1.noarch

Complete!
[root@stitch ~]# ▯
```

Figure 4-19. The output of the localinstall command

6. By default, CentOS restricts connections to most ports. You'll need to open up port 10000, by issuing the commands `firewall-cmd --zone=public --add-port=10000/tcp` and `firewall-cmd --runtime-to-permanent` as root.

7. You should now be able to navigate to the login address listed at the end of the installation. For me, this was https://stitch.jonwestfall.net:10000. It's possible that you'll get an error. This is because, while the connection is cryptographically secure, the cryptographic certificate was generated by your VPS. Your browser is warning you that the only computer telling you that it's your VPS is your VPS itself. Basically no other computer has verified it actually is the computer it claims to be. We'll fix that later. For now, you'll need to make an exception on your computer to visit the Webmin's login page (see Figure 4-6).

8. Once you've logged in with your root username and password, you will see the Webmin Dashboard (see Figure 4-7).

Installing a Trusted SSL Certificate on CentOS

On CentOS, installing a trusted SSL certificate is still an easy process, although there are a few more steps because CentOS doesn't make some of the same assumptions that Debian does. This will clear up the certificate errors you're receiving when you try to log into Webmin. To do so, follow these steps:

1. First, install the Apache Web Server. This is required so that the encryption service we're going to use, Let's Encrypt, requires a way to verify the server's identity by placing a file in the web server's document root. To do this, click "Un-used Modules" in Webmin and then "Apache Webserver" (see Figure 4-8).

2. Click "Install Now" to install the Apache Web Server (similar to Figure 4-9).

3. Webmin will then tell you which packages it will download and install. Click "Install Now" again to confirm that you'd like to install those packages. You'll now need to configure the Apache Web Server's secure virtual host – the configuration portion that tells it what to do when someone asks for the https version of your website.

4. Click "Refresh Modules" to have Webmin rescan which modules should be active (because you just installed Apache, it should move from Un-used Modules to Servers), then "Servers," and "Apache Webserver."

5. You'll need to modify the virtual host information for the secure version of your website. To do this, click the globe icon (Figure 4-20) next to the second option, which lists the port served as 443.

Figure 4-20. The globe icon indicating that you'll edit the virtual server configuration

6. At the bottom, in the Virtual Server Details section, you'll want to add your hostname (mine is stitch.jonwestfall.net) in both places and change the Document Root from "Default" to /var/www/html (see Figure 4-21). Click Save, and then restart the Apache Web Server by clicking the "Start" button (Figure 4-22) or the "Apply Changes" button (Figure 4-23) in the upper right.

Figure 4-21. The virtual host configuration options

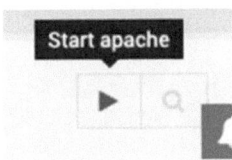

Figure 4-22. The Start button in the upper right of the Apache Web Server configuration

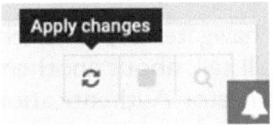

Figure 4-23. The Apply Changes button in the upper right of the Apache Web Server configuration

7. Finally, you'll need to open port 443 using a similar command to the one you used earlier to open port 10000. The command is firewall-cmd --zone=public --add-port=443/tcp and then firewall-cmd --runtime-to-permanent to make the change permanent.

8. We're finally ready to set up the SSL Encryption. In Webmin, go to the Webmin menu, and then choose "Webmin Configuration" (see Figure 4-13).

9. Choose "SSL Encryption" (see Figure 4-14).

10. Choose the "Let's Encrypt" tab. Let's Encrypt is a free service that will install an industry-recognized SSL certificate onto your machine. I recommend using similar settings as in Figure 4-24, changing the server name to be the same as what you've set for your own domain.

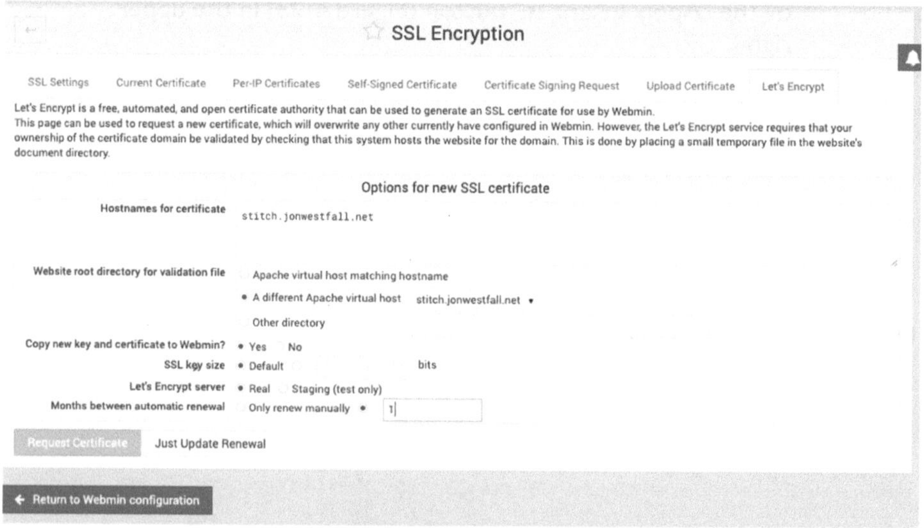

Figure 4-24. Let's Encrypt settings for CentOS

11. Restart Webmin and refresh your web browser.

You should now be able to navigate to your Webmin login page without any certificate errors. Next, we'll talk about another step you may want to take for security – enabling Two-Factor Authentication (2FA).

Installing Two-Factor Authentication (2FA) for Webmin

Webmin includes support to generate and use Google Authenticator Two-Factor Authentication tokens, which I would highly suggest looking into in order to better secure your server, especially if you plan on leaving Webmin running at all times (see the following for a discussion on this). You'll need the Google Authenticator app or a compatible authentication application to generate a code each time you'd like to log into your server, which you'll provide alongside your username and password.

Enabling Two-Factor Authentication

1. Go to the Webmin menu and then "Webmin Configuration."

2. Click "Two-Factor Authentication."

3. Choose "Google Authenticator."

4. Click "Save." You'll likely receive an error about Authen::OATH not being installed; click the "Perl Modules" link to install it automatically. On Debian, this installation should go fairly easily. CentOS may require multiple modules be downloaded and compiled.

5. Go back to the Two-Factor Authentication screen, Choose "Google Authenticator" and then choose "Save."

6. Click the "Webmin Users" link under the Webmin menu.

7. Click the "Two-Factor Authentication" button.

8. Click the "Enroll for Two-Factor Authentication" button. You'll need an authenticator client, such as Google Authenticator, on your mobile device to complete enrollment or a compatible authenticator application. I strongly suggest Google Authenticator at least to start as other clients might not be fully compatible.

9. Log out and then log back in using your Two-Factor Authentication key in addition to your usual username and password.

Having Two-Factor Authentication enabled helps secure your Webmin installation. However, you may also want to simply shut down Webmin when you aren't using it or elect not to have it start up by default. The next section will discuss how you can accomplish that goal.

Starting and Stopping Webmin

By default, Webmin is set to start up when your VPS starts up. If you're concerned about security, you may wish to only start Webmin when you are going to use it and to shut it down when you aren't using it. We can use the systemctl command to start, stop, enable, and disable Webmin using the following commands:

Action	Command
`systemctl enable webmin.service`	Enable Webmin to start whenever your VPS starts.
`systemctl disable webmin.service`	Disable auto-starting Webmin when your VPS starts. Note: If Webmin is currently running, this command won't stop it.
`systemctl start webmin.service`	Start Webmin. If Webmin is disabled, the next time the system reboots, Webmin won't start automatically.
`systemctl stop webmin.service`	Stop Webmin.
`systemctl status webmin.service`	See what the current status of Webmin is.

Now that we know how to start and stop Webmin and how to enable and disable it, let's walk through the basic modules that ship with Webmin and discuss what they do.

Basic Modules

Webmin uses a modular architecture that allows you to not only control all aspects of your VPS but also customize access to only particular aspects, if you so desire. We'll discuss this more later in this chapter. For now, let's take a look at the Webmin modules that ship by default and which are enabled.

When Webmin is installed for the first time, it scans your VPS to see what other software you have installed. If you have software installed that it can manage, for example, an Apache Web Server or a MySQL database server, it will automatically enable those modules. If you do not have these enabled, it will place the unused modules in a special menu named "Un-used Modules," just in case you need them. You can also trigger this process of scanning and enabling by clicking the "Refresh Modules" button. Otherwise, modules are nested in groups. Let's look at each group and what modules it contains.

Webmin Group

The Webmin group contains items that allow you to customize the Webmin software. It begins with a Backup Configuration Files option, which will let you back up your Webmin settings and configurations. You can choose to either back these up once or on a regular schedule. This is very useful in situations where you may want to have a "snapshot" of the configuration at one time that you can revert to later, or if you are going to be setting up multiple VPSs, you might want to have a configuration file that you can keep as the "master" configuration to be restored each time you set up a new

VPS. This module also provides robust destinations for the backup – you can save it to the VPS itself, but also configure it to save to an FTP server or SSH server or download directly in your browser. One great option for saving backups would be to have Webmin make a backup weekly and upload it to another server using SSH, thus allowing you to restore even if your VPS becomes corrupt.

The next option, Change Language and Theme, provides customization for the look and language of Webmin. The Webmin Actions Log will let you look at what yourself, and perhaps others, have been using Webmin to do over the past several days or since installation (see Figure 4-25). This can be very useful to help audit changes that yourself or another administrator may have made. It can also let you see what tasks you do most frequently, thus perhaps inspiring you to learn how to do them manually, if you're using Webmin as a learning tool.

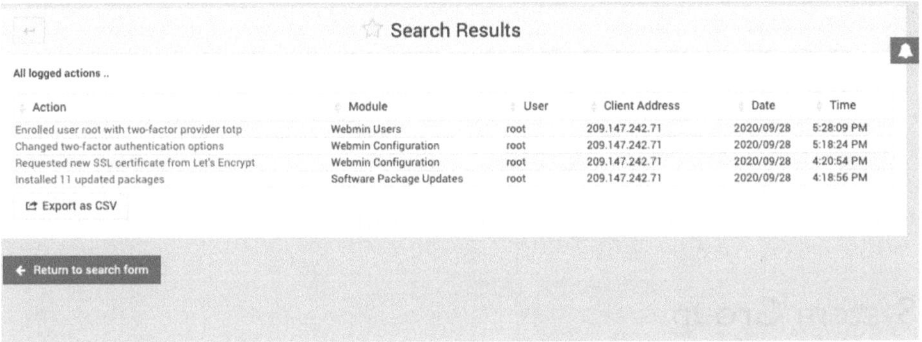

Figure 4-25. *The Webmin Actions Log*

The next three options all allow you to customize Webmin in more advanced detail. Webmin Configuration can be used to set up a variety of options regarding how Webmin is accessed and the functions it can automate, such as sending email. Webmin Servers Index allows you to add other VPSs to your current Webmin installation (they must be running Webmin as well). This is handy if you have a number of VPSs that you want to administer, to provide shortcuts to them. You can also use the cluster features, which we'll discuss later, to run the same task on multiple VPSs at the same time!

Finally, the last option, Webmin Users, allows you to add different user accounts that have access to Webmin and to customize them to only allow access to specific modules or specific areas of modules (see Figure 4-26). We'll discuss this more later in this chapter, as it's a powerful tool enabling multiple administrators to use Webmin, ensuring that each only has access to what they are required to administer and nothing more.

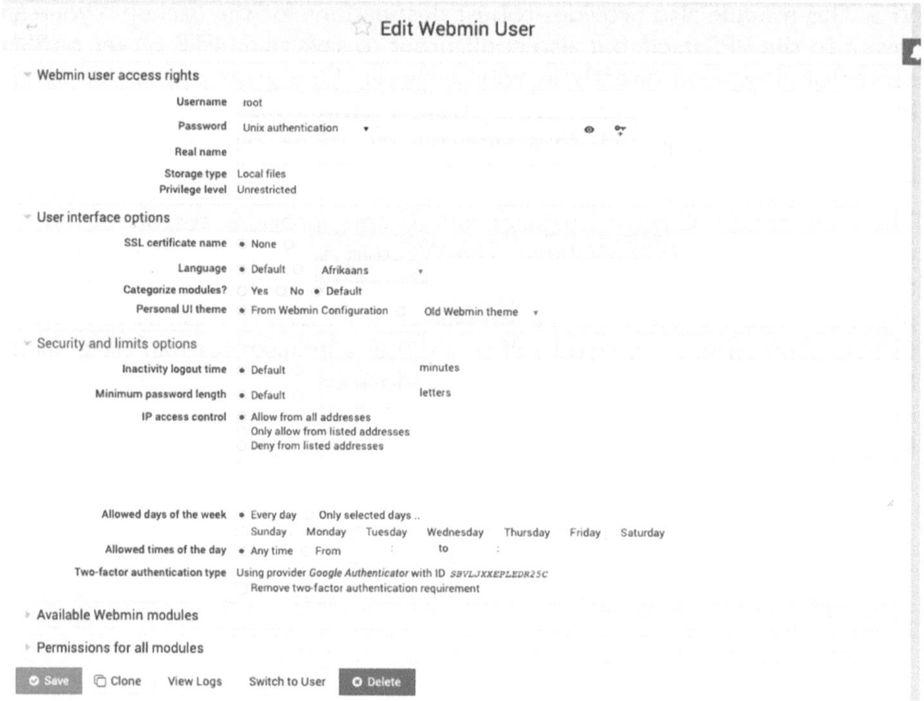

Figure 4-26. The root user account settings in Webmin Users

System Group

The System group has a number of options that enable us to customize the basic operation of our VPS. The Bootup and Shutdown screen gives a visual representation to the system services that we typically use the systemctl command to view or modify (see Figure 4-27). The Change Passwords option allows you to quickly change a user's password, similar to what root can do using the passwd command. Notably you can also change passwords in the Users and Groups option at the bottom of this menu.

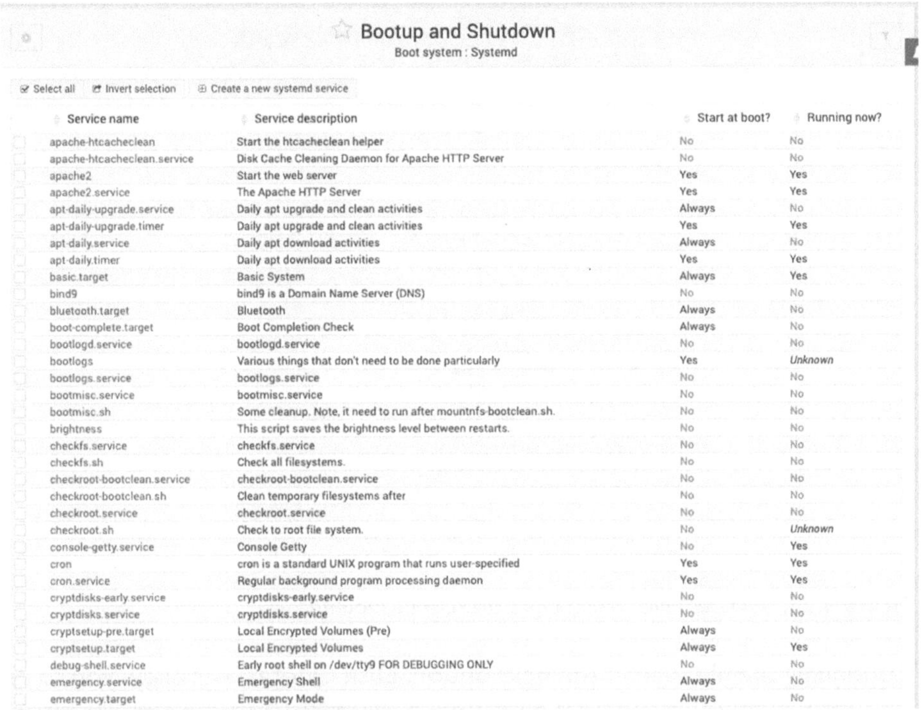

Service name	Service description	Start at boot?	Running now?
apache-htcacheclean	Start the htcacheclean helper	No	No
apache-htcacheclean.service	Disk Cache Cleaning Daemon for Apache HTTP Server	No	No
apache2	Start the web server	Yes	Yes
apache2.service	The Apache HTTP Server	Yes	Yes
apt-daily-upgrade.service	Daily apt upgrade and clean activities	Always	No
apt-daily-upgrade.timer	Daily apt upgrade and clean activities	Yes	Yes
apt-daily.service	Daily apt download activities	Always	No
apt-daily.timer	Daily apt download activities	Yes	Yes
basic.target	Basic System	Always	Yes
bind9	bind9 is a Domain Name Server (DNS)	No	No
bluetooth.target	Bluetooth	Always	No
boot-complete.target	Boot Completion Check	Always	No
bootlogd.service	bootlogd.service	No	No
bootlogs	Various things that don't need to be done particularly	Yes	Unknown
bootlogs.service	bootlogs.service	No	No
bootmisc.service	bootmisc.service	No	No
bootmisc.sh	Some cleanup. Note, it need to run after mountnfs-bootclean.sh.	No	No
brightness	This script saves the brightness level between restarts.	No	No
checkfs.service	checkfs.service	No	No
checkfs.sh	Check all filesystems.	No	No
checkroot-bootclean.service	checkroot-bootclean.service	No	No
checkroot-bootclean.sh	Clean temporary filesystems after	No	No
checkroot.service	checkroot.service	No	No
checkroot.sh	Check to root file system.	No	Unknown
console-getty.service	Console Getty	No	Yes
cron	cron is a standard UNIX program that runs user-specified	Yes	Yes
cron.service	Regular background program processing daemon	Yes	Yes
cryptdisks-early.service	cryptdisks-early.service	No	No
cryptdisks.service	cryptdisks.service	No	No
cryptsetup-pre.target	Local Encrypted Volumes (Pre)	Always	No
cryptsetup.target	Local Encrypted Volumes	Always	Yes
debug-shell.service	Early root shell on /dev/tty9 FOR DEBUGGING ONLY	No	No
emergency.service	Emergency Shell	Always	No
emergency.target	Emergency Mode	Always	No

Figure 4-27. The Bootup and Shutdown screen

Disk and Network Filesystems shows all of the file systems that are currently either in use on your system or saved in your `/etc/fstab` file. Unlike Windows computers, Linux tends to have many different partitions that are mounted at various places in the file system. For example, you might want to store all of your user's data files (under `/home`) on a separate hard drive than the files for the operating system, and this screen will allow you to set up different mounts to accomplish this. You can also take advantage of the different mounting options (see Figure 4-28) to connect this machine to file servers elsewhere, although this likely won't be a scenario you frequently use with a VPS.

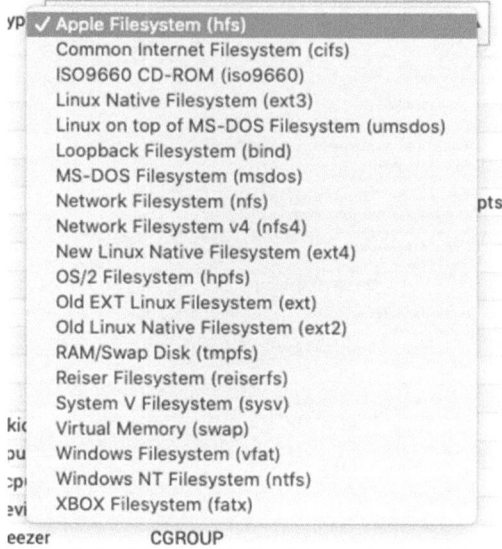

Figure 4-28. Different file system types that can be mounted

Continuing the file theme, the next option, Disk Quotas, will allow you to set up a certain amount of space each user is allowed to use, if the file system supports it. Filesystem Backup provides a basic backup and restore option for specific files (and allows for scheduling as well, which we'll discuss more in future chapters). Finally, the Log File Rotation option allows you to tell the system how frequently to rotate (discard old) log files, including how long to keep archived logs. This menu option is sometimes confused for the "System Logs" option later in this menu – this screen doesn't let you view the logs, just configure their rotation. System Logs will let you view them.

Next, we get into a few items that you typically would rarely interact with. MIME Type Programs allows you to specify the default program to handle a specific type of content, whether it be text, application data, image files, or anything else. The defaults here typically work very well and don't need to be tweaked. Similarly, the PAM Authentication screen is also not one to mess with. PAM stands for Pluggable Authentication Modules – anytime you do something that the system requires you to be authorized for or authenticated for (think anytime you need to type your password), it consults the PAM configuration to determine how to go about doing the authorization or authentication. If you decide to do something to authentication, such as add system-wide Two-Factor Authentication, you may need to modify PAM. Otherwise, look, but don't touch!

The next option in the group, Running Processes, can be an extremely useful tool. It shows all of the processes that are running on the VPS and who started them. As can be seen in Figure 4-29, on my system, the `root` user started the system with the command `init -z` – from there, all of the other processes started. Each process is given a PID, or process ID, number. You can use this number with the `kill` command to terminate any process, although you will want to be careful with this ability!

ID	Owner	Started	Command
1	root	2 hours ago	init -z
79	root	2 hours ago	/lib/systemd/systemd-journald
110	root	2 hours ago	/lib/systemd/systemd-udevd
121	systemd-network	2 hours ago	/lib/systemd/systemd-networkd
127	root	2 hours ago	/usr/sbin/rsyslogd -n -iNONE
129	root	2 hours ago	/usr/sbin/cron -f
253	root	2 hours ago	/sbin/agetty -o -p – \u –noclear –keep-baud console 115200,38400,9600 linux
254	root	2 hours ago	/sbin/agetty -o -p – \u –noclear tty2 linux
255	root	2 hours ago	/usr/sbin/sshd -D
256	root	2 hours ago	/usr/sbin/apache2 -k start
257	www-data	2 hours ago	/usr/sbin/apache2 -k start
258	www-data	2 hours ago	/usr/sbin/apache2 -k start
337	root	2 hours ago	/usr/bin/perl /usr/share/webmin/miniserv.pl /etc/webmin/miniserv.conf
14457	root	a minute ago	sh -c ps --cols 2048 -eo user:80,ruser:80,group:80,rgroup:80,pid,ppid,pgid,pcpu, ...
14458	root	a minute ago	ps --cols 2048 -eo user:80,ruser:80,group:80,rgroup:80,pid,ppid,pgid,pcpu,vsz,ni ...

Figure 4-29. *Running Processes*

One useful thing to do periodically is to record the list of running processes. By knowing what is supposed to be running on your machine, it's easier to detect when software you weren't aware of decides to take up residence. A list of known good processes is useful to have in your administrator's notebook.

The next option, Scheduled Cron Jobs, lets you access the Crontab scheduling software typically installed in Linux. Cron allows you to perform commands on a regular basis, either at a given time or given interval. Think about the Task Scheduler in Windows – it's the same basic idea. Cron syntax can be a bit daunting at first, so having a graphical way to control it is very useful.

Moving along, the next two options, Software Package Updates and Software Packages, can be used to automate updating packages and to list the packages of software you currently have installed, respectively. I typically advise administrators to avoid scheduled upgrades or updates, in lieu of doing them manually on a set schedule – otherwise, if an upgrade or update goes wrong, you might find your machine unresponsive at a critical time or on a critical day. As long as you are diligent about updating on a regular schedule, you'll reap the same benefits without the uncertainty. We'll talk more about that in Chapters 5 and 9.

The remaining items in the System group include System Documentation, which will let you access the manual pages installed, as well as in other documentation. System Logs, as mentioned earlier, allows you to view any of the log files that the system maintains (auth.log is useful to see if anyone has tried to log into your box and failed, and the apache error.log is useful when troubleshooting web server issues). And finally, Users and Groups allows you to set up new user accounts and manage group memberships.

A lot of important content is in this group, and in general I advise a look but don't touch attitude for most of it when you're starting out. Exploring each option and seeing what is available can be a great way to learn about basic administration. Once you're ready, you can then progress onto the Servers group.

Servers Group

By default, there aren't a lot of options enabled under the Servers menu if you've just installed Webmin on a new VPS. On CentOS, you'll see Procmail Mail Filter, Read User Mail, Sendmail Mail Server, and SSH Server. Debian will likely show Procmail, Read User Mail, and SSH Server. As you install more server software, such as the Apache Web Server, and use the "Refresh Modules" option, more will appear in this menu.

If you're wondering about the mail options, they're present because the Linux operating system was built to be multiuser from the start, and that meant allowing some way to communicate between users. This was the first implementation of email, and while we think of email today as being global, it originated on a much smaller level, existing on just individual machines that would eventually be networked together. Thus, each user on a Linux machine has a mailbox and can set up rules to process their mail or filter it (using Procmail). As an administrator, you can view all of the user mailboxes if you wish. Although if you use this mail feature within your group, you might not want to for privacy purposes!

Finally, the last default option is the SSH Server. We've already covered connecting to SSH, although the actual protocol is very flexible. We'll talk about securing SSH in the future, and this module gives you access to some of the most common tweaks, such as disabling root access (not something you want to do until you have at least one other user account on the VPS!), through the "Authentication" menu. You'll see options in there that allow you to disable password authentication altogether, requiring you to use cryptographic keys only.

Others Group

The Others group includes useful features that Webmin includes that don't neatly fit under the other options. These include

- Command Shell, which lets you execute commands by typing them in and clicking "Execute Command" – an easy way to run a specific command, without having to log in via SSH.

- File Manager, a graphical file manager that lets you upload, download, copy, move, create, and delete files.

- HTTP Tunnel, which allows you to open a web page *through* your VPS. This is useful if you are behind a firewall or content filter that prevents you from viewing the content directly.

- Perl Modules, as Webmin is written in Perl, which you can use to install specific modules that you might find useful. Typically not a common module to use, but handy when you need it.

- Protected Web Directories, which can automate the ability to set up password-protected areas of a website.

- SSH Login, which uses a Java SSH client to connect to the VPS through SSH. This is only available if you are running Debian and have the Java client installed in your browser.

- System and Server Status, a very basic monitoring system that can keep an eye on various aspects of your server and contact you if something breaks, either through email or another means.

- Text Login, which is a console login written in HTML and JavaScript, allowing you to use the VPS similar to how you would via SSH.

- Upload and Download, which includes a series of options to download files from the Web to your VPS, upload files to your VPS, or download files from your VPS. This could be useful to automate moving of files during non-peak times or to download a specific large file to your VPS so that you can retrieve it later when you are on a more stable connection.

These are all useful tools that can be helpful, although they are fairly narrow in scope.

Networking Group

The Networking group contains modules that will help you set up and manage the network connections you have to the outside world. By default, VPS providers typically already set up your network connections, so in practice, you are not likely to ever need a lot of these features. You can generally safely ignore the Network Configuration, Kerberos5, NIS Client and Server, and TCP Wrappers options if you have them.

However, you will want to be aware of the Bandwidth Monitoring and Firewall options. The first is easy to understand — it allows you to track all of the connections to and from your VPS. Be aware though that this log can get very large very quickly, so you'll likely only want to do this for a limited time.

The Firewall option specifies what ports should be open on the VPS to accept connections, as well as what connections the machine may make outgoing. By default on Debian, if you use the Linux Firewall command, you'll see that everything is allowed. CentOS does start with a more restrictive firewall and should be administered with the FirewallD module. We'll cover firewall configuration more in Chapter 5.

Hardware Group

Because your VPS is a virtual machine, it doesn't really have hardware to manage. The two options under this menu are typically Printer Administration (which you can use to set up connections to printers or printer-like devices) and System Time, which allows you to manually specify the current time and the server's time zone. The System Time module is also useful in that it will let you set up a synchronization schedule between your computer and an NTP Time Server, such as pool.ntp.org which is a public time server. I have seen dozens of situations in the past where the wrong time set on a server has caused very strange and bizarre errors. It's often something so minor we fail to check it, so having your VPS synchronize time regularly can be very useful in heading off problems.

Cluster Group

Finally, the last group of modules all relate to clustering multiple VPSs together, with all of them running Webmin. Each of these modules will let you run a single command, such as a file copy, a Cron job setup, updating software packages, and more, on multiple machines at the same time. This can be very useful for a seasoned system administrator to automate their work; however, it's not likely you'll be using it as you start out. But knowing it's there might make you less hesitant to launch additional VPSs, as you know you can manage them from a central machine.

We've now gone through most of the Webmin interface, and it's a useful time to talk about two advanced topics — creating other administrative users that can help share the load and a special version of Webmin that's targeted toward users of your system, vs. administrators, named Usermin.

Advanced Topics

Because Webmin is open source software, you can customize it in many different ways. Since we don't have that much space, I want to highlight two specific functions of Webmin that I think are worth exploring — the first, to create other administrative users that can help you and, the second, to build your own "portal" for your friends, family, or coworkers, whoever might need certain services.

Creating Other Webmin Users

Being a system administrator is a hard job, and sometimes you wish you could just delegate certain tasks. For example, say we have a friend named Bob. Bob is loyal and true, but somewhat easy to fluster. You've decided to go out of town for the weekend, but want to make sure that if something happens to your VPS, Bob can shut it down and wait for you to return to take a look.

On one hand, you could give Bob the root password and let him log into Webmin or SSH and hope that they don't get overwhelmed by the choices or the command line. This is probably not a good option for Bob. Another option would be to set up a program such as sudo that will let a user account (bob) issue just one command — shutdown. This might still be a lot for Bob — he's never used a command line before.

You decide on yet another option — creating a Webmin user account for Bob which can only shut down the machine. To do this, you'll

1. Go to the Webmin Users module, under the Webmin menu.

2. Choose "Create a New Privileged User" (see Figure 4-30).

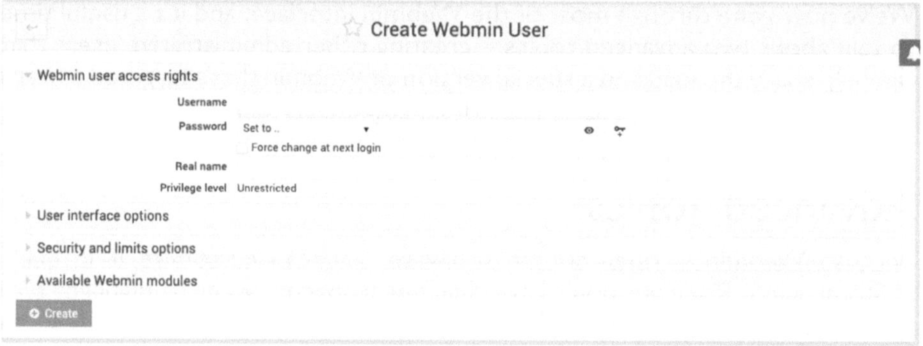

Figure 4-30. The new privileged user screen

3. Create a username and password for Bob. If you've previously created an account for Bob on the server (e.g., through the adduser command or through the Users and Groups module), you can set the password to "Unix Authentication," and it will use Bob's regular password. However, if you want Bob to only be able to access Webmin, just keep it at "Set to..." and generate a secure password to give to Bob.

4. Now we need to restrict Bob's account and make it more comfortable. Under "User interface options," I'm going to change the "Categorize Modules" to "No," since Bob won't have many modules to manage. Under "Security and limits options," I'm going to allow Bob only in on Saturdays and Sundays, and under "Available Webmin modules," I'm going to leave everything unchecked except "Bootup and Shutdown." Once I'm set, I'll click "Create."

5. I can now see that I have two user accounts, root and Bob (see Figure 4-31). I'm going to click the red arrow in the lower left of the screen to log out as root, and I'll log back in as Bob.

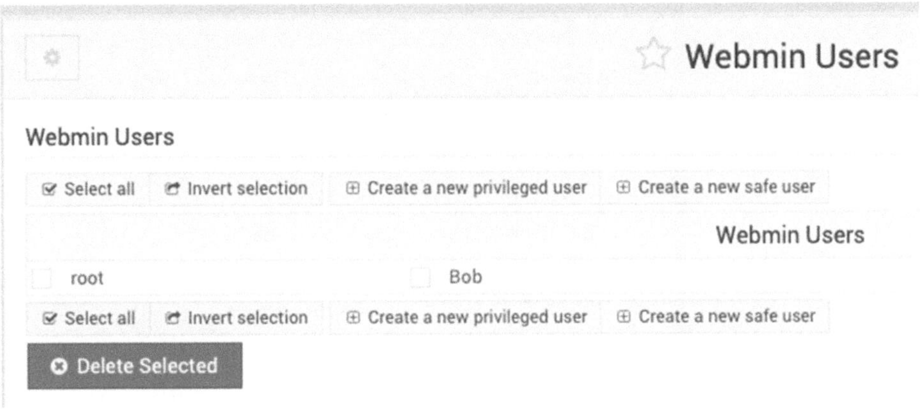

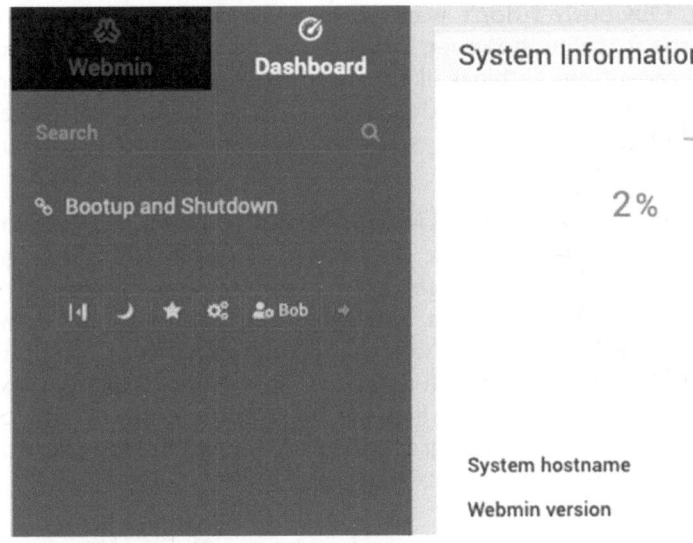

Webmin Users
Webmin Users
Select all
Invert selection
Create a new privileged user
Create a new safe user
Webmin Users
root
Bob
Select all
Invert selection
Create a new privileged user
Create a new safe user
Delete Selected

Figure 4-31. Additional user created

As you can see in Figure 4-32, Bob only has one option in his left-hand menu, Bootup and Shutdown. Clicking it and scrolling to the bottom, there is a "Shutdown System" button (see Figure 4-33). Now all I have to do when I go on vacation is tell Bob, "Visit this website (`https://lilo.jonwestfall.net:10000`), log in with your username and password, click 'Bootup and Shutdown,' and choose the 'Shutdown System' button at the bottom." This should be simple enough and also secure enough, since the most Bob could do is change some of my startup and shutdown options with permission to the Bootup and Shutdown tab.

Webmin
Dashboard
Search
Bootup and Shutdown
Bob
System Informatio
2%
System hostname
Webmin version

Figure 4-32. Bob's left-hand menu

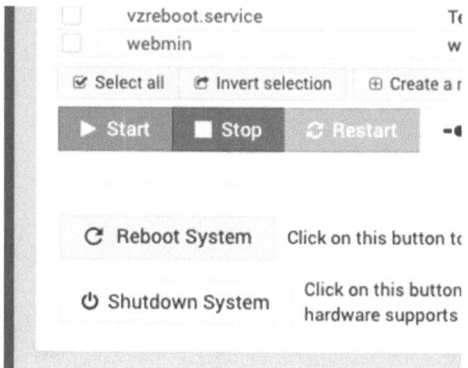

Figure 4-33. The Shutdown System button

Thinking about it, you could now see how you might be able to delegate very basic commands or even configuration tasks such as adding new protected web directories or file download jobs by creating custom sub-administrators! But what about a situation where you have a lot of users and you want them all to have some level of access. Enter the Usermin service!

Usermin

Webmin is a great control panel for administrators, but remember how I said that Linux is a multiuser operating system? That means that I could have dozens or hundreds of users on my machine that also need to access various resources. Obviously I don't want to give them unrestricted administrator access to the machine; however, I might want to let them log in and perform basic user operations – things like manage their own database, if I'm running a database server, or manage their website files or send and receive email. Thankfully there is a similar system to Webmin that they can use, called Usermin.

To install Usermin, go to the "Un-used Modules" menu in Webmin and click "Usermin Configuration." Click the "Install Usermin RPM Package" or the "Install Usermin tar.gz Package" to install the appropriate version (see Figure 4-34). You should get a message saying that you can now log into Usermin at the same address as your Webmin server, except instead of running on port 10000, Usermin defaults to run on port 20000. Now you just need to start Usermin – you'll find the "Usermin Configuration" option has now moved to the "Webmin" group in the left-hand menu. Click it, and then click "Start Usermin" at the bottom.

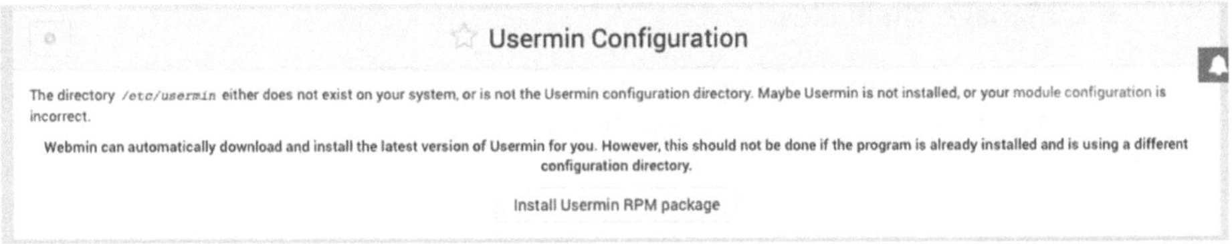
Usermin Configuration
The directory /etc/usermin either does not exist on your system, or is not the Usermin configuration directory. Maybe Usermin is not installed, or your module configuration is incorrect.
Webmin can automatically download and install the latest version of Usermin for you. However, this should not be done if the program is already installed and is using a different configuration directory.
Install Usermin RPM package

Figure 4-34. The Install Usermin option

If you're running Debian, you can go there straight away. However, if you're on CentOS, you'll need to first open port 20000 by going to the FirewallD options under the Network menu, clicking "Add Allowed Port" and putting port 20000 in the Single Port box, and then clicking "Create" (see Figure 4-35). From the main FirewallD screen, click "Apply Configuration," and now you should be able to open the Usermin login.

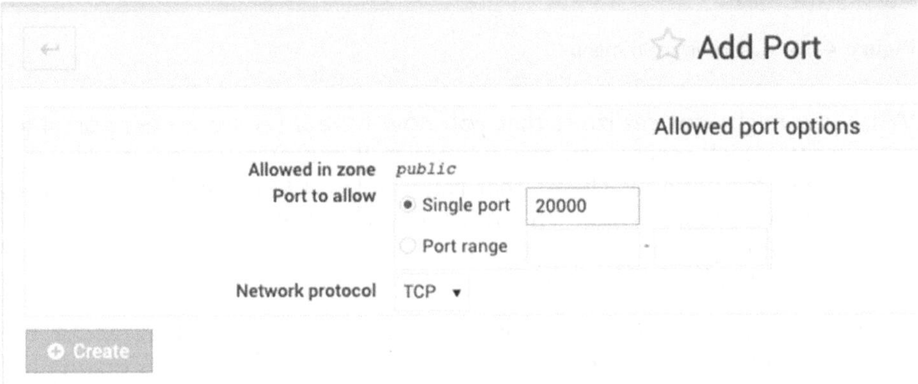
Add Port
Allowed port options
Allowed in zone
public
Port to allow
Single port
20000
Port range
Network protocol
TCP
Create

Figure 4-35. Allowing access to port 20000

And what do you find when you go there? That same pesky connection error you got way back at the start of the chapter when you installed Webmin. To fix this, choose SSL Encryption in the Usermin Configuration, and change it to use the same values as SSL Encryption in the Webmin module – to do this, click the "Copy Certificate from Webmin" button at the bottom. Then click "Restart Usermin," and you should be able to log in to Webmin.

Logging in, you'll see (Figure 4-36) that your regular users have the ability to do the following:

- Filter and forward mail.
- Change their password.
- Encrypt, decrypt, sign, and verify files with GnuPG.

- Manage their files.

- Manage their MySQL and PostgreSQL databases, assuming they have access to them.

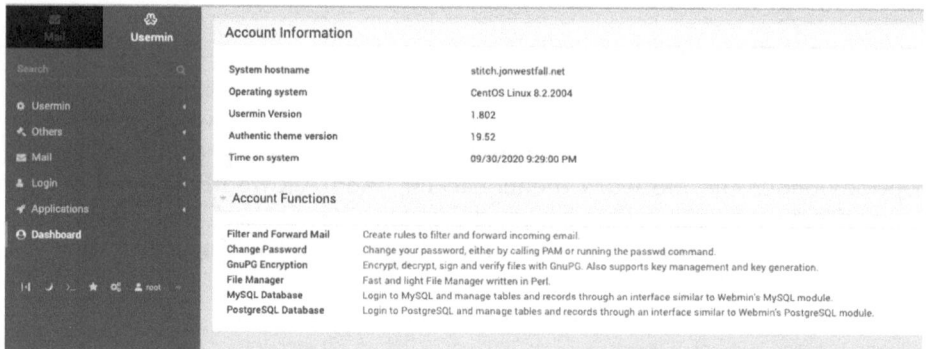

Figure 4-36. Usermin main menu

What you might not realize is that you now have a secure access portal for your users, which means you can customize it out as much as you like. I've built "hubs" for previous clients that rely solely on Usermin, heavily utilizing the Custom Commands (https://download.webmin.com/download/modules/custom.wbm.gz) and Custom Link (www.webmin.com/download/modules/link.wbm.gz) modules.

Hopefully, these two advanced use scenarios get you thinking about the possibilities that you can create using Webmin. As we've seen, Webmin is a tool that will allow you to not only administer your server but also learn about Linux administration as well as empower others to manage their own portions of the server! But as we've gone through, we've started to see the creeping mention of something completely vital to today's survival on the Internet: good security practice. In the next chapter, we will talk about the basics of Linux security and how to protect your server from the bad actors seeking to mess up your good time!

Basics of Linux Security

It isn't hard to find examples of data security issues in the world today. It seems like every few days we're hearing about data theft from the businesses that we work with (through mandatory disclosure emails), ransomware attacks in the news, and our own concerns over the privacy of our data on our computers. We hear companies talk about encryption and security policies, and we create passwords that are eight or more characters including uppercase, lowercase, symbols, numbers, and probably soon emoji. In this chapter, we'll cover the basics of securing your VPS and considerations that you should have while working not only to manage it but also to make it harder for someone else to take advantage of an always-on machine. We'll cover three big areas in this chapter: "physical" security (of a virtual device!), network security, and how to keep track of what's going on by checking your log files regularly.

Physical Security, Console Access, and File Permissions

Straight away, let's remember that you have very little to do with the actual physical security of your VPS. Your provider is responsible for the hardware that your VPS lives on, and presumably they care about security and aren't

© Jon Westfall 2021
J. Westfall, *Set Up and Manage Your Virtual Private Server*,
https://doi.org/10.1007/978-1-4842-6966-4_5

running the physical box mounted below the counter at a gas station, next to the Icee machine with a big sign that says "Play with me"! That being said, some providers will provide more details about their physical security setup, namely, in the form of discussing if they run their physical security compliant with various government regulations that some of their clients might require. You can always ask about physical security before you set up an account.

Console Access

From a VPS perspective, the closest you can get to physically accessing your VPS is using a feature called "console" access. Gained by logging into your provider's management interface, console access allows you to directly connect to your VPS as if you had hooked up a keyboard, monitor, and mouse directly to it. It's the equivalent of a KVM switch mentioned in earlier chapters. Some providers give you a direct interface on the web page, while others allow access to the console over the Secure Shell (SSH) protocol. In Figure 5-1, we see the screen that my provider uses to enable console access, which warns us that this is not to be used as a replacement for SSH. I can then enable the console (Figure 5-2).

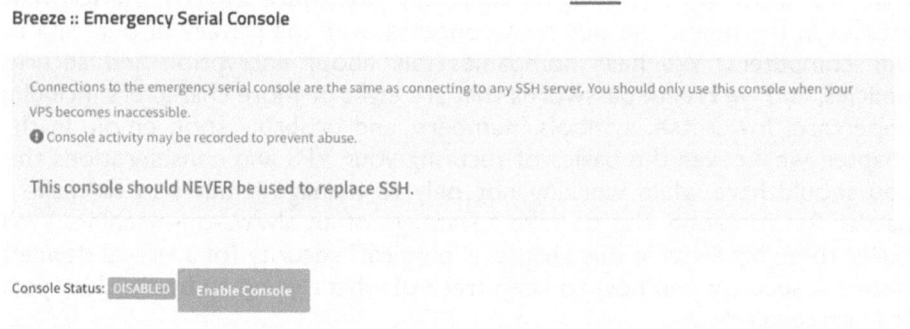

Breeze :: Emergency Serial Console

Connections to the emergency serial console are the same as connecting to any SSH server. You should only use this console when your VPS becomes inaccessible.

 Console activity may be recorded to prevent abuse.

This console should NEVER be used to replace SSH.

Console Status: DISABLED   Enable Console

Figure 5-1. The Console Access Screen

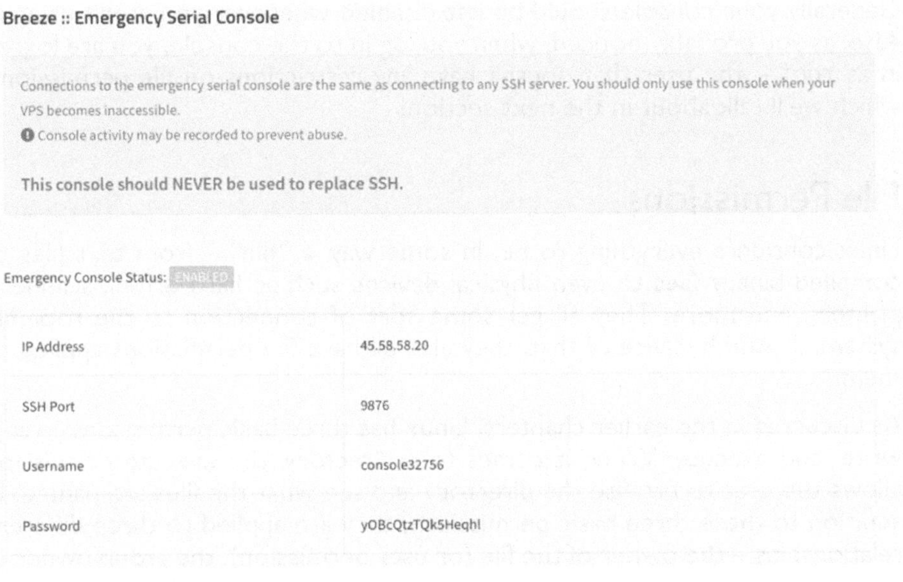

Breeze :: Emergency Serial Console

Connections to the emergency serial console are the same as connecting to any SSH server. You should only use this console when your VPS becomes inaccessible.

ⓘ Console activity may be recorded to prevent abuse.

This console should NEVER be used to replace SSH.

Emergency Console Status: ENABLED

IP Address	45.58.58.20
SSH Port	9876
Username	console32756
Password	yOBcQtzTQk5Heqhl

Figure 5-2. The console, enabled

To connect to the console, I can use the provided IP address, port, username, and password. The command on my MacBook would look like the following:

```
ssh -p 9876 console32756@45.58.58.20
```

We can see the connection in Figure 5-3. From here I can "fix" any problem I might have, such as restarting SSH (assuming that's the reason I didn't connect to it in the first place), fixing the firewall (in case I accidentally locked myself out), or resetting a password as the root user using the passwd command.

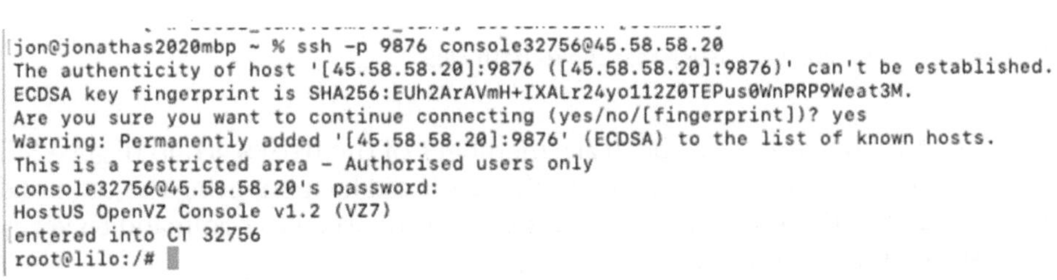

```
jon@jonathas2020mbp ~ % ssh -p 9876 console32756@45.58.58.20
The authenticity of host '[45.58.58.20]:9876 ([45.58.58.20]:9876)' can't be established.
ECDSA key fingerprint is SHA256:EUh2ArAVmH+IXALr24yo112Z0TEPus0WnPRP9Weat3M.
Are you sure you want to continue connecting (yes/no/[fingerprint])? yes
Warning: Permanently added '[45.58.58.20]:9876' (ECDSA) to the list of known hosts.
This is a restricted area - Authorised users only
console32756@45.58.58.20's password:
HostUS OpenVZ Console v1.2 (VZ7)
entered into CT 32756
root@lilo:/# 
```

Figure 5-3. Logging into the console

You may have noticed that my provider explicitly tells me that, due to the power of the console access, the password is only shown once. Indeed, as soon as I disable the console, the login credentials no longer work, and I would need to reenable it. And when I do, it is a different generated password.

Generally your console should be left disabled whenever you aren't using it. Also, as you probably noticed, when you log in to the console, you are logged in as root – the user that doesn't have any restrictions on file permissions, which we'll talk about in the next section!

File Permissions

Linux considers everything to be, in some way, a "file" – from text files to compiled binary files to even physical devices such as hard drives, scanners, printers, and more. They all get some sort of connection to the root file system, /. And because of that, they also all have file permissions applied to them.

As discussed in the earlier chapters, Linux has three basic permissions – read, write, and execute. When it comes to a directory, the execute permission allows the user to browse the directory and see what the files are named. In addition to these three basic permissions, they are applied to three different relationships – the owner of the file (or user permission), the group owner of the file (or group permission), and everyone else (other). Imagine the following scenario:

Jon has two files in his home directory, file1 and file2. As we can see in Figure 5-4, the file permissions are set to -rw-r--r-- which indicates that jon can read and write the files, other members of the jon group can read the files, and everyone else who is not jon or in the jon group can read the files.

```
jon@lilo:~$ ls -l
total 0
-rw-r--r-- 1 jon jon 0 Oct 16 16:36 file1
-rw-r--r-- 1 jon jon 0 Oct 16 16:36 file2
```

Figure 5-4. The directory listing that shows both files

Imagine that jon and steve both are members of the users group (Figure 5-5 will actually make this happen and verify that it did happen, using the usermod command to add them to the users group and the groups command to verify they are members of users).

```
root@lilo:/home# usermod -a -G users jon
root@lilo:/home# usermod -a -G users steve
root@lilo:/home# groups jon
jon : jon users
root@lilo:/home# groups steve
steve : steve users
root@lilo:/home# ▮
```

Figure 5-5. Adding jon and steve to the users group

Jon would like to allow Steve to edit `file1`. To do that, he needs to do the following:

1. Change the group owner of `file1` to `users` from `jon`, his private group.

2. Change the file permissions on `file1` to allow other `users` group members, like Steve, to edit it.

He can accomplish that with the following code: chown `jon:users file1` chmod `664 file` or chmod g+w `file1`.

As we can see in Figure 5-6, the file permissions line has now changed to add the w permission to the group, and the user/group owner has changed from jon jon to jon users, so Steve, being a member of `users`, could now access it and write to it.

```
jon@lilo:~$ chown jon:users file1
jon@lilo:~$ chmod 664 file1
jon@lilo:~$ ls -l
total 0
-rw-rw-r-- 1 jon users 0 Oct 16 16:36 file1
-rw-r--r-- 1 jon jon   0 Oct 16 16:36 file2
jon@lilo:~$ ▮
```

Figure 5-6. Updated file permissions

Now if I log into the VPS as `steve`, I can access and write to `file1`, as seen in Figure 5-7, but I cannot write to `file2`.

```
$ echo "I'm writing to file 1" > /home/jon/file1
$ echo "I'm writing to file 2" > /home/jon/file2
sh: 3: cannot create /home/jon/file2: Permission denied
$ ▮
```

Figure 5-7. The steve user can write to file1, but gets an error writing to file2

Knowing about file permissions is vital to securing your Linux system for several reasons, namely:

- If you intend to collaborate with other users, you'll need to create directories and files that all can access. For example, if multiple people are going to be editing the web server files in /var/www, you'll want to create a new group (perhaps web-authors) using the groupadd command, then add your users to that group (using the usermod command shown earlier), and then finally change the group owner of /var/www to web-authors.

- This also reminds us that programs on the system tend to run under their own user accounts, for security. For example, on Debian, the Apache Web Server runs under the user www-data and the group www-data (CentOS uses apache for both). The default permissions on /var/www allow all users to read and execute, which means that the web server can serve pages properly. However, if you were to remove those permissions, perhaps in an attempt to secure the system, you'd errantly also prevent the web server from doing its job!

- Be careful in changing permissions in an attempt to secure the machine. Years ago as a young administrator, I wondered about why the file that stored all of the users on the machine, /etc/passwd, was readable by everyone. Being naive, I took away the world read permission and promptly crashed the system. Turns out this wasn't a security hole – the file needed to be able to be read by several people, and thus, taking that away became a problem.

- Finally, in a collaborative environment, remember that each user on the system, when they create a file, will be creating it as owned by them and their primary group. As primary groups are generally the same as the user's name (e.g., jon is the primary group for jon), in a shared directory, I might set up a situation where new files are only writable by the original owner. There are a few ways to prevent this, including having users' primary groups changed or changing the umask that the user creates files in by default (the standard umask is 0022, which is interpreted as the number of permission bits to remove from various groups – it takes away w from group and other and takes nothing away from the user). Another method, which I've used with success, is writing a scheduled job that goes through shared directories and changes the file permissions en masse to something all authorized users can access and write. Running this script once per hour or so generally ensures that anyone who didn't set their file permissions properly will find them set properly before the next user tries to edit or access the file.

SetUID, SetGID, and SELinux

In addition to what is discussed earlier, there are three additional advanced topics that you'll want to have, at least, passing awareness of and what they do. Two relate to how the system treats specific files, while the third relates to a radical change to how Linux treats security.

First, we have the concepts of SetUID and SetGID, which stand for "set user ID" and "set group ID." These special permissions allow a regular user (such as jon) to run a command as if they were the owner of the command, typically an administrative user such as root. There are a few different reasons why we might use these. First, you might want to allow users to do things normally reserved for just root, such as mount and unmount file systems, shut down the system, or start the web server process. Second, you may want a program to always write its files as the owner of the program, vs. the user currently running, to facilitate easier collaboration. Finally, you may have a program shared among several users that needs to always run with the same preferences and settings, and thus SetUID or SetGID would be a good option. To set it, you would use the chmod command but include either an additional starting number (e.g., chmod 6666 would SetUID and SetGID and allow read and write for all) or use +s, such as chmod u+s, which would SetUID, but not SetGID.

To determine if SetUID or SetGID is set on a file, you can either look at the long format of the directory listing (using -l with the ls command) to see if you see s in the permission string (e.g., /bin/su, the command to switch users, has -rwsr-xr-x as its permission string, vs. /bin/sync, which has -rwxr-xr-x), or you can use the stat command, as seen in Figure 5-8, which shows both the s in the permission string and the octal (numeric) notation of 4755 in this case.

```
root@lilo:/etc/apache2# stat /bin/su
  File: /bin/su
  Size: 63568          Blocks: 128        IO Block: 4096    regular file
Device: 4410b641h/1141945921d   Inode: 394131      Links: 1
Access: (4755/-rwsr-xr-x)  Uid: (    0/    root)  Gid: (    0/    root)
Access: 2020-10-16 16:36:19.376650213 +0200
Modify: 2019-01-10 09:30:43.000000000 +0100
Change: 2020-07-02 12:10:13.876812876 +0200
 Birth: -
root@lilo:/etc/apache2# stat /bin/sync
  File: /bin/sync
  Size: 35488          Blocks: 72         IO Block: 4096    regular file
Device: 4410b641h/1141945921d   Inode: 394067      Links: 1
Access: (0755/-rwxr-xr-x)  Uid: (    0/    root)  Gid: (    0/    root)
Access: 2020-07-02 12:10:06.000000000 +0200
Modify: 2019-02-28 16:30:31.000000000 +0100
Change: 2020-07-02 12:10:06.959821211 +0200
 Birth: -
```

Figure 5-8. The stat command showing one file with SetUID and another without

In general, you won't need to use SetUID or SetGID very often; however, where you may get into trouble is if they've been set and you accidentally change them. Thus, before issuing any permissions change command, you'll want to use the `ls -l` command to determine what the existing permissions are, in case you'd need to change them.

Second, we have SELinux, or Security-Enhanced Linux. This is a kernel extension, disabled by default, that can be used to greatly limit the ability for programs to interact with each other on a Linux system. Inspired by work done by the National Security Agency (NSA), SELinux "sandboxes" the user and software into areas where they cannot easily hijack or compromise the entire system. This is great when properly set up and running, but it can be very complicated to get the permissions properly set. Thus, for most purposes, SELinux will be more trouble than it's worth, unless you are working with extremely sensitive information or information that would have a high value to attackers. Because most users reading an entry-level book on Linux administration aren't in that group, I won't go any further on it here. However, I felt it was important to highlight, in case you saw mentions of it and wondered if it was something you should enable. The short answer to that is: Probably not…but maybe in the future!

Speaking of something you might want to enable, especially if you have multiple people administering your machine and you aren't using a graphical interface such as Webmin, let's talk about sudo!

Securing Administrative Access Using sudo

Ever need to tell an administrator to do something? Then sudo is your tool – as the name literally means "super user do" as in the way one might give a command. We can use sudo to create access rules that let regular user accounts perform specific functions.

To get started, you'll need to install sudo as the root user, using the command apt-get install sudo or yum install sudo depending on if you're on Debian or CentOS. Once you've installed sudo, you can edit its configuration file. Unlike most software, you need to use a special command to edit sudo's configuration, visudo. Running this command will open your default text editor application (on Debian, it opens in nano; on CentOS, it opens in vim) and display /etc/sudoers – the configuration file. We can then set up a variety of very granular rules to control who can access what, on which machines, using which commands. It's worth noting that the default version of /etc/sudoers on CentOS is much longer than on Debian, giving many more example commands that you might use, but likely do not need to.

The simplest way to use sudo is to allow certain users to execute any command as if they were root. They do this by simply adding sudo before the command they wish to execute. Let's first allow the user jon to execute any command as root and then see sudo in action.

First, we'll add the following line in the User privilege section (although technically it could go anywhere):

```
jon ALL=(ALL:ALL) ALL
```

This tells sudo that the user jon can access all commands on all hosts. Saving the file and switching to the jon user, I can reboot the machine by using the command sudo shutdown -r now. As seen in Figure 5-9, it will prompt me for my user password, and assuming I provide it, it will reboot the server.

```
jon@lilo:/root$ sudo shutdown -r now

We trust you have received the usual lecture from the local System
Administrator. It usually boils down to these three things:

    #1) Respect the privacy of others.
    #2) Think before you type.
    #3) With great power comes great responsibility.

[sudo] password for jon:
jon@lilo:/root$ ▊
```

Figure 5-9. Rebooting the system using sudo

You'll notice that it prompted me for my password, as a security measure so that if I were to leave my jon account logged in and someone were to come to my machine and see this, they couldn't start executing commands without knowing my password. If this isn't a scenario you foresee happening, you could add an option to the jon entry in /etc/sudoers to read

```
jon ALL=(ALL) NOPASSWD: ALL
```

This NOPASSWD option tells sudo that you do not need to enter your user password, although it does degrade overall security.

You could, at this point, add entries for every person that you want to have access. However, sudo also allows you to specify all members of a group to have permissions. If I trusted all of my users, I could add the following line that would give them all the ability to use sudo:

```
%users ALL=(ALL:ALL) ALL
```

And once I'd added them all to the users group, they'd have access.

We have just scratched the surface of what sudo can do — it has robust support to create groups of commands, groups of servers, and more in order to centralize and finely tune what super user commands one can perform. Generally what I've discussed here is what a new administrator needs so that they don't have to run under the root command regularly, which, as we've discussed earlier, is dangerous. Equally as dangerous is the practice of using the command sudo bash to launch a shell that runs as root — this means you can execute commands without the need to use sudo. However, you may also fall into the same trap that you would running as the root user. Be cautious.

A final note before we move on to network security: sudo allows access control and auditing. Other solutions to share administrative access aren't as secure yet just as useful. Years ago, I ran across a machine where the administrators had edited the /etc/passwd file to set the user ID number for each administrative user to 0. The root user account always has the user ID of 0, so the system, in essence, thought there were several root users. Each admin could log in with their own username and password, but essentially they were all root. This meant if one admin changed a setting, any auditing software or logging software would have identified it as root and thus made it very hard to track down which admin made the change. If you see this sort of behavior recommended, I would strongly advise using sudo, for the more fine-tuned abilities it offers.

Now that we've discussed console security, it's time to move on to the area that's most likely to be compromised: your network connection to the Internet!

Network Security

When it comes to security of an Internet-connected machine, we run into a fundamental issue – the most secure machine on the planet is "air gapped," meaning it isn't connected to any other system or, in some strictest sense, any sort of input/output device at all. However, as you can imagine, this greatly limits the usefulness of the computer! So assuming you have to connect to the Internet, like most of us do, how do you do it in a secure way? In this section, we'll discuss two primary means of security: firewalls and removing login via password.

Open Ports and Firewalls

Years ago I asked a group of students in a computer repair course what they thought a firewall did. One especially humorous student replied that it "burned" the hacker's computer. Sadly, this is much more interesting than what a firewall actually does. In reality, a firewall is simply a set of rules that determines which "doors" on a computer can be opened and which are closed and locked.

Recall our earlier discussion of port numbers from Chapter 1. In it, we discussed that web servers listened for requests on a specific port number, either 80 (for http) or 443 (for https). If someone attempted to communicate with your computer on that port, the web server was free to answer. On our VPS, when we start the web server, it "binds" to that particular port or ports.

At any time, we can see what software on our VPS is bound to a particular outgoing port by using the command `netstat -tulpn | grep LISTEN` – this will use the `netstat` command to tell us all of the software attempting to listen for network connections. On a fresh install of CentOS 8, we have three items listening, as seen in Figure 5-10:

- sshd, the Secure Shell software that we're logged into, on the IPv4 network that is still most commonly used today

- sendmail: accep, software that accepts email deliveries for users on the box

- sshd, on tcp6 – the Secure Shell software accepting connections on the IPv6 network, the next generation of the Internet Protocol (IP)

```
[root@stitch ~]# netstat -tulpn | grep LISTEN
tcp        0      0 0.0.0.0:22              0.0.0.0:*               LISTEN      503/sshd
tcp        0      0 127.0.0.1:25            0.0.0.0:*               LISTEN      518/sendmail: accep
tcp6       0      0 :::22                   :::*                    LISTEN      503/sshd
[root@stitch ~]# 
```

Figure 5-10. Output of the netstat command on CentOS

On Debian Linux, the output is very similar (see Figure 5-11), with the only exception being that Sendmail isn't installed by default.

```
root@lilo:~# netstat -tulpn | grep LISTEN
tcp        0      0 0.0.0.0:22           0.0.0.0:*              LISTEN      311/sshd
tcp6       0      0 :::22                :::*                   LISTEN      311/sshd
```

Figure 5-11. Output of the netstat command on Debian

Now that we know we have software listening on TCP ports 22 and 25, we normally could connect to those ports directly with the appropriate software – an email client for port 25, to send mail, and a secure host client like PuTTY or ssh on port 22. It's worth noting that there are two types of IP connections – TCP (Transmission Control Protocol) used for most communications that require both sides to acknowledge each bit of data and UDP (User Datagram Protocol) which is used when bits of data can safely be lost (e.g., during streaming music or video).

A firewall sits between the program that wants to receive or send information on a given port and the network connection to the machine. It's a set of rules that determine if the software waiting to be connected to is allowed to be connected to. Imagine it sort of like a child who's always ready to come out and play with their friends (the software), but a parent is there to say, "Nope, it's past your bedtime" (the firewall).

By default, CentOS and Debian treat firewall rules a bit differently, as mentioned in previous chapters. Figure 5-12 shows the default CentOS firewall rules on a fresh install, and Figure 5-13 shows the default Debian rules. As you can see, CentOS creates a number of zones and rules by default, whereas Debian does not.

```
[root@stitch ~]# iptables -L
Chain INPUT (policy ACCEPT)
target     prot opt source              destination
nat_PREROUTING_ZONES_SOURCE all -- anywhere              anywhere
nat_PREROUTING_ZONES all -- anywhere              anywhere
nat_PRE_public all -- anywhere              anywhere              [goto]
nat_PRE_public all -- anywhere              anywhere              [goto]
nat_POSTROUTING_ZONES_SOURCE all -- anywhere              anywhere
nat_POSTROUTING_ZONES all -- anywhere              anywhere
nat_POST_public all -- anywhere              anywhere              [goto]
nat_POST_public all -- anywhere              anywhere              [goto]
nat_PRE_public_pre all -- anywhere              anywhere
nat_PRE_public_log all -- anywhere              anywhere
nat_PRE_public_deny all -- anywhere              anywhere
nat_PRE_public_allow all -- anywhere              anywhere
nat_PRE_public_post all -- anywhere              anywhere
nat_POST_public_pre all -- anywhere              anywhere
nat_POST_public_log all -- anywhere              anywhere
nat_POST_public_deny all -- anywhere              anywhere
nat_POST_public_allow all -- anywhere              anywhere
nat_POST_public_post all -- anywhere              anywhere

Chain FORWARD (policy ACCEPT)
target     prot opt source              destination
nat_PREROUTING_ZONES_SOURCE all -- anywhere              anywhere
nat_PREROUTING_ZONES all -- anywhere              anywhere
nat_PRE_public all -- anywhere              anywhere              [goto]
nat_PRE_public all -- anywhere              anywhere              [goto]
nat_POSTROUTING_ZONES_SOURCE all -- anywhere              anywhere
nat_POSTROUTING_ZONES all -- anywhere              anywhere
nat_POST_public all -- anywhere              anywhere              [goto]
nat_POST_public all -- anywhere              anywhere              [goto]
nat_PRE_public_pre all -- anywhere              anywhere
nat_PRE_public_log all -- anywhere              anywhere
nat_PRE_public_deny all -- anywhere              anywhere
nat_PRE_public_allow all -- anywhere              anywhere
nat_PRE_public_post all -- anywhere              anywhere
nat_POST_public_pre all -- anywhere              anywhere
nat_POST_public_log all -- anywhere              anywhere
nat_POST_public_deny all -- anywhere              anywhere
nat_POST_public_allow all -- anywhere              anywhere
nat_POST_public_post all -- anywhere              anywhere

Chain OUTPUT (policy ACCEPT)
target     prot opt source              destination
nat_PREROUTING_ZONES_SOURCE all -- anywhere              anywhere
nat_PREROUTING_ZONES all -- anywhere              anywhere
nat_PRE_public all -- anywhere              anywhere              [goto]
nat_PRE_public all -- anywhere              anywhere              [goto]
nat_POSTROUTING_ZONES_SOURCE all -- anywhere              anywhere
nat_POSTROUTING_ZONES all -- anywhere              anywhere
nat_POST_public all -- anywhere              anywhere              [goto]
nat_POST_public all -- anywhere              anywhere              [goto]
nat_PRE_public_pre all -- anywhere              anywhere
nat_PRE_public_log all -- anywhere              anywhere
nat_PRE_public_deny all -- anywhere              anywhere
nat_PRE_public_allow all -- anywhere              anywhere
nat_PRE_public_post all -- anywhere              anywhere
nat_POST_public_pre all -- anywhere              anywhere
nat_POST_public_log all -- anywhere              anywhere
nat_POST_public_deny all -- anywhere              anywhere
nat_POST_public_allow all -- anywhere              anywhere
nat_POST_public_post all -- anywhere              anywhere
# Warning: iptables-legacy tables present, use iptables-legacy to see them
```

Figure 5-12. Default CentOS firewall rules

```
root@lilo:~# iptables -L
Chain INPUT (policy ACCEPT)
target      prot opt source                    destination

Chain FORWARD (policy ACCEPT)
target      prot opt source                    destination

Chain OUTPUT (policy ACCEPT)
target      prot opt source                    destination
```

Figure 5-13. Default Debian firewall rules

The reason for this is due to the firewall management tools each distribution ships with. Debian does not ship with any firewall management tool other than the `iptables` command, which I've used earlier to output these lists. The tool that CentOS uses, and that we will install on Debian, is `firewallD`. Before moving on to the next step, you'll want to install `firewallD` on Debian by using the following commands:

```
apt-get install firewalld systemctl enable firewalld
systemctl start firewalld systemctl status firewalld
```

This last command, on Debian, should show you the status of FirewallD. If you see an error message that says the software failed to start, try the following solution from `https://vander.host/knowledgebase/operating- sys-tems/failed-to-load-nf_conntrack-module-when-starting-firewalld/`:

```
mkdir /lib/modules/$(uname -r) touch /lib/modules/$(uname -r)/modules.
{builtin,order} for i in /sys/module/*; do echo kernel/${i##**/}.ko; done >>
/lib/modules/$(uname - r)/modules.builtin depmod -a
```

Then restart FirewallD with `systemctl start firewalld`.

Once FirewallD is installed, you can get the status of it by running the command

```
firewall-cmd --state
```

It should return "running." Let's first see what rules are in place and then add a few basic rules and then enable the firewall.

First off, we can discuss the concept of "zones" – FirewallD allows you to create several different zones that refer to the other computers that are going to connect to your VPS. In an environment where you might have several trusted servers, all talking to each other, you might set up a "home" or "private" zone that has looser security requirements than the "public" zone. We'll focus exclusively on the "public" zone here, since that's the most regular use case. Let's see what rules apply to the "public" zone:

```
firewall-cmd --zone=public --permanent --list-services
```

On Debian, we see "dhcpv6-client" and "ssh" are enabled; on CentOS, we see "cockpit," "dhcpv6-client," and "ssh" are enabled. Cockpit is a web management tool, similar to Webmin. Dhcpv6-client is needed if you are using your IPv6 connection on your VPS, and ssh is the Secure Shell protocol. By default, even if other software is waiting to hear a connection (e.g., the child waiting for their friends to come by and ask to play), the firewall won't let any other traffic through.

We can add rules to our firewall pretty easily. The following command will permanently add a web server, http on port 80, to the firewall:

```
firewall-cmd --zone=public --permanent --add- service=http
```

We can also open arbitrary ports, if we like, using the following command that would allow Webmin:

```
firewall-cmd --zone=public --permanent --add- port=10000/tcp
```

Using the preceding combinations, you can allow only what you absolutely need to connect to your box to the public zone. It's worth noting that you can also configure a firewall to only allow certain programs to connect to the Internet, although that's a bit more complex and can lead to frustration if vital programs are prevented from accessing the network. For now, you'll want to make sure your firewall is configured and that you have allowed access to only what you need. One of those is nearly always ssh, the protocol you use to secure your server, so let's talk about securing it a little bit more – by using keyfiles to access SSH and turning off password authentication.

Securing SSH by Using Keyfiles

Passwords are great, aren't they? I mean that extremely sarcastically. Easy to forget, requiring frequent changes to be secure, and oddly arcane in their construction, they are not the best method of securing access to your VPS. And not to mention that anyone who has your password can pretend to be you. Further adding to the fact that we've all probably committed a few password sins in our lives (e.g., easy-to-guess passwords), and you're setting up for a bad situation.

Thankfully, SSH allows us to authenticate through a cryptographic keyfile pair. These key pairs, with one file residing on your computer and one residing on your VPS, share a common cryptographic element, which allows your VPS to verify that the other file is you and not someone else. Let's set this up on our VPS first by generating the keyfile and then authenticating with it. These steps are designed to be used on a Mac or Linux computer. If you are running Windows, see the following section on PuTTY.

First, issue the following command to create your keyfile. You can accept all of the defaults and are free to choose a passphrase or leave it blank:

ssh-keygen

As seen in Figure 5-14, my key was generated. The private keyfile was saved in /home/jon/.ssh/id_rsa, and the public key was saved as /home/jon/.ssh/id_rsa.pub.

```
jon@lilo:~$ ssh-keygen
Generating public/private rsa key pair.
Enter file in which to save the key (/home/jon/.ssh/id_rsa):
Created directory '/home/jon/.ssh'.
Enter passphrase (empty for no passphrase):
Enter same passphrase again:
Your identification has been saved in /home/jon/.ssh/id_rsa.
Your public key has been saved in /home/jon/.ssh/id_rsa.pub.
The key fingerprint is:
SHA256:5YzPDjER8FJ1JpDTd/GjuBGMS33WFt9KpojRpVrJgYo jon@lilo.jonwestfall.net
The key's randomart image is:
+---[RSA 2048]----+
|     ..+*+ + .o  |
|      o++=0. o.+ |
|     ...++B= +o++|
|    E ...@..=+o..|
|       S.+o...   |
|        = o      |
|       . o.      |
|        o        |
|         .       |
+----[SHA256]-----+
```

Figure 5-14. Generating a keyfile

Using the cat function, I can open my private keyfile, as seen in Figure 5-15. Once I have the output on my screen, I can then use the copy function and then paste the private key into a new file on my computer named "mykey." Remember where you store this key on your computer, if you decide to move it, as you'll need it later.

```
[root@stitch ~]# cat .ssh/id_rsa
-----BEGIN OPENSSH PRIVATE KEY-----
b3BlbnNzaC1rZXktdjEAAAAABG5vbmUAAAAEbm9uZQAAAAAAAABAAABlwAAAAdzc2gtcn
NhAAAAAwEAAQAAAYEAz3ZNY9SvF9N5APki/hEFBaoXeisWSTziof7GKRfZq0XCNcasGgKF
TsfGQumN3Jt1bXPg0McD19eeetGrCX3Spo35jLlERQOXt+qVOl0yWhftT/FIEWglf4RPBU
rYnZqU2XXcH25SqRTLwiuAR17LbGOqwFL63ccOu72KqaCoIuwKgiAx8BEwNkUpQggSfcDV
V8ZF8ChNw1JJsg03Nkx1bwLpWlhE4Fjp1AGMdURqjymAZ+O7wwmcvV+Ltuhl4Y+sjIEIUM
lB20NS6q2rFgkMviii/FuwGm0T6j5YIl0nCYMf0luRAmDHh1pXT9gc4yYcWDAOvlvyVxlX
gY+BpgzlLxS4EMkPYJUEL4HW7XKIsjVwb63iqOv4Qpj/QeKRewrU16MRThgFiZQx952W4t
arlkuTc8phPjo19DFwAbp0fARvmYmrSYpn/bd53o6gwPZPvq6D3jz9gfq/B0s/G8rx6ArQ
8LrOBtLKCXKdYs+20NgPYS7lIZCmp9clUomqk2yFAAAFmDFGVVsxRlVbAAAAB3NzaC1yc2
EAAAGBAM92TWPUrxfTeQD5Iv4RBQWqF3orFkk84qH+xikX2atFwjXGrBoChU7HxkLpjdyb
dW1z4NDHA9fXnnrRqwl90qaN+Yy5REUDl7fqlTpdMloX7U/xSBFoJX+ETwVK2J2alNl13B
9uUqkUy8IrgEdey2xjqsBS+t3HDru9iqmgqCLsCoIgMfARMDZFKUIIEn3A1VfGRfAoTcNS
SbINNzZMdW8C6VpYROBY6dQBjHVEao8pgGfju8MJnL1fi7boZeGPrIyBCFDJQdtDUuqtqx
YJDL4oovxbsBptE+o+WCJdJwmDH9JbkQJgx4daV0/YHOMmHFgwDr5b8lcZV4GPgaYM5S8U
uBDJD2CVBC+B1u1yiLI1cG+t4qjr+EKY/0HikXsK1NejEU4YBYmUMfedluLWq5ZLk3PKYT
46NfQxcAG6dHwEb5mJq0mKZ/23ed6OoMD2T76ug948/YH6vwdLPxvK8egK0PC6zgbSygly
nWLPttDYD2Eu5SGQpqfXJVKJqpNshQAAAAMBAAEAAAGAEdNJXP2GOdbau8GsRwYxV0ZBFC
clmA9aLa8VWayJ8FRjFnnGicmTqKwzlcY5gS3+TfQ56dZftyj4nfbr6jncYqEqQvQcMI3Z
eFz4i3Y8gE8z/b1ugshfCHDW1U6UBB6nEXQ2AKFbCtoVk85nDDrR4bNClZnLokibNHhZtK
9wIugDEyEvCUCA0vjoTZsh85og+pS3p6Xe4JxuZpUKHGk/YdVvNWsGJ/ybwrKLXfwN59Ua
ClMf6+ckh4TxHTsknafZRMO4abFRWvZpa67q+NEdV4ukILOhTG2QMhYQMeiGkPRNSud6JL
vwtBZwLCETpNvOsgGVIqiR88l+M9jJP42FSVAM20L5/BCEvAmajHB5Z6TU1AFt8abYrsbI
tCkvqgK3oqQVbJ0tk9ag7Lh24TlT7nx27eAcH6hmIt3bTu2nGUFDqQCOciywMPWu8YXvdT
urbEmJ9AtOsGXd6KBi0DQWvqmbLTEFQQNB9C0022+KHXofHMq7C1zcFlRvUAUsoZ+BAAAA
wQDVdUpOmAx5MYZPbLPGkzlIWU0WbvDjnyNXVvpduf6i8eOpwhbPVYQvlvytoN+nu/LfxJ
DK0jZwZVhtlOZK1H80pfkCJWC9Bp/oBu6Qea0pjJS8kPIXVZ+C2HM4bRsKZkqqCMTYUYh5
pgjWHP8ASrxPQUce5kwpnnhVWTchZrQho3GwyHehrcUxyDxTuBePtsOaSXrZjZQBHIHJgZ
jQ5ASbwVYgkAvG2iUuQWTX03dAOiQQYyr2kJvSSagL8lOYgkkAAADBAP3OxzfJMIBlnVZB
7GMcoJEOjLAIG8yfRhpBEbyPClQ3QnYmMFaP8+owOXYl/fSuNdHVcUSlZKa/wZctbfxvU+
dTKkkAfQ+tHmxFrCmo1kRny90iL63DyklbM5O1N7HMrxJ5UhjmINpbWo9NAr5Ayz3Jbey7
jr4Dwve0ywTxU0m+Vdjhuvzge2+LUZJbE5he/rKDpN5niPBz2//YLRS7AiglzgV/DIEMbV
JwgeuPFOpqild+OIDX5j9NL6+ADAeC5QAAAMEA0UELV5GusDXAwl5CGRL3t2ZjYx1AYJYV
ejwutoOTzGW4wN+KwosRK0YzX7VQQurZqtkKTU88ETXl3m1NP4/MtR+zAAdA2FyQUCddLk
5F5374mEMkokl9DNwqYasnW+7sG3bB8wT3r+UE5lHHZLlI32xlhgKvDPDyOVyV27DOUn2F
/KglRpDP4mugrFw9xe5wSEVRxBWGOKrsvFT0RKsl88wDp82rsvEB9BR5bjubQwY/TVh7+o
PEZOPK+OTyY4khAAAAG3Jvb3RAAc3RpdchGNoLmpvbndlc3RmYWxsLm5ldAEcAwQFBgc=
-----END OPENSSH PRIVATE KEY-----
```

Figure 5-15. Cat'ing the file output

On the server, I'll copy the private key to my authorized_keys file by using the following command:

```
cp ./.ssh/id_rsa.pub ./.ssh/authorized_keys
```

As seen in Figure 5-16, when I connect using my MacBook and the "mykey" file, I can now authenticate without using a password, using the command

```
ssh -i ./mykey jon@lilo.jonwestfall.net
```

```
[root@stitch ~]# cat .ssh/id_rsa
-----BEGIN OPENSSH PRIVATE KEY-----
b3BlbnNzaC1rZXktdjEAAAAABG5vbmUAAAAEbm9uZQAAAAAAAABAAAABlwAAAAdzc2gtcn
NhAAAAAwEAAQAAAYEAz3ZNY9SvF9N5APki/hEFBaoXeisWSTziof7GKRfZq0XCNcasGgKF
TsfGQumN3Jt1bXPg0McD19eeetGrCX3Spo35jLlERQOXt+qVOl0yWhftT/FIEWglf4RPBU
rYnZqU2XXcH25SqRTLwiuAR17LbGOqwFL63ccOu72KqaCoIuwKgiAx8BEwNkUpQggSfcDV
V8ZF8ChNw1JJsg03Nkx1bwLpWlhE4Fjp1AGMdURqjymAZ+O7wwmcvV+Ltuhl4Y+sjIEIUM
lB20NS6q2rFgkMviii/FuwGm0T6j5YIl0nCYMf0luRAmDHh1pXT9gc4yYcWDAOvlvyVxlX
gY+BpgzlLxS4EMkPYJUEL4HW7XKIsjVwb63iqOv4Qpj/QeKRewrU16MRThgFiZQx952W4t
arlkuTc8phPjo19DFwAbp0fARvmYmrSYpn/bd53o6gwPZPvq6D3jz9gfq/B0s/G8rx6ArQ
8LrOBtLKCXKdYs+20NgPYS7lIZCmp9clUomqk2yFAAAFmDFGVVsxRlVbAAAAB3NzaC1yc2
EAAAGBAM92TWPUrxfTeQD5Iv4RBQWqF3orFkk84qH+xikX2atFwjXGrBoChU7HxkLpjdyb
dW1z4NDHA9fXnnRqwl90qaN+Yy5REUDl7fqlTpdMloX7U/xSBFoJX+ETwVK2J2alNl13B
9uUqkUy8IrgEdey2xjqsBS+t3HDru9iqmgqCLsCoIgMfARMDZFKUIIEn3A1VfGRfAoTcNS
SbINNzZMdW8C6VpYROBY6dQBjHVEao8pgGfju8MJnL1fi7boZeGPrIyBCFDJQdtDUuqtqx
YJDL4oovxbsBptE+o+WCJdJwmDH9JbkQJgx4daV0/YHOMmHFgwDr5b8lcZV4GPgaYM5S8U
uBDJD2CVBC+B1u1yiLI1cG+t4qjr+EKY/0HikXsK1NejEU4YBYmUMfedluLWq5ZLk3PKYT
46NfQxcAG6dHwEb5mJq0mKZ/23ed6OoMD2T76ug948/YH6vwdLPxvK8egK0PC6zgbSygly
nWLPttDYD2Eu5SGQpqfXJVKJqpNshQAAAMBAAEAAAGAEdNJXP2G0dbau8GsRwYxV0ZBFC
clmA9aLa8VWayJ8FRjFnnGicmTqKwzlcY5gS3+TfQ56dZftyj4nfbr6jncYqEqQvQcMI3Z
eFz4i3Y8gE8z/b1ugshfCHDW1U6UBB6nEXQ2AKFbCtoVk85nDDrR4bNClZnLokibNHhZtK
9wIugDEyEvCUCA0vjoTZsh85og+pS3p6Xe4JxuZpUKHGk/YdVvNWsGJ/ybwrKLXfwN59Ua
ClMf6+ckh4TxHTskndfZRMO4abFRWvZpa67q+NEdV4ukILOhTG2QMhYQMeiGkPRNSud6JL
vwtBZwLCETpNvOsgGVIqiR88l+M9jJP42FSVAM20L5/BCEvAmajHB5Z6TU1AFt8abYrsbI
tCkvqgK3oqQVbJ0tk9ag7Lh24TlT7nx27eAcH6hmIt3bTu2nGUFDqQCOciywMPWu8YXvdT
urbEmJ9AtOsGXd6KBi0DQWvqmbLTEFQQNB9C0022+KHXofHMq7C1zcFlRvUAUsoZ+BAAAA
wQDVdUpOmAx5MYZPbLPGkzlIWU0WbvDjnyNXVvpduf6i8eOpwhbPVYQvlvytoN+nu/LfxJ
DK0jZwZVhtlOZK1H80pfkCJWC9Bp/oBu6Qea0pjJS8kPIXVZ+C2HM4bRsKZkqqCMTYUYh5
pgjWHP8ASrxPQUce5kwpnnhVWTchZrQho3GwyHehrcUxyDxTuBePtsOaSXrZjZQBHIHJgZ
jQ5ASbwVYgkAvG2iUuQWTX03dAOiQQYyr2kJvSSagL8lOYgkkAAADBAP3OxzfJMIBlnVZB
7GMcoJEOjLAIG8yfRhpBEbyPClQ3QnYmMFaP8+owOXYl/fSuNdHVcUSlZKa/wZctbfxvU+
dTKkkAfQ+tHmxFrCmo1kRny90iL63DyklbM5O1N7HMrxJ5UhjmINpbWo9NAr5Ayz3Jbey7
jr4Dwve0ywTxU0m+Vdjhuvzge2+LUZJbE5he/rKDpN5niPBz2//YLRS7AiglzgV/DIEMbV
JwgeuPFOpqild+OIDX5j9NL6+ADAeC5QAAAMEA0UELV5GusDXAwl5CGRL3t2ZjYx1AYJYV
ejwutoOTzGW4wN+KwosRK0YzX7VQQurZqtkKTU88ETXl3m1NP4/MtR+zAAdA2FyQUCddLk
5F5374mEMkokl9DNwqYasnW+7sG3bB8wT3r+UE5lHHZLlI32xlhgKvDPDy0VyV27D0Un2F
/KglRpDP4mugrFw9xe5wSEVRxBWGOKrsvFT0RKsl88wDp82rsvEB9BR5bjubQwY/TVh7+o
PEZoPK+OTyY4khAAAAG3Jvb3RAc3RpdGGNoLmpvbmdldlc3RmYWxsLm5ldAECAwQFBgc=
-----END OPENSSH PRIVATE KEY-----
```

Figure 5-16. *Connecting without a password*

If you run into trouble or are asked for the password again, you may have a permissions issue on either your computer or the VPS. Changing file permissions on your computer (if you're running macOS or Linux) will be the first to check – myfile should only be readable and writable by you, so a quick chmod 600 myfile will likely fix that.

On the VPS, you'll need to make sure that the .ssh directory is only readable by you (chmod 700 .ssh) and that your authorized keys file is only readable by you (chmod 600 .ssh/authorized_keys). That should then allow you to authenticate without a password.

PuTTY

If you are on a Windows PC, then you'll need to use PuTTY to connect to your VPS, and the steps will be slightly different than the preceding steps to add an SSH keyfile. Here's what you'll need to do:

1. Use the PuTTYgen command, which installs with PuTTY, to generate your keyholes on your computer.

2. Copy the public key to your VPS by pasting it into your ./.ssh/authorized_keys file. You can use the nano text editor.

3. Make sure your .ssh and authorized_keys file have the proper permissions as indicated earlier.

4. Finally, when you connect with PuTTY, you'll need to choose "SSH" under the "Category" menu on the left and navigate to the location of your private key that you saved earlier with the PuTTYgen command. This will tell PuTTY to use the keyfile instead of the password.

Locking It All Down

Once you can reliably get into your VPS without a password, you can turn off password authentication completely. To do this, use the following command to edit the SSH configuration:

```
nano /etc/ssh/sshd_config
```

Find the line that reads PasswordAuthentication and change it from yes to no. Then save the file and restart SSH:

```
systemctl restart ssh
```

Your VPS now only allows you to connect with the keyfile, so you'll want to keep it safe. You can also usually connect through the console, as discussed earlier, in situations where you have an emergency and only have the password to your VPS provider account.

Securing the firewall and SSH are two steps that should be done on all VPSs for security. Next, we'll discuss how to keep an eye on security throughout the time we use the VPS by checking log files.

Log File Management

Part of running a VPS is knowing how to find information out when things go wrong or to proactively determine a problem is happening before it becomes a bigger issue. To do this, you'll want to know where to find information, specifically in log files.

Viewing and Rotating Logs

Your VPS stores its log files in /var/log, and by default, only root can read them. The following table lists the most common log files, their names on both Debian and CentOS, and what you'll find in them:

Log File Name (CentOS)	Log File Name (Debian)	Description
secure	auth.log	A listing of login attempts, whether they were successful, and the IP address where they originated.
btmp	btmp	A binary log file that records all failed login attempts. It will look pretty ugly using cat or nano — it's designed to be read using the last command.
cron	A portion of /var/syslog	The Cron scheduler enters information regarding jobs run and errors logged.
dmesg	dmesg	System messages that are logged during bootup prior to the system logging software initializing.
messages	messages	Messages logged by the system logging software.

In addition to those log files, you'll also find logs that are specific to software you've installed and used, such as apt or apache2 on Debian (http on CentOS). In general, log files are your first line of defense in figuring out what might be happening on your box. I typically back them up as part of my disaster recovery plan, so that if a machine breaks or is hacked, I have some idea of what's going on.

You may also think about how fast log files can add up, especially the files that track brute-force login attempts (another good reason to disable password authentication in SSH). Linux has a tool, logrotate, that can automatically rotate logs. By default, it is installed and set up on both CentOS and Debian, and you can find its configuration in /etc/logrotate.d — each file in that directory corresponds to the name of a log file in /var/log and tells logrotate how often to rotate the old logs out. For example, btmp is set to rotate monthly, meaning at the end of the month you'll find a file named btmp.1.gz, which is a Gzipped archive of the btmp file from last month. Eventually it will be deleted at the start of the next month, meaning you always have between 30 and 60 days of log entries in btmp. Depending on your installation, important logs such as secure may never be rotated. Thus, if you find yourself running out of space on your VPS, checking /var/log is not a bad idea — it can fill up quickly!

Assuming that you're checking your log files often, you may wonder how to proactively look for problems before they start. After all, the log files will only tell you that a problem is happening. To proactively look, you'll need to engage in some form of proactive administration (e.g., looking for problems before they start!). Chapter 9 should be helpful in this regard, our administrator's weekly checklist.

Final Thoughts on Security

Security is an evolving landscape, and what's provided in this chapter is the starting point and absolute minimum that you need to be aware of. From this point, I suggest following websites that discuss security exploits, such as The Hacker News (https://thehackernews.com), which will tell you about recent exploits and discuss how best to secure systems for them. In the end no system is hack-proof, which is why we'll want to pay particular attention to the next chapter on backups and version control and Chapter 9, our weekly checklist!

Basics of Backups and Version Control

Running your own VPS can be challenging when everything is going right, but it can be downright frustrating and stressful when things go wrong. One of the most common things that goes wrong is when a file is corrupted or accidentally modified or deleted. It's times like that system administrators really enjoy having a robust backup or version control system. Without one, you may find that this is easily enough to sink your entire VPS. Nothing worse than building out a system that you really come to rely on and enjoy using and then to have it all seemingly go up in virtual flames because you're missing the key phrase in a configuration file – the phrase you added 3 years ago and didn't bother to write down!

In this chapter, I'm going to talk about backups and version control, how they are different, and how each plays a role in the process. I'll also talk about some things you may be tempted to do, such as use file synchronization tools, and how they aren't always the best option. By the end of this chapter, you'll be able to determine what you need to back up and how to do it. I'll also provide a few example scripts that you can use to back up your files regularly.

© Jon Westfall 2021
J. Westfall, *Set Up and Manage Your Virtual Private Server*,
https://doi.org/10.1007/978-1-4842-6966-4_6

Backup Basics: What to Back Up, Where to Back It Up, and How Often to Back Up

One of the great benefits of Linux is that everything is a file held in a few common locations. Configuration files are, generally, always under /etc, users' personal data is generally stored under /home, and your web server files are generally under /var/www. This means it's generally easy to find the files you'll need to back up, vs. the files that you can always reinstall (such as system software packages) when setting back up a crashed server or moving to a new server.

The following table shows the directories that I typically back up on my VPSs and a rationale for each one, as well as how far back I typically keep copies of the files:

Directory	Rationale	Length to Retain
/etc	This directory takes up less than 10 megabytes and typically has all of your configuration files, with the possible exception of software used by just one user (which then might have its configuration under /home). Definitely a small amount of space to pay for having those backups.	1 year, typically sufficient in case it isn't until later I find that a configuration change has caused a problem.
/home	On my personal blog's server, this entire directory takes up just under 800 megabytes. Most of that is my home directory, which has copies of installers, test configuration files, files I needed to keep safe, and my .bash_history file that contains all of the commands I've entered. This is extremely useful and the directory that typically will have the most personal information.	3 months. By then, typically you'll notice if you deleted something you needed!
/var/log	System log files. These can get large depending on how often you rotate them; however, they are essential when trying to determine why certain programs aren't working properly. Also useful if you find yourself having strange issues overall with your system, as the individual files can help you systematically rule out each piece of software.	3 months.
/var/www	The files on the web server. This is where all of the public HTML files that you serve will live, and thus you'll want to make sure you have backup copies.	3 months.
/var/lib/mysql	The database files for your MySQL database server. If you're running any sort of application that requires a MySQL database, such as WordPress or another database-driven web application, you'll want to back these up regularly so that you can recover the data.	3 months.

(continued)

Directory	Rationale	Length to Retain
/root	The root user's home directory. Useful for the same reason other home directories are needed – you never know what you stored here when you were setting things up initially!	3 months.

Once you've decided what to back up, you then need to think about where you want to back it up to. There are a few options you might have, depending on your own personal setup and where you store files in your home or office setup. Let's walk through some of the most common:

1. On the VPS Itself (perhaps in a directory such as /backup) – This is generally a very poor idea for the simple fact that if something happens to your VPS, it's likely not going to preserve the backup directory unscathed. The only thing this really guards you against is an accidental modification or file deletion – you could restore the file in question from the backup directory's copy. Later in this chapter, we'll talk about synchronizing directories to a cloud service or to your own home computer, and in that case, you might use a local backup directory to be a temporary home for your backups. But they should never be the only home for them.

2. Another VPS – This option can work very well if you have the space required on the other VPS to store the backup files. You may wish to talk to your hosting provider, however, and request another VPS on a different physical machine and perhaps a different physical data center. While you'll use bandwidth to transfer the files (both to the destination machine and away from the source machine), you do gain an "off-site" backup by having the files physically in another machine in potentially another region of the country.

3. Your Computer at Home – This option works well if you have a lot of storage on your computer(s) at home and don't mind scheduling a job to back up directly to it. In the next section, we'll talk about scheduled vs. on-demand backups, which may require you to have a computer that is always on to receive files, something you may need to specifically configure if you don't typically leave a computer running and connected to the Internet at all times.

4. A cloud storage provider, such as Dropbox, OneDrive, or Google Drive. This can be a viable option assuming you have the space on the cloud provider and you have an account that allows you to easily move the files to the cloud provider. Typically paid cloud accounts can store files of various sizes; however, free accounts typically have size restrictions that make it hard to store backups.

Wherever you store your backups, you'll want to make sure that it's easy for you to get to in an emergency and that you have the information easily accessible. For my VPS backups, I typically use the second backup method discussed in the following (using the Duplicati open source package) and back up to a dedicated "backup" VPS – a VPS I purchased that specifically had 1 terabyte of space. I pay $45 a year for this; however, as a premium subscriber of Microsoft Office (for $100 a year), I could also use my OneDrive space. I've actually thought about backing up to both, since I tend to be on the paranoid side (as you'll see from my discussions in the following!). You only have to be burned by missing backups once to see a clear need and urgent desire to have them very well established and reliable.

My advice: If you would literally cry over missing data, it needs to be backed up in at least three ways/places: previous versions, multiple virtual locations, and multiple physical locations! However, doing this can be tedious, which is why we typically automate the process. Let's talk about why that is important in the following section.

Scheduled vs. On-Demand Backups

Backing up your server can seem like something you'll want to do manually or on-demand. After all, it allows you to easily see that the backup was done, and you can make it part of your weekly administrative checklist (see Chapter 9). However, I would argue that *checking* backups should be part of your weekly checklist, not *making* backups. Here are the simple reasons why:

1. Humans are fallible – we forget to do things even if we are aware they are important. When it comes to going down a checklist, such as your weekly administrator's list of tasks, you may be interrupted at one point and believe you completed something you hadn't. In Chapter 9, I provide a number of things for you to keep an eye on, but none of them, by themselves, will spell disaster if you forget them every so often. Backups, though, are items you do not want to have even 1 day less of.

2. Backups need to be kept very up to date – daily if possible. While it might be useful to have the backup from last week, if your server crashes, you have to retrace your steps, metaphorically. Did you install anything new since the last backup? Did you modify any files? And if you have users who are using your system for email or for data storage, did they have any files that weren't backed up? Email servers are especially important in this regard – recall my ticket system from Chapter 1. If I only back it up every week, it's likely that all the tickets I'm backing up were for historical record. All of the active tasks that have come in and are still being worked on will likely not last more than a week, and thus the data my users need most (what do I have to do today?) will be the data that isn't backed up.

3. Backups also can fail in strange ways, even reporting that they are successful. It is much better to carve out time regularly to check your backups to make sure they are working, vs. using that time to make backups and assume they're good.

Therefore, I would not recommend relying on yourself to make on-demand backups. You need a backup solution that runs regularly, preferably nightly or even hourly if you have data that changes very quickly, and runs in an automated fashion. In the next two sections, I'll go over a very simple backup method using software already on your VPS and a more complex yet full-featured solution using an open source package named Duplicati.

Backup Method 1: Gzipped Tar Files and Shell Scripts

Your VPS contains two Linux utilities, tar and gzip. tar is an archiving utility that can take several files or directories and bundle them up into a single "tarball." gzip is a file compression utility that can then shrink that tarball in size, making it easier to move over the network. Sometimes you'll also see references to the program bzip2, another file compression utility. You can recognize tarred and zipped files by the extensions tar.gz, .tgz, or tar.bz2.

The simplest backup method would be to run the `tar` command, such as the one in the following, to create a new archive file named "backup.tar" containing the contents of the /etc directory. Note that all of these commands were run as the `root` user, so if you get a permission denied error, add `sudo` to each command's start:

```
tar -cvf backup.tar /etc
```

Changing this to include an additional argument, z, will also compress the file using `gzip`:

```
tar -cvzf backup.tar.gz /etc
```

To restore files, you'd simply use the `tar` command with the x or extract argument:

```
tar -xvf backup.tar
```

Sometimes this can, however, set off what is jokingly called a "tarbomb" – dumping all of the files out into the current directory and causing a mess. To untar your files to another directory, you can add the -C option:

```
tar -xvf backup.tar -C /tmp/backup.
```

There are a plethora of scripts on the Internet that will create tar files in an automated fashion, such that you can schedule them using the `cron` scheduler. `cron` is set up by editing your own `crontab` file, and we can schedule a simple backup by directly calling `tar`. To do so, type `crontab - e` and you'll be brought to your default text editor and an empty Crontab file. Cron entries have five numbers at the start of them, for the minute, hour, day of the month, month, and day of the week. Putting the following command in your Crontab will tell the system to back up the /etc directory to /home/jon/etc.tar each night at midnight:

```
0 0 * * * /bin/tar -cvf /home/jon/etc.tar /etc
```

At this point, you have your backups on the VPS, and your job is to move them wherever you want to store them. The `rsync` utility can be helpful in this fashion, copying files from one machine to another. However, if you prefer a more intuitive interface, you may be happier with the next solution: backing up your VPS via a program named Duplicati.

Backup Method 2: Duplicati GUI

Duplicati (http://duplicati.com) is a free open source backup software product. It incorporates an easy-to-use web graphical user interface and supports tons of backup destinations.

To get started with it, you'll first need to install it. Head over to https:// duplicati.readthedocs.io/en/latest/02-installation/ and look for the installation instructions for your version of CentOS or Debian; they all differ slightly. Once installed, Duplicati is only accessible by going to port 8200 on the VPS *from the VPS itself* – this is a security measure, intended to prevent unauthorized use. We'll need to tunnel our connection through, mapping port 8200 on our local machine to port 8200 on our VPS. On a Mac or Linux machine, the following command will do the trick, replacing "yourvps" with the domain name or IP address of your VPS and "yourusername" with the username you use for SSH:

```
ssh -L 8200:localhost:8200 yourusername@yourvps
```

On a Windows machine, you can accomplish this in PuTTY by going to the "Tunnels" section (under the Connection ➤ SSH option) and adding a new forwarded port. Put "8200" in as the source port and "localhost:8200" in as the destination. Choose "Local" and "Auto" for your connections and choose "Add." Once added, connect as normal.

Now visiting http://localhost:8200 will take you to the Duplicati home screen (see Figure 6-1). The first time, it will ask you if you are using a multiuser environment or single. Most of the time, unless you'd like your users to each be able to use Duplicati to set up their own backups, you'll choose "No, my machine has only a single account." Once you've dismissed that prompt, you now can access the Duplicati configuration (Figure 6-2).

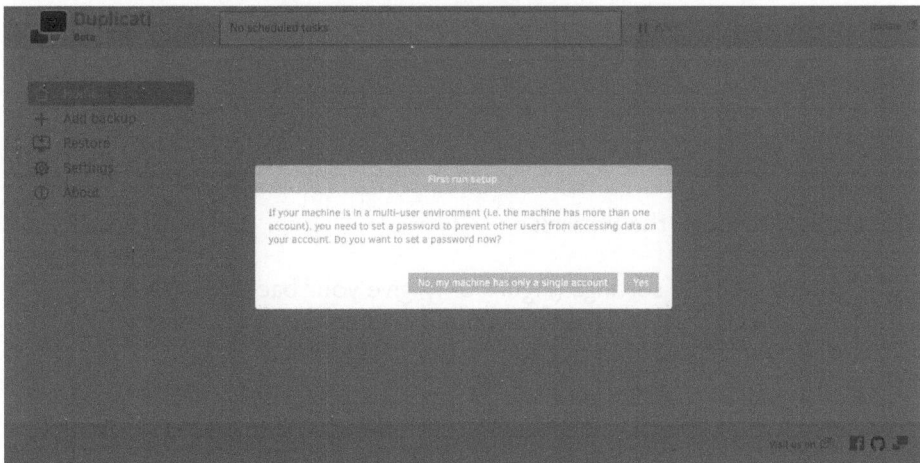

Figure 6-1. Duplicati home screen on first run

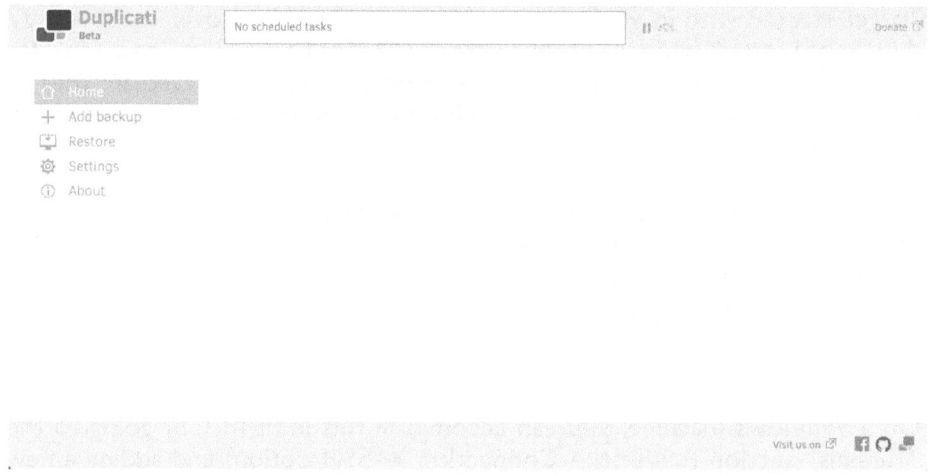

Figure 6-2. Duplicati home screen

To get started, choose "Add backup" and then "Configure a new backup" (see Figure 6-3) and click Next.

Add a new backup

○ Configure a new backup
    Enter configuration details

○ Import from a file
    Load a configuration from an exported job or a storage provider

Figure 6-3. New backup prompt

Then follow through the wizard:

    1. In General settings (Figure 6-4), give your backup a name, and choose a backup passphrase that can securely encrypt your backup. Do not forget the passphrase!

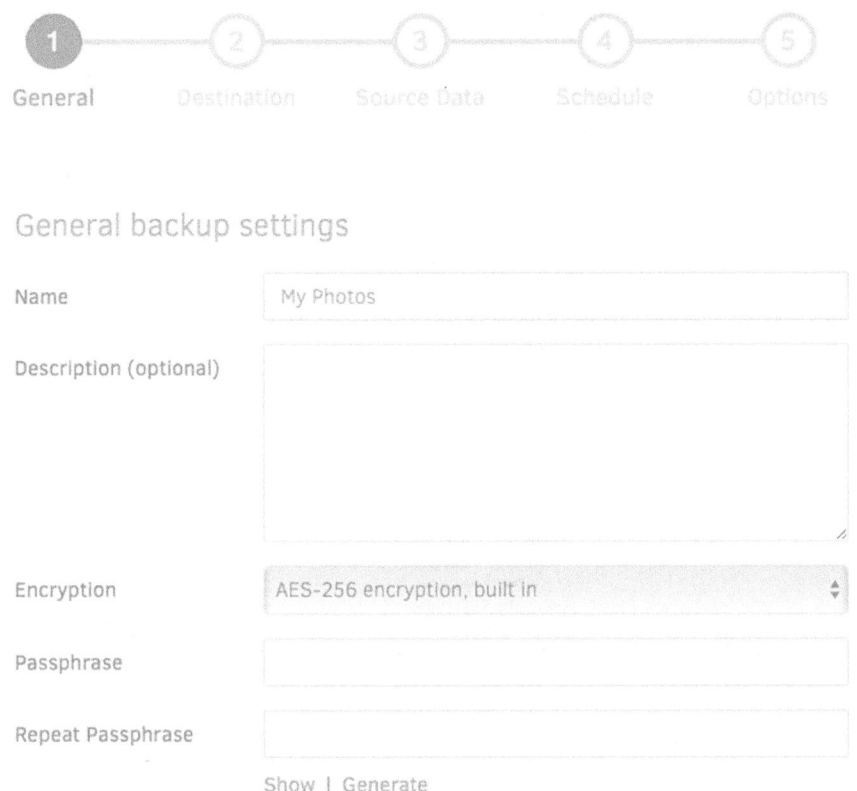

Figure 6-4. General backup settings

2. Next, in Destination (Figure 6-5), choose where you want to store your backups. Duplicati defaults to a local directory; however, you can choose to move the files over FTP or SFTP to another machine or store them on a number of cloud services, such as Dropbox, Microsoft OneDrive, Google Drive, and more.

Backup destination

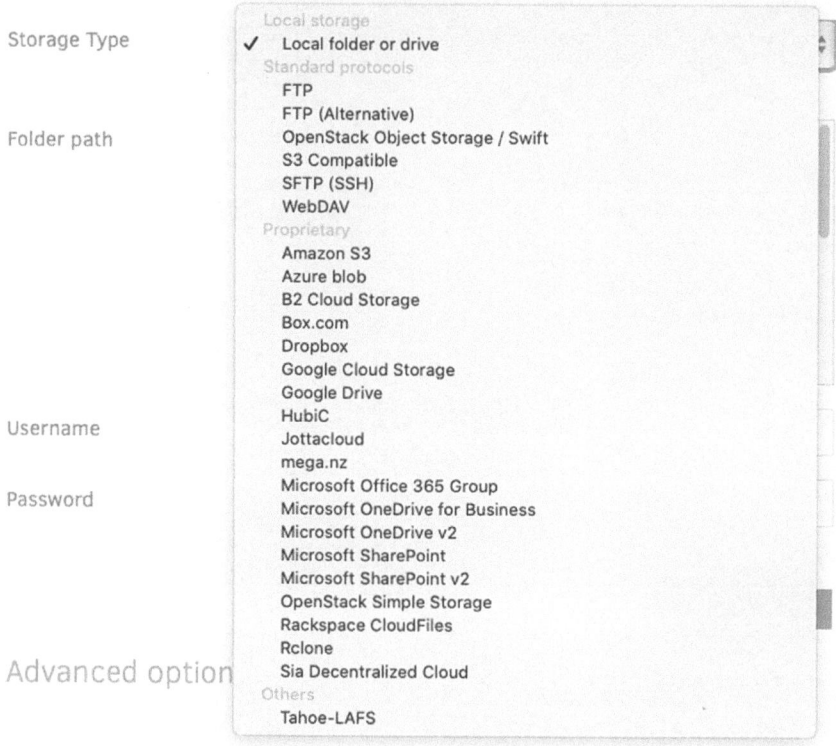

Storage Type

Local storage

✓   Local folder or drive

Standard protocols

    FTP

    FTP (Alternative)

Folder path   OpenStack Object Storage / Swift

    S3 Compatible

    SFTP (SSH)

    WebDAV

Proprietary

    Amazon S3

    Azure blob

    B2 Cloud Storage

    Box.com

    Dropbox

    Google Cloud Storage

    Google Drive

Username   HubiC

    Jottacloud

    mega.nz

Password   Microsoft Office 365 Group

    Microsoft OneDrive for Business

    Microsoft OneDrive v2

    Microsoft SharePoint

    Microsoft SharePoint v2

    OpenStack Simple Storage

    Rackspace CloudFiles

    Rclone

Advanced option   Sia Decentralized Cloud

Others

    Tahoe-LAFS

Figure 6-5. Backup destinations

3.   Then, select the source data (Figure 6-6) you'd like to back up. I typically select all of the folders that I mentioned earlier.

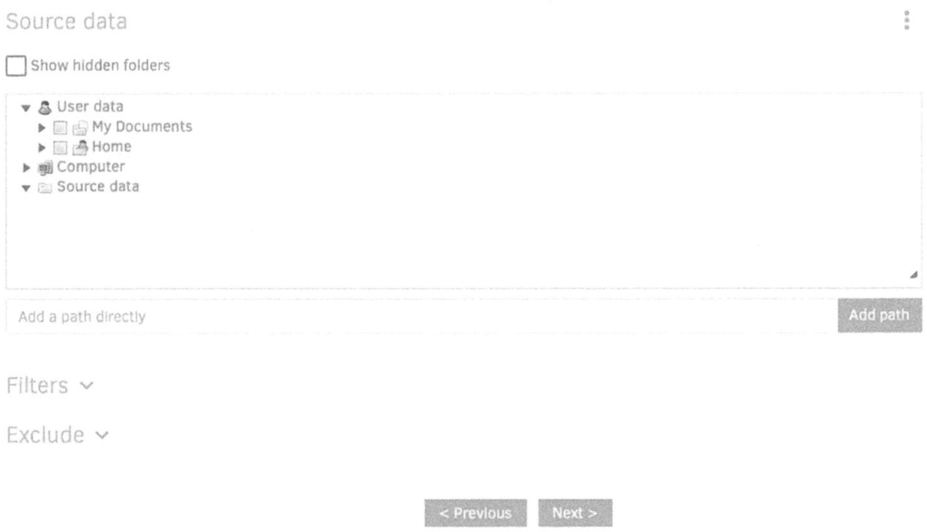

Source data   ⋮

☐ Show hidden folders

▾ 👤 User data
   ▸ ☐ 📁 My Documents
   ▸ ☐ 📁 Home
 ▸ 💻 Computer
▾ 📁 Source data

Add a path directly	Add path

Filters ⌄

Exclude ⌄

< Previous | Next >

Figure 6-6. Source data selection

    4.   Finally, you'll set your backup schedule (Figure 6-7).

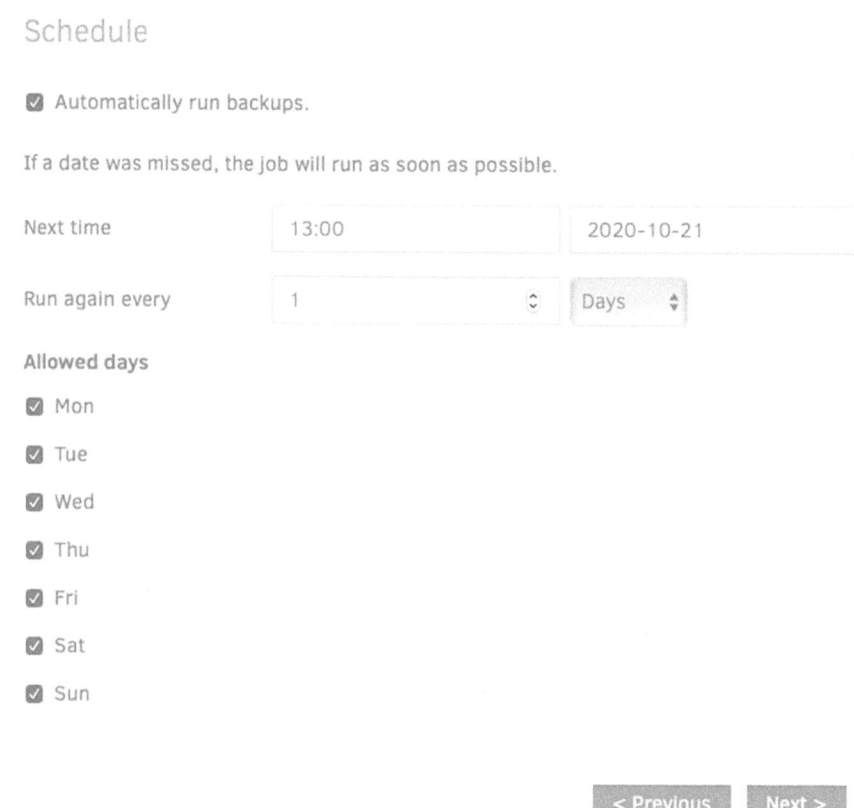

Schedule

☑ Automatically run backups.

If a date was missed, the job will run as soon as possible.

| Next time | 13:00 | 2020-10-21 |

| Run again every | 1 | Days |

Allowed days

☑ Mon

☑ Tue

☑ Wed

☑ Thu

☑ Fri

☑ Sat

☑ Sun

< Previous   Next >

Figure 6-7. The backup schedule

5. And you can configure any advanced options you need, including retention, and choose Save (Figure 6-8).

General options

Remote volume size   50   MByte

This option does not relate to your maximum backup or file size, nor does it affect deduplication rates. See this page before you change the remote volume size.

Backup retention   Keep all backups

Nothing will be deleted. The backup size will grow with each change.

Advanced options ⌄

< Previous   Save

Figure 6-8. The General options and Advanced options screen

From there, Duplicati is set up and will start backing up your data on the schedule you specified. One nice feature of Duplicati is that it stores incremental, versioned backups. This means that if you tell it to keep the last 3 months of backups, you can restore the version of a file from any point in that last 3 months. This, itself, can be useful when trying to track down when a file was changed or was deleted, since you can roll back to any earlier version. It's a rudimentary form of version control, which we'll talk about in the next section!

Version Control Using Git

Sometimes backups aren't exactly what you need when you have a lot of changes happening to a given file or set of files. Perhaps you simply need to be able to "walk back" to an earlier time in that file's history and see what it read at that point. This is especially helpful for groups that have multiple users collaborating on the same set of files. Thankfully, the well-known and established Git version control system can easily be used on a Linux server to allow you to keep track of changes to files, either in a shared directory among several users or in your own directory.

To see this in action, let's first install Git using the following commands:

Debian: `apt-get install git` CentOS: `yum install git`

Next, let's imagine that I have a directory in /home/jon named updates. In this directory, I keep information about every change I make to my VPS, which is a great thing to do in general. Each time I change a file in updates, I also want to make a note of what I changed and the significance.

First, let's create the updates directory and then initialize Git (Figure 6-9):

```
mkdir updates cd updates git init
```

```
jon@lilo:~$ mkdir updates
jon@lilo:~$ cd updates
jon@lilo:~/updates$ git init
Initialized empty Git repository in /home/jon/updates/.git/
jon@lilo:~/updates$
```

Figure 6-9. The setup of my Git updates directory

From this point, Git is watching what I do in that directory and tracking changes. Let's make an update – I'll create a new file named "installed-git" and pipe in what we did:

```
echo "Installed git, and set it up for demonstration purposes" >
installed-git
```

If I type the command git status, I can see that it noticed my new file (Figure 6-10).

```
jon@lilo:~/updates$ git status
On branch master

No commits yet

Untracked files:
  (use "git add <file>..." to include in what will be committed)

        installed-git

nothing added to commit but untracked files present (use "git add" to track)
jon@lilo:~/updates$ ▊
```

Figure 6-10. git status

Git expects that every so often, I'm going to add files that I've created and "commit" the changes, basically making a note of what I've done to the file. I'll do this now by running the following commands:

```
git add . git commit
```

The first time I try to commit (Figure 6-11), Git asks me, politely, who I am. I'll set that and then commit again:

```
jon@lilo:~/updates$ git add .
jon@lilo:~/updates$ git commit

*** Please tell me who you are.

Run

  git config --global user.email "you@example.com"
  git config --global user.name "Your Name"

to set your account's default identity.
Omit --global to set the identity only in this repository.

fatal: empty ident name (for <jon@lilo.jonwestfall.net>) not allowed
```

Figure 6-11. Git prompting for identifying information

```
git config --global user.email
"jon@lilo.jonwestfall.net" git config --global user.name
"Jon Westfall" git commit
```

Git now launches my default text editor and asks me to enter a commit message (Figure 6-12). I'll tell it that I was noting that we had installed Git and save the file.

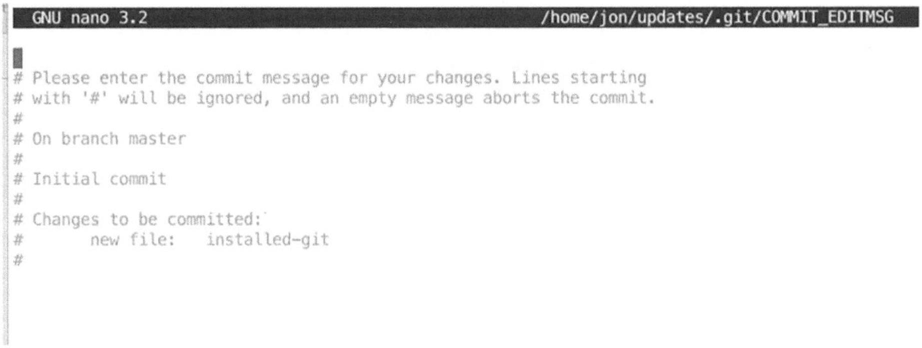

```
GNU nano 3.2                                        /home/jon/updates/.git/COMMIT_EDITMSG

# Please enter the commit message for your changes. Lines starting
# with '#' will be ignored, and an empty message aborts the commit.
#
# On branch master
#
# Initial commit
#
# Changes to be committed:
#       new file:   installed-git
#
```

Figure 6-12. The blank Git commit prompt in my default text editor

I now get a message saying that the commit happened (Figure 6-13). I'm now going to make a few edits and commits to the file, such that the file that originally said "Installed git, and set it up for demonstration purposes" now has updates, such that I might enter each time I changed something about the system.

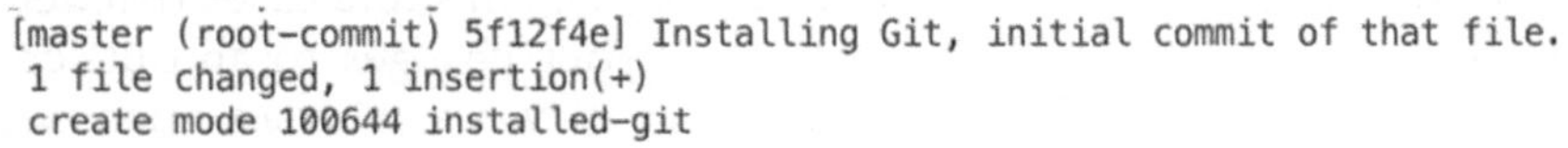

```
[master (root-commit) 5f12f4e] Installing Git, initial commit of that file.
 1 file changed, 1 insertion(+)
 create mode 100644 installed-git
```

Figure 6-13. A successful Git commit message

After several changes and commits, I can see the entire string of file history by using the command git show installed-git. As you can see in Figure 6-14, it will show me that the most recent update removed Update 1 and that since installed-git was created, Update 1 was removed, Updates 2 and 3 were added, and the top of the file remained unchanged.

```
jon@lilo:~/updates$ git show installed-git
commit c4bb4ea85b6299bc5a26a275b9a8e7d5ff50c743 (HEAD -> master)
Author: Jon Westfall <jon@lilo.jonwestfall.net>
Date:   Wed Oct 21 18:27:59 2020 +0200

        Removed Update 1

diff --git a/installed-git b/installed-git
index 3e35add..cd01489 100644
--- a/installed-git
+++ b/installed-git
@@ -1,5 +1,5 @@
 Installed git, and set it up for demonstration purposes

-Update 1: Added new users
-
 Update 2: Another update into this file.
+
+Update 3: Removed Update 1!
```

Figure 6-14. The changes to the installed-git file

This is just the tip of the iceberg with Git – you can also create different "branches" of files (in case you make major changes and want to have two different working sets of files) and push your files to a Git server, such as the publicly available GitHub. I believe version control plays a role in backup and disaster recovery strategy, mostly as a frontline method to track changes within files on your server. However, you may find in some cases that version control is all you need, assuming you push your changes to an outside Git server or another VPS. If you do any sort of work with an open source development program, you'll also likely come into contact with Git, as most source code today is managed using version control of some kind, and the Git clone feature makes it very easy to pull entire directories of source code to your computer.

This brings us to an intersection between file backups, version control, and a newer strategy: data synchronization. In the next section, I'll talk about how data can be synchronized and if it's useful or potentially dangerous.

The Great Synchronization Debate: Delight or Disaster Waiting to Happen?

Originally, computer systems did not have a lot of "spare" storage dedicated to storing duplicates of existing files. Tape backup drives required you to store backups as one continuous stream of data that could be unpacked if necessary, but weren't easy to pluck a single file or directory out of. Today we have a great deal of space available to us, which has made directory synchronization very attractive. From one of the first implementations consumers saw (Windows 95's Briefcase feature, which synchronized a local directory to a floppy disk) to modern cloud storage solutions such as Dropbox and OneDrive, synchronization has been useful and also potentially problematic.

At a glance, it may seem to be a great advantage. Rather than worry about backing up files, simply have software on either end look for changes in the files, and as soon as a change happens, zip it off to the other side. However, while this sounds tempting, there are some downsides to it.

First, many synchronization systems do make it instantly available, which means if you make a mistake on the file you're working with, you can't simply open the copy on the other side and get the original version. Or at least you probably can't unless you work faster than the cloud! This has led many synchronization providers to provide version histories, which are helpful, keeping past versions of files so that any accidental changes can be reverted. Most limit the number of revisions, especially for customers who are on the "free" tier of service.

Adding on to that, what if you've made additions/modification/deletions to several files or directories? Now you not only need to recover the right version of one file, but of several. At this point, having a proper backup data set, such as one we discussed earlier, is much more attractive.

Finally, a growing problem today is intentional file corruption in the form of ransomware. Ransomware refers to the malicious encrypting of your own files on your own machine, and once the files are encrypted, you are told you need to pay a certain nontrivial amount of money for the decryption key; otherwise, your files are useless. And if you pay, there is no guarantee that you have "honest" criminals who will actually give you the key.

Backups do not fully guard against ransomware, as if they are stored on networked servers, it is possible that they will be encrypted too. However, synchronization services are especially vulnerable given how fast changes sync up. This is why having multiple backup destinations, and destinations that are not always accessible or mounted, can be very useful. My paranoid state also has me making various snapshot backups on network-attached servers (NASs) and even occasional "air-gapped" backups (e.g., backup to an external drive that I keep locked in a fireproof safe). You can never have enough backup copies of your sensitive data. And you also can never have enough successful tests of recovering that data. In the last section of this chapter, we'll talk about a simulated disaster recovery and steps to migrate to a new server should the need arise.

Simulated Disaster Recovery and Migration to a New Server

Backups are only good if they work. Testing them regularly is something you should attempt to do fairly often, perhaps once a month at the least. You also might want a checklist of items should you decide to move from one VPS to another.

Test Restorations

Testing a restoration can be as easy as untarring a file in a test directory, using the preceding commands, or installing Duplicati on another machine and using it to restore the files it creates. The reason to do this typically relates to how backups fail. In my career, I've seen the following issues affect backups, some of which are easier to spot than others:

- The backup job simply fails to run due to lack of disk space, lack of processor time, and so on. You'll notice that your backup files have old timestamps (using the `ls -l` command to see the date created). In this case, the backup file is likely fine, but you might not be able to get much use out of it if it's very old.

- The backup job runs, but isn't backing up what you think it is. This might be because you've left a directory out, or you never updated the backup command after installing a new piece of software that is writing its data somewhere new. This is why fully restoring a backup into a new directory, and verifying you have everything you need to set up a new VPS, can be very useful.

- The backup job runs, but is somehow corrupted in copying or transporting. This can occur if you're trying to use forms of compression or encryption that are incorrectly set up. If you set up your backups to use compression or encryption, make sure you restore from those files and not the original backup (or tar file) that you compressed or encrypted. In some cases, you may think everything is fine, not realizing that the encryption or compression applied after the backup is to blame. This is also a good case for trying to restore the files on a new or different computer or VPS, to make sure that there isn't something that the software is depending on that is only installed on your VPS.

By regularly testing restorations, you'll also be more confident when trouble arises. Nothing is better than having a user come to you in a panic and say "I accidentally deleted this file" and you can confidently reply "No problem, I'll just restore it from last night's backup!" And nothing more terrifying than thinking you can restore it only to find that the backup isn't from last night — it's from last year, and it also is corrupt!

VPS Migration Checklist

At one point in my life, after I found out about low-end Virtual Private Servers, I jumped around quite a bit between hosting companies. Sometimes it was for a better price. Other times it was because the technology wasn't as stable at a company as I'd hoped. And still other times it was to consolidate down to one company instead of using two or three. In that time, I came up with the following list for myself of things I needed to do when moving to a new VPS. I've put it in the following table, with a column for you to check off as you go and a column for your own notes. I suggest using it as a guide if you would need to move VPSs or are testing your disaster recovery scenario.

Check When Complete	Step	Explanation	Your Notes
✓	Install operating system	This is typically done for you, although you may need to rebuild the VPS if you're starting over with the same company. Rebuilding wipes the current operating system and starts with a "fresh slate."	*Use this area as a space for your own notes as you complete this step, including configuration you tweak, important addresses, and important login information.*
✓	Install software	Install the following software if you need it or regularly use it: Webmin, MySQL, Apache, PHP, Postfix mail server.	
✓	Copy backup files from the old server to new.	Either copy the files via SFTP, or you can use the following command on the *old* server to copy a directory to the *new* server (in this case, the /var/www/ directory). Replace username with your username on the new server and *newserver.example.com* with the address of the *new* server: `rsync -avz -e "ssh" "/var/www" username@newserver.example.com:'/var/www.`	

(continued)

Check When Complete	Step	Explanation	Your Notes
✓	Copy MySQL databases	Copy the database files from /var/lib/mysql from the old server to the new server, or restore from backup.	
✓	Create user accounts	If you create a series of user accounts for yourself and others, make sure you make the same accounts on the new machine, so that you can copy over your home directories easily.	
✓	Create MySQL users and passwords	In some cases, depending on how you restore your MySQL databases, you may need to also restore your users and passwords.	
✓	Set up backups	Set up the backups that you'll need for the new machine, using either tar or Duplicati.	
✓	Restore configuration files	Restore specially written configuration files from /etc to your new machine. Back up original files first, in case you need to revert to the base install.	
✓	Monitor for issues	For the first few weeks, log in regularly to make sure that everything is reading and writing as it should. Check log files for errors.	

Hopefully you will find this a good guide for migrating servers as needed. However, you'll also want to create your own list of recovery steps in case you find yourself in a scenario that requires a rebuild.

Overall this chapter has gone over the basics of backups and version control, which ideally you'll never need to know more than preparing for a disaster. But if a disaster does strike, it's good to know you have everything you need in place, and have tested plans, that can get you back to a normally functioning VPS!

Basics of Server Software Administration

A VPS is really only useful if it provides services to you that enrich your productivity and professional life. In this chapter, we're going to talk about several possible services that your VPS can provide, through the installation of various *servers*. At first this may seem strange in that, thus far, we've used the term "server" to refer to the entire VPS. However, technically any software that provides a service to a *client* is a *server*; thus, many of the products we will talk about in this chapter have the word "server" in their name. Those products include

- The Apache 2 Web Server, which serves web pages over ports 80 and 443 – what we typically think of as "http" and "https"

- The MySQL database server, or its offspring MariaDB, which is a popular relational database product, able to store the data that either powers your web pages or other servers

© Jon Westfall 2021
J. Westfall, *Set Up and Manage Your Virtual Private Server*,
https://doi.org/10.1007/978-1-4842-6966-4_7

- The Postfix mail server, which allows you to handle receiving and sending email from your VPS

- An additional feature of Webmin (see Chapter 4), which allows you to keep an eye on everything with a unified status dashboard and handle early detection of issues

It's not likely you'll need all of these servers; in fact, most will be happy with just the first two or three. However, the discussion here is not only to help you with what you need but also to help you think of ways in which these systems might be useful later. And there is always the chance you'll run across them when looking up a problem later, so an introduction can be very helpful. So let's get started with probably the most well-known of these, Apache.

The Apache 2 Web Server

The Apache HTTP Server Project started in 1995 and has grown to be one of the best-known and most used web servers in the world. HTTP, standing for hypertext transfer protocol, is the format that allows your web browser to request a stream of HTML (Hypertext Markup Language) from the web server and then display or render it properly on your screen. HTML is a markup language in that the content also includes "tags" that tell the web browser how to display the data, so at its core, the web server's job is pretty simple – send long strings of text to the clients that request them and make available any other asset (such as a picture or video file) that needs to be available. In theory simple, but in practice complex in the abilities that Apache can perform. In this section, we'll install Apache and get it up and running and then talk about how to extend it by installing PHP and a free SSL (Secure Sockets Layer) certificate from Let's Encrypt.

Installation and Basic Configuration

Installing Apache is a pretty simple affair. On CentOS, run the command yum install httpd and then systemctl enable httpd and systemctl start httpd. On Debian, run the command apt-get install apache2, and the server will be started automatically.

Next, we open up the appropriate firewall rules by using the command firewall-cmd -- zone=public --permanent --add-service=http and then restart the firewall with systemctl restart firewalld.

And we can then test our work by going to our VPS in our web browser. In my case, the address of my Debian test machine, Lilo, is http://lilo. jonwestfall.net, and the address of my CentOS test machine, Stitch, is http://stitch.jonwestfall.net. Opening this will lead to the default Apache landing page for CentOS (Figure 7-1) or Debian (Figure 7-2).

Test Page

This page is used to test the proper operation of the Apache HTTP server after it has been installed. If you can read this page it means that this site is working properly. This server is powered by CentOS.

Just visiting?

The website you just visited is either experiencing problems or is undergoing routine maintenance.

If you would like to let the administrators of this website know that you've seen this page instead of the page you expected, you should send them e-mail. In general, mail sent to the name "webmaster" and directed to the website's domain should reach the appropriate person.

For example, if you experienced problems while visiting www.example.com, you should send e-mail to "webmaster@example.com".

Important note:

The CentOS Project has nothing to do with this website or its content, it just provides the software that makes the website run.

If you have issues with the content of this site, contact the owner of the domain, not the CentOS project. Unless you intended to visit CentOS.org, the CentOS Project does not have anything to do with this website, the content or the lack of it.

For example, if this website is www.example.com, you would find the owner of the example.com domain at the following WHOIS server: http://www.internic.net/whois.html

Are you the Administrator?

You should add your website content to the directory /var/www/html/ .

To prevent this page from ever being used, follow the instructions in the file /etc/httpd/conf.d/welcome.conf .

Promoting Apache and CentOS

You are free to use the images below on Apache and CentOS Linux powered HTTP servers. Thanks for using Apache and CentOS!

The CentOS Project

The CentOS Linux distribution is a stable, predictable, manageable and reproduceable platform derived from the sources of Red Hat Enterprise Linux (RHEL).

Additionally to being a popular choice for web hosting, CentOS also provides a rich platform for open source communities to build upon. For more information please visit the CentOS website.

© 2019 The CentOS Project | Legal | Privacy

Figure 7-1. Default landing page on CentOS

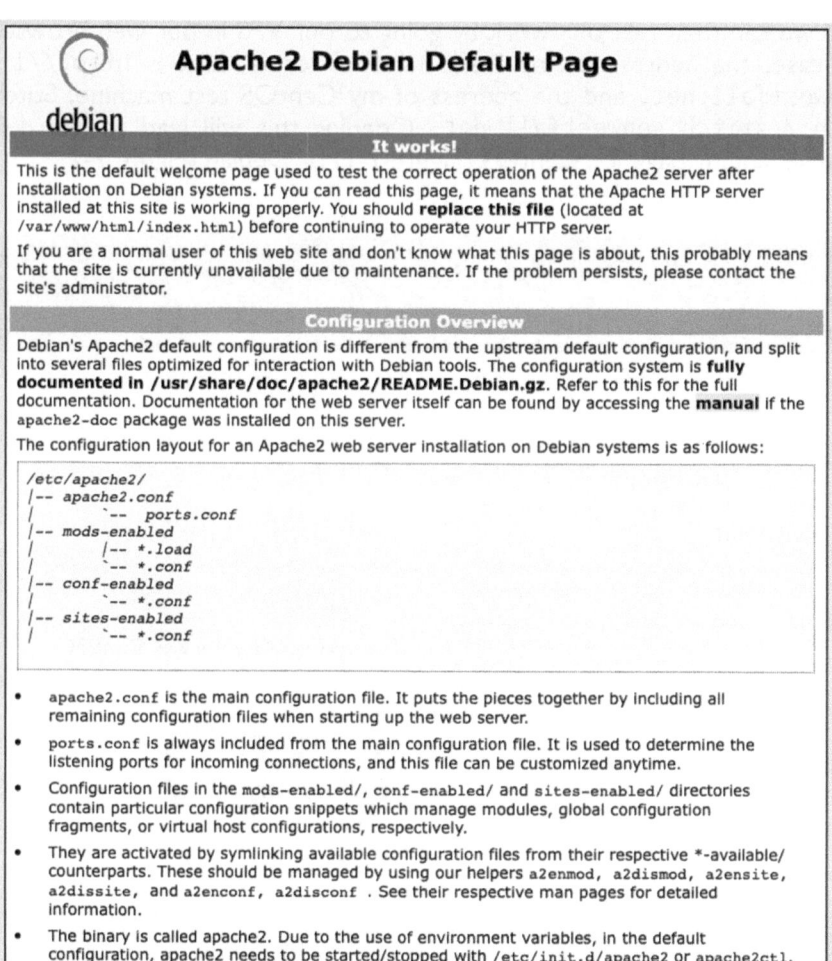

Figure 7-2. Default landing page on Debian

Each page gives you some basic information about the web server, about where configuration files are stored, and about how to get started with your files. When you install Apache, it stores a series of files under the directory /var/www/html. If you go there on your Debian VPS, you'll see a file named index.html – opening it will show you the HTML that created Figure 7-2. On CentOS, things are handled a little differently – you won't find any files in /var/www/html by default, as the image shown in Figure 7-1 is actually housed in a special directory, /usr/share/httpd/noindex/. You might wonder what it means by "noindex."

By default, Apache looks for a file it refers to as the index in any given directory and displays that first. We usually name this file something like index.html, although technically it can be called anything you like. In this way, people can visit our website by going to an address that contains just the root directory or directory name (e.g., http://lilo.jonwestfall.net) instead of http://lilo.jonwestfall.net/index.html, which is the exact same file.

At this point, Apache is up and running, and we can host a very simple website by placing HTML files and assets (e.g., images) in the /var/www/html directory. By naming the first file we want people to see index.html, we have our website up and running.

Apache, though, has a number of things we can do in terms of customization and enabling features. Briefly, here are some things to be aware of:

- Apache stores its configuration files at /etc/httpd (CentOS) or /etc/apache2 (Debian). Some common reasons you may modify them would be to add virtual hosts (e.g., the ability to have multiple websites on the same machine, each responding to a different domain name) or to customize Apache to your liking (e.g., renaming the directory index, adding password protection to a folder, etc.). Entire books are written about Apache configuration, so we won't go in depth here other than to say this: before modifying your Apache configuration, be sure to back it up in case there are issues. Also, before restarting Apache to make changes, it's helpful to run apachectl configtest to make sure there are no errors!

- Apache has a number of modules that can be enabled or disabled (using the a2enmod and a2dismod commands on Debian; on CentOS, you'll need to modify the configuration files). Apache modules extend the functionality of the server in order to do things such as connect to other software (we'll see this with the following PHP extension) or allow the web server to modify web pages as it serves them.

- Apache normally requires all configuration to be in these configuration files with one exception – what's referred to as the "distributed configuration file," "hypertext access" file, or simply the file name .htaccess. These files, when placed in a directory the web server is displaying (such as /var/www/html), can override the regular Apache configuration for just that directory. Commonly you see this for specific index files or password protection.

Again, a bit beyond the scope of this book, but if you see .htaccess as you browse the Web, you'll know what it is referring to. As a VPS administrator, you can likely accomplish everything you'd need to do with .htaccess by just changing the configuration files under /etc/ directly.

It's worth noting that as a new administrator, a tool such as Webmin (see Chapter 4) can be very helpful when learning how to use the Apache Web Server. It will handle writing and updating configuration files for you, thus helping to prevent typos or other easy errors.

Extending Capabilities with PHP

PHP, or the PHP Hypertext Preprocessor (yes, the first P stands for PHP... wonderful recursive acronyms), extends the capabilities of Apache by allowing your VPS to modify HTML files before they are sent to the web browser. Anytime you've seen "dynamic" content on a web page (e.g., you've logged into it, it displays your name, etc.) that the programmer didn't put in "statically," there has been some form of preprocessing done with it. PHP is one of the most popular preprocessors, although many others exist.

To give a demonstration of PHP, let's install it and then write a simple PHP file that displays the date. On Debian, use the command apt-get install php; it will automatically install the software and enable the Apache module. On CentOS, the command is yum install php; then restart Apache with systemctl restart httpd (Debian restarts Apache on its own).

Next, create a new file under /var/www/html using this command:

```
nano /var/www/html/date.php
```

And type the following into that file:

```
<?php
echo date('l jS \of F Y h:i:s A');
?>
```

Save the file by pressing Ctrl+O and then Ctrl+X. Now if you visit the file in your web browser by adding date.php to the end of your address (e.g., http://lilo.jonwestfall.net/date.php), you'll see the date displayed, instead of the code you wrote (see Figure 7-3). The code roughly told PHP to echo the current date, in the format shown, and is one of the many examples found in the PHP documentation on the date function (www.php.net/manual/en/function.date.php).

Tuesday 27th of October 2020 03:58:47 PM

Figure 7-3. date.php rendered in the web browser

PHP is one of the most common languages that open source software is written in, meaning that having it installed on your server (likely alongside MySQL) is going to greatly enhance all of the capabilities you have. We'll see one such open source project in Chapter 8, when we talk about WordPress.

Finally, before we leave Apache, let's secure things up a little bit by installing an SSL certificate, allowing us to have encrypted communications between our server and our users. We'll do this with the superbly useful service Let's Encrypt.

Installing a Free SSL Certificate with Let's Encrypt

Prior to October 2016, if you wanted to secure your web pages with SSL (Secure Sockets Layer, the s in *https*), you needed to purchase a cryptographic certificate from one of the handful of companies that issued them. This typically cost somewhere in the range of $10–100 a year, depending on the certificate, and had to be renewed regularly. Then the nonprofit Let's Encrypt service started, allowing us to easily add SSL to our web server for free.

To do so, issue these commands:

CentOS:

```
yum install epel-release
yum install letsencrypt
yum -y install mod_ssl
firewall-cmd --zone=public --permanent --add-service=https systemctl restart
firewalld
systemctl stop httpd
```

Debian:

```
apt-get install letsencrypt
firewall-cmd --zone=public --permanent --add-service=https systemctl restart
firewalld
systemctl stop apache2
```

Next, we need to configure Let's Encrypt by verifying our server. We'll do this by using the certbot certonly command. Issue the command, and then choose the first option (1). Walk through the prompts, and at the end you should see a message that tells you "Congratulations" under the Important Notes section and gives you the address of your certificate files. You'll want to write those down or keep them handy (see Figure 7-4).

```
Waiting for verification...
Cleaning up challenges

IMPORTANT NOTES:
 - Congratulations! Your certificate and chain have been saved at:
   /etc/letsencrypt/live/stitch.jonwestfall.net/fullchain.pem
   Your key file has been saved at:
   /etc/letsencrypt/live/stitch.jonwestfall.net/privkey.pem
   Your cert will expire on 2021-01-25. To obtain a new or tweaked
   version of this certificate in the future, simply run certbot
   again. To non-interactively renew *all* of your certificates, run
   "certbot renew"
 - If you like Certbot, please consider supporting our work by:

   Donating to ISRG / Let's Encrypt:   https://letsencrypt.org/donate
   Donating to EFF:                     https://eff.org/donate-le
```

Figure 7-4. *The Congratulations message*

Now you have your certificates, you need to install them on your server and then restart your server. To do this on CentOS, run nano /etc/httpd/ conf.d/ssl.conf to open the SSL configuration file. Find the line that reads SSLCertificateFile and put in the address to the first certificate listed in the Congratulations message (for me, this is /etc/letsencrypt/live/stitch. jonwestfall.net/fullchain.pem). On the SSLCertificateKeyFile line, you'll put the second address. See Figure 7-5.

```
 GNU nano 2.9.8 /etc/httpd/conf.d/ssl.conf

#   ciphers, etc.)
#   Some ECC cipher suites (http://www.ietf.org/rfc/rfc4492.txt)
#   require an ECC certificate which can also be configured in
#   parallel.
SSLCertificateFile /etc/letsencrypt/live/stitch.jonwestfall.net/fullchain.pem

#   Server Private Key:
#   If the key is not combined with the certificate, use this
#   directive to point at the key file.  Keep in mind that if
#   you've both a RSA and a DSA private key you can configure
#   both in parallel (to also allow the use of DSA ciphers, etc.)
#   ECC keys, when in use, can also be configured in parallel
SSLCertificateKeyFile /etc/letsencrypt/live/stitch.jonwestfall.net/privkey.pem
```

Figure 7-5. *The edits to the SSL.conf file on CentOS*

Finally on CentOS we need to enable the SSL module. To do this, save the file and issue the command `systemctl restart httpd`.

To do this on Debian, run nano /etc/apache2/sites-available/default-ssl.conf, find the areas of the file with the SSLCertificateFile and SSLCertificateKeyFile, and replace them with the appropriate information from the Congratulations message. See Figure 7-6. Then run the command a2ensite and choose default-ssl (see Figure 7-7).

```
#   A self-signed (snakeoil) certificate can be created by installing
#   the ssl-cert package. See
#   /usr/share/doc/apache2/README.Debian.gz for more info.
#   If both key and certificate are stored in the same file, only the
#   SSLCertificateFile directive is needed.
SSLCertificateFile /etc/letsencrypt/live/lilo.jonwestfall.net/fullchain.pem
SSLCertificateKeyFile /etc/letsencrypt/live/lilo.jonwestfall.net/privkey.pem
```

Figure 7-6. *The configuration file on Debian*

```
root@lilo:/etc/apache2/sites-available# a2ensite
Your choices are: 000-default default-ssl
Which site(s) do you want to enable (wildcards ok)?
```

Figure 7-7. *The a2ensite command on Debian*

Finally on Debian we need to enable the SSL module. To do this, run a2enmod and type `ssl` at the prompt (see Figure 7-8). Finally restart Apache by typing `systemctl restart apache2`.

```
root@lilo:/etc/apache2/sites-available# a2enmod
Your choices are: access_compat actions alias allowmethods asis auth_basic auth_digest auth_form authn_anon authn_core authn_dbd authn_dbm auth
n_file authn_socache authnz_fcgi authnz_ldap authz_core authz_dbd authz_dbm authz_groupfile authz_host authz_owner authz_user autoindex brotli
buffer cache cache_disk cache_socache cern_meta cgi cgid charset_lite data dav dav_fs dav_lock dbd deflate dialup dir dump_io echo env expires
ext_filter file_cache filter headers heartbeat heartmonitor http2 ident imagemap include info lbmethod_bybusyness lbmethod_byrequests lbmethod_
bytraffic lbmethod_heartbeat ldap log_debug log_forensic lua macro md mime mime_magic mpm_event mpm_prefork mpm_worker negotiation php7.3 proxy
 proxy_ajp proxy_balancer proxy_connect proxy_express proxy_fcgi proxy_fdpass proxy_ftp proxy_hcheck proxy_html proxy_http proxy_http2 proxy_sc
gi proxy_uwsgi proxy_wstunnel ratelimit reflector remoteip reqtimeout request rewrite sed session session_cookie session_crypto session_dbd set
envif slotmem_plain slotmem_shm socache_dbm socache_memcache socache_shmcb speling ssl status substitute suexec unique_id userdir usertrack vho
st_alias xml2enc
Which module(s) do you want to enable (wildcards ok)?
ssl
```

Figure 7-8. *Enabling the SSL module*

Now, if we've followed all the commands, we can visit our VPS and add the "s" after "http" to get the secure version. Visiting https://lilo. jonwestfall.net now shows me the lock icon at the top, and clicking it, I see the certificate information shown in Figure 7-9.

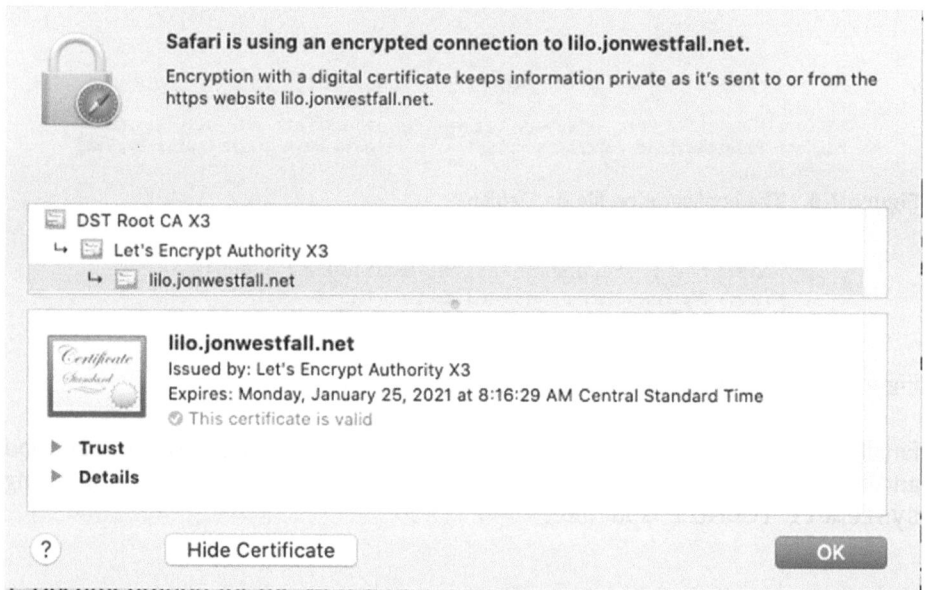

Figure 7-9. The Certificate Information on my Lilo Server

Now that SSL is up and running, the last thing we need to do is provide a mechanism to automatically renew the certificate. By default, the certificates are only valid for a short time. Here's how to get the Cron scheduler to do this for us regularly.

Start by typing crontab -e to edit your server's Cron file. In that file, put the line 0 0 * * * /usr/bin/certbot renew at the bottom. Save the file, and now each day your server will check and renew the certificate if necessary.

Now that you have a fancy web server up and running, let's think about the data we might store on it, using the MySQL database!

The MySQL or MariaDB Database Server

Imagine having five spreadsheets on your computer, tracking orders, inventory, customers, complaints, and billing information for your business. In each spreadsheet, you track specific information, but you also have links that connect to other spreadsheets. For example, in your order spreadsheet, you'll have a customer ID number that links to your customer spreadsheet. In your complaints, you might have an order ID number that links to the order in question. This concept of linked relationships is what powers a relational database management system, or RDBMS. MySQL, the name being a combination of the cofounder's eldest daughter's name (My) and the term "Structured Query Language," the method used to store and retrieve data in the database, is one of the most popular RDBMSs in the world today, thanks to its robust developer community and its very attractive price tag (Free). In 2010, Sun Microsystems purchased MySQL and began to create commercial versions (the base version is still free). At that time, the cofounder and others created a new version using the open source code named MariaDB (this time after his younger daughter's name). Today both maintain compatibility with each other for the most part, so you can generally use the terms MySQL and MariaDB interchangeably.

For our purposes, MySQL most commonly is used to store user data so that it can be used to power web pages. For instance, a blog might have a database set up to power it, with posts being stored in one table, comments being stored in another, and blog author bios stored in a third. A web page that tracks orders for a company may have the same tables that we talked about earlier. In this section, we'll install MySQL and show how it integrates in a web page.

Installation

First, let's get the appropriate software installed. We'll need the MySQL database, and we'll need the module that connects MySQL to PHP. Use the following commands to install both of these.

```
CentOS:yum install mariadb-server php-mysqlnd.x86_64
systemctl enable mariadb
systemctl start mariadb

Debian:apt-get install mariadb-server php-mysql
```

By default, both CentOS and Debian install MySQL with a blank database root password. This means we can run the command `mysql -u root` on either and get into the database directly. In Figure 7-10, I'm using the commands `show databases;` and `quit` to log into the database server, show the list of databases (there are three), and then exit back to my command prompt.

```
root@lilo:~# mysql -u root
Welcome to the MariaDB monitor.  Commands end with ; or \g.
Your MariaDB connection id is 50
Server version: 10.3.23-MariaDB-0+deb10u1 Debian 10

Copyright (c) 2000, 2018, Oracle, MariaDB Corporation Ab and others.

Type 'help;' or '\h' for help. Type '\c' to clear the current input statement.

MariaDB [(none)]> show databases;
+--------------------+
| Database           |
+--------------------+
| information_schema |
| mysql              |
| performance_schema |
+--------------------+
3 rows in set (0.000 sec)

MariaDB [(none)]> quit
Bye
root@lilo:~# ▊
```

Figure 7-10. Querying the database list on Debian Linux

Having a blank root password is not very secure, and we can use the following command to help us tighten up security a bit on our server before we move on to the next section. Run mysql_secure_installation in your console, leave the password blank when asked, and then choose "Y" when asked if you want to change the root password. Change it to something secure, and then accept the default options as you move through the program, as I've done in Figure 7-11.

```
[root@stitch ~]# mysql_secure_installation

NOTE: RUNNING ALL PARTS OF THIS SCRIPT IS RECOMMENDED FOR ALL MariaDB
      SERVERS IN PRODUCTION USE!  PLEASE READ EACH STEP CAREFULLY!

In order to log into MariaDB to secure it, we'll need the current
password for the root user.  If you've just installed MariaDB, and
you haven't set the root password yet, the password will be blank,
so you should just press enter here.

Enter current password for root (enter for none):
OK, successfully used password, moving on...

Setting the root password ensures that nobody can log into the MariaDB
root user without the proper authorisation.

Set root password? [Y/n] Y
New password:
Re-enter new password:
Password updated successfully!
Reloading privilege tables..
 ... Success!


By default, a MariaDB installation has an anonymous user, allowing anyone
to log into MariaDB without having to have a user account created for
them.  This is intended only for testing, and to make the installation
go a bit smoother.  You should remove them before moving into a
production environment.

Remove anonymous users? [Y/n] Y
 ... Success!

Normally, root should only be allowed to connect from 'localhost'.  This
ensures that someone cannot guess at the root password from the network.

Disallow root login remotely? [Y/n] Y
 ... Success!

By default, MariaDB comes with a database named 'test' that anyone can
access.  This is also intended only for testing, and should be removed
before moving into a production environment.

Remove test database and access to it? [Y/n] Y
 - Dropping test database...
 ... Success!
 - Removing privileges on test database...
 ... Success!

Reloading the privilege tables will ensure that all changes made so far
will take effect immediately.

Reload privilege tables now? [Y/n] Y
 ... Success!

Cleaning up...

All done!  If you've completed all of the above steps, your MariaDB
installation should now be secure.
[root@stitch ~]#
Thanks for using MariaDB!
[root@stitch ~]#
```

Figure 7-11. *Securing the MySQL Installation*

Now that we have MySQL installed, in the next section, I'll show you a few
simple commands to see how MySQL databases are created, accessed, and
displayed in a web page.

Basic Commands

A database server is useful only if it holds data. In this section, we're going to walk through

- Adding a database

- Adding a table to that database

- Adding data to that table

- Adding a user account that can access the database

- Writing a simple web page that displays the data we put in the table

Each step of the way, I'll provide example code that you can type in. Be careful to make sure you include all of the punctuation – commas, semicolons, and case can sometimes matter.

Let's start by logging into the MySQL server with the command mysql -u root -p. We set a password, so we need to add the -p option to the command so that it will prompt us to enter our password.

Now we'll tell MySQL that we want to create a database named "friends," using the command create database friends;. In Figure 7-12, we can see the database has been created, as it appears when we use the show databases; command.

```
[root@stitch ~]# mysql —u root —p
Enter password:
Welcome to the MariaDB monitor.  Commands end with ; or \g.
Your MariaDB connection id is 20
Server version: 10.3.17-MariaDB MariaDB Server

Copyright (c) 2000, 2018, Oracle, MariaDB Corporation Ab and others.

Type 'help;' or '\h' for help. Type '\c' to clear the current input statement.

MariaDB [(none)]> create database `friends`;
Query OK, 1 row affected (0.000 sec)

MariaDB [(none)]> show databases;
+--------------------+
| Database           |
+--------------------+
| friends            |
| information_schema |
| mysql              |
| performance_schema |
+--------------------+
4 rows in set (0.002 sec)
```

Figure 7-12. Creating the friends database

Now that we have the database, we simply need to switch to it by typing use database friends. Let's create a table to store all of my friends in, by then typing CREATE TABLE IF NOT EXISTS myfriends (name VARCHAR(255), description text);. As you can see in Figure 7-13, MySQL reports that this has been done.

```
MariaDB [(none)]> use friends;
Database changed
MariaDB [friends]> CREATE TABLE IF NOT EXISTS myfriends (name VARCHAR(255), description te
xt);
Query OK, 0 rows affected (0.011 sec)
```

Figure 7-13. Creating the table

You can think of the table as a spreadsheet, and now we'll enter two rows by typing INSERT into myfriends(name,description) VALUES ("Steve","Steve is my best friend"), ("Karey", "Karey is my wife");. Pressing Enter, we get confirmation that this has been successfully done (Figure 7-14).

```
MariaDB [friends]> INSERT into myfriends(name,description) VALUES ("Steve","Steve is my bes
t friend"), ("Karey", "Karey is my wife");
Query OK, 2 rows affected (0.002 sec)
Records: 2  Duplicates: 0  Warnings: 0
```

Figure 7-14. Rows entered into the myfriends table

Finally we can confirm that the data was entered by issuing a *select* statement, which asks MySQL to show us the data. In this case, we want all of the data in the table, denoted by using an asterisk: SELECT * from myfriends;. Figure 7-15 confirms that the data is there.

```
MariaDB [friends]> SELECT * from myfriends;
+-------+-------------------------+
| name  | description             |
+-------+-------------------------+
| Steve | Steve is my best friend |
| Karey | Karey is my wife        |
+-------+-------------------------+
2 rows in set (0.000 sec)
```

Figure 7-15. Data successfully retrieved

Congratulations! You've now made your first table inside your first database and written your first few rows. Next, we just need to have a way to access it. Let's create a new user named 'friendviewer', with password 'friendly', and give it access to the friends database. The following commands will do this for us (you may omit the first command if you are still logged into MySQL):

```
mysql -u root -p
CREATE USER 'friendviewer'@'localhost' IDENTIFIED BY 'friendly';
GRANT SELECT ON friends.* to 'friendviewer'@'localhost';
FLUSH PRIVILEGES;
quit;
```

After running those commands, I can now log in as 'friendviewer', as seen in Figure 7-16. This user, because it only has the SELECT permission (in the preceding GRANT statement), can only view data. It cannot enter or update. This is good practice for accounts that just need to access data, but shouldn't be able to modify it.

```
[root@stitch ~]# mysql -u friendviewer -p
Enter password:
Welcome to the MariaDB monitor.  Commands end with ; or \g.
Your MariaDB connection id is 24
Server version: 10.3.17-MariaDB MariaDB Server

Copyright (c) 2000, 2018, Oracle, MariaDB Corporation Ab and others.

Type 'help;' or '\h' for help. Type '\c' to clear the current input statement.

MariaDB [(none)]> show databases;
+--------------------+
| Database           |
+--------------------+
| friends            |
| information_schema |
+--------------------+
2 rows in set (0.000 sec)

MariaDB [(none)]> use friends;
Reading table information for completion of table and column names
You can turn off this feature to get a quicker startup with -A

Database changed
MariaDB [friends]> select * from myfriends;
+-------+-----------------------+
| name  | description           |
+-------+-----------------------+
| Steve | Steve is my best friend |
| Karey | Karey is my wife      |
+-------+-----------------------+
2 rows in set (0.000 sec)
```

Figure 7-16. The friendviewer account logging in and viewing the friend list

Now let's wrap it all up. We'll create a simple PHP page that displays the friend list. To do so, run the command nano /var/www/html/friendlist.php to create and edit a new file under your web root directory. Put the following code in that file:

```
<?php
$connection = new mysqli("localhost","friendviewer","friendly","friends");
$data = $connection->query("SELECT * from myfriends"); while ($line = $data-
>fetch_assoc()) {
        echo "<p>Friend's Name: " . $line["name"] . ",<br> A description: "
        . $line["description"];
}
$connection -> close();
?>
```

Saving the file and then browsing to it in your web browser (e.g., http:// stitch.jonwestfall.net/friendlist.php) should display the results of the database query, as I've done in Figure 7-17.

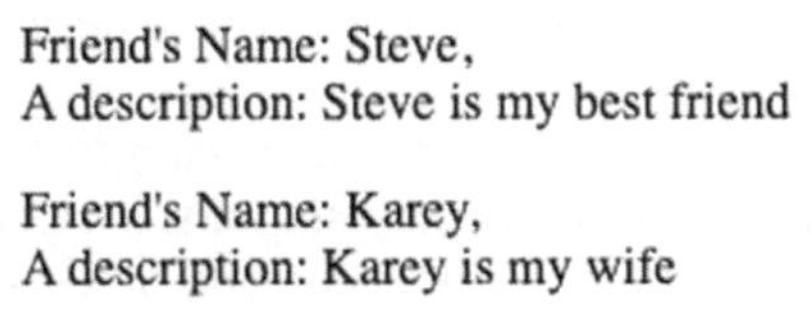

Friend's Name: Steve,
A description: Steve is my best friend

Friend's Name: Karey,
A description: Karey is my wife

Figure 7-17. *Displaying the database rows*

Again, congratulations! You've now shown data from your database on a web page! Thinking about it, you can now see how the connections you're making on the back end between web server and database server are formed and the possibilities that this can have. In the next chapter, we'll look at a software product that heavily utilizes this relationship, WordPress, in order to create a rich blog interface. But before we do that, let's briefly talk about the other servers that you might run into – Postfix and how to monitor the whole situation using Webmin.

The Postfix Mail Server

Since its inception, Linux has bundled an electronic mail system with its various distributions, most frequently Sendmail, a program dating back to 1983. While reliable and useful, it can be a bit prickly to configure. This has led to alternatives, such as the Exim mail server in 1995 and Postfix in 1998. In this section, I'll talk about setting up and configuring Postfix, which I tend to choose as it has a high emphasis on security, is actively developed, and has robust documentation. Additionally it also supports a wide range of add-ins so that you can customize your mail server as needed.

Installation

To get started, let's install Postfix. On CentOS, you'll need to do the following:

```
yum install postfix
systemctl enable postfix
systemctl start postfix
```

On Debian, you'll run apt-get install postfix. At the end of the installation, you'll be given a Postfix configuration screen (Figure 7-18). Accept the default of "Internet Site," and in System mail name, make sure you use the full server address for your server (e.g., lilo.jonwestfall.net for mine).

At this point, Postfix is now set up to send and receive email. However, you now need to make sure that the path is cleared to Postfix by

- Making sure that your server has a valid MX record in its DNS configuration. If you're using a third-party registrar for DNS, such as Network Solutions or GoDaddy, you'll need to add this. In my case, for lilo.jonwestfall. net, I would need to add an A record (if you don't have one already) and a MX record by logging into GoDaddy, my registrar, going to my domain manager, and adding the DNS record as seen in Figure 7-19. This tells the Internet that mail for @lilo.jonwestfall.net addresses should go to (unsurprisingly) lilo.jonwestfall.net!

- You also need to open your firewall to allow servers on the Internet to directly connect to your server's port 25, the port used to receive mail. You can do this by running the command firewall-cmd --zone=public --permanent --add-service=https and then systemctl restart firewalld.

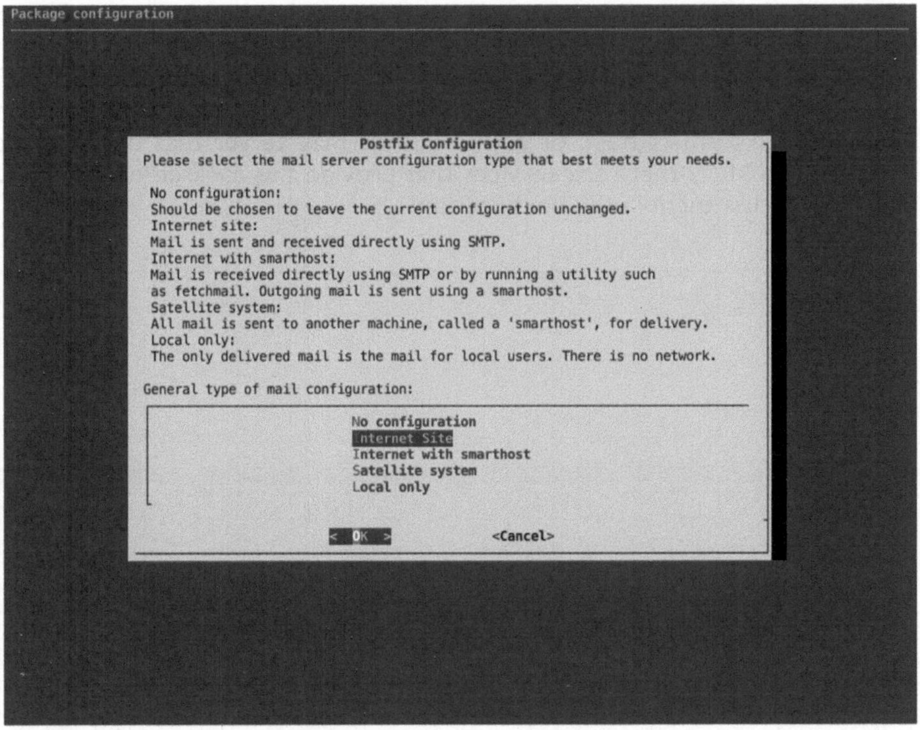

Figure 7-18. The Postfix configuration window on Debian

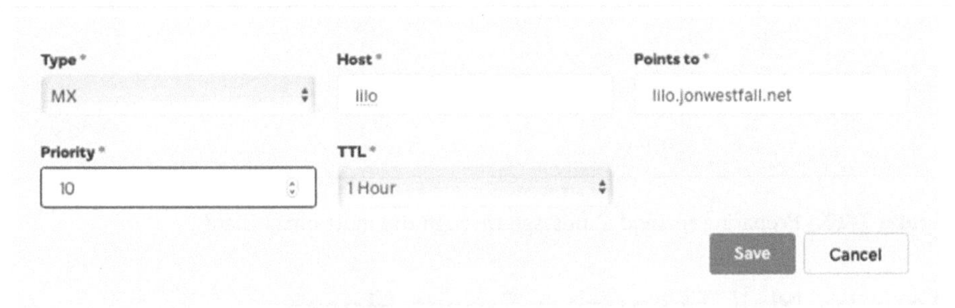

Figure 7-19. Adding a DNS MX record

At this point, you can send and receive mail by using the `mail` command or using a simple email client such as `mutt` (`yum install mutt` or `apt-get install mutt`), as seen in Figure 7-20. One thing you may notice, though, is that your test emails don't go through properly. They may get marked as spam or not go through at all. Why is that? Well, it's because you have a relatively new mail server that most of the Internet doesn't know…and that's suspicious to most of the Internet. This leads many receiving mail servers to consider your server suspect – a possible spam powerhouse that the receiver wants to protect its users from. So how do you gain "respect"? Well, you could either go through a lot of trouble to establish yourself, from using special DNS records to establishing regular mail sending habits, or you can route your email through a smart host, or an established mail server that the Internet "trusts." Thankfully there are services that provide this for free or low cost, and we'll discuss them in the next section!

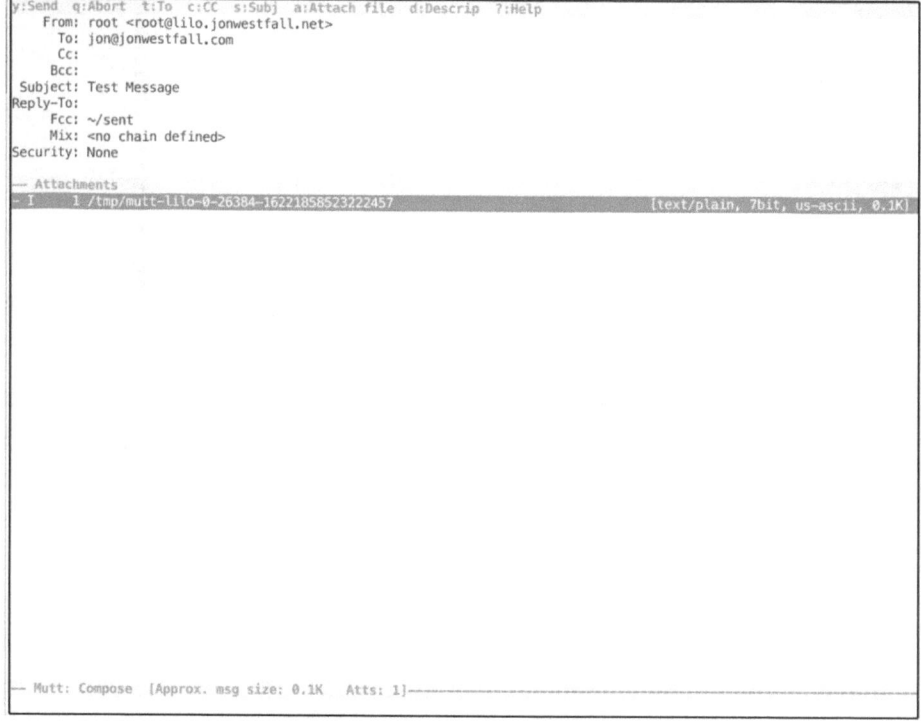

Figure 7-20. Preparing to send a message through the mutt email client

Routing Mail Through a Smart Host

As mentioned, a smart host allows you to route your outgoing email through an established mail host that is trusted by other servers on the Internet. For small traffic, services such as Smtp2Go (www.smtp2go.com) allow you to do this for free, charging you if you go over 1,000 emails per month. This isn't usually a problem if you're running a VPS for a small business that doesn't do a lot of email marketing. If you do decide to send email in bulk, you'll typically pay somewhere under $100 a month depending on the amount you'd like to send.

To get started, you'll typically need a username, password, and server address and port number of the smart host. Once you have those, follow these steps:

1. Create a new file in your /etc/postfix directory named relay_passwd by using the command nano /etc/postfix/relay_passwd.

2. Add the following information to the file in this order: server address:port number username:password. So if the server is mail.test.com and you're to send on port 25, with username testuser and password testpassword, your file will look like this:

   ```
   mail.test.com:25 testuser@testpassword
   ```

3. Save the file (Ctrl+O) and exit (Ctrl+X).

4. Run the postmap command to encode the file: postmap /etc/postfix/relay_passwd. This will generate the file relay_passwd.db.

5. Edit the file main.cf (e.g., nano /etc/postfix/main.cf).

6. Add the following information to the end of the file, changing mail.test.com to the server address from #2.

   ```
   relayhost = mail.smtp2go.com:2525
   smtp_use_tls = yes smtp_sasl_auth_enable = yes
   smtp_sasl_password_maps = hash:/etc/postfix/relay_passwd
   smtp_sasl_security_options =
   ```

7. If you are on CentOS, you'll need to install the SASL library, by running yum install cyrus-sasl-plain.

8. Save the file, and then restart Postfix with the command systemctl restart postfix.

Note If you find you are having issues with the preceding configuration, you may also need to find the line that reads inet_protocols = all and change it to inet_protocols = ipv4. Save and restart Postfix.

Congratulations! You now have email flowing out of your server, and you should be able to receive it as well. There are some useful things you can now do, including

- Running your own small mail server for your users.

- Receiving email and then sending it to a web page or web service – like my ticket board example from Chapter 1. Users can simply email back replies, and it will appear in the ticket board software.

- Running a small mailing list with archive, using the open source Mailman program.

- Sending automated emails to yourself as reminders!

Email, love it or hate it, is one of the most common methods of communication we have. You now have the tools to help master it! In the next section, we'll cover one more element you might want to enable – system monitoring within Webmin.

Server Monitoring Within Webmin

In Chapter 4, we discussed how to set up and use Webmin to help administer your server. I briefly mentioned the System and Server Status option: however, it is likely something you'll want to explore more, now that you've installed some other services on your VPS.

To refresh your memory, you access the System and Server Status by first logging into Webmin and then clicking the option under the "Tools" or "Others" menu. It should bring up something similar to Figure 7-21.

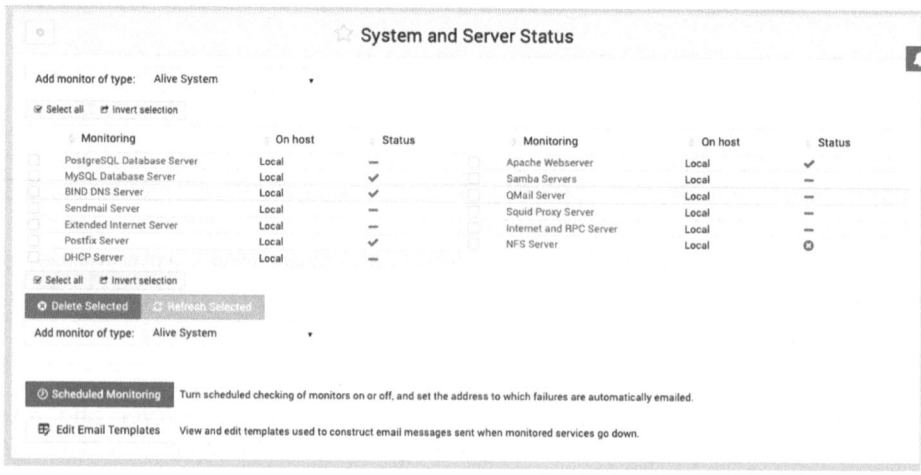

Figure 7-21. System and Server Status in Webmin

You'll notice that you have several entries for servers that are not installed or enabled, such as PostgreSQL Database Server, Sendmail Server, and Extended Internet Server. The status will simply show a dash. You should also have monitors for servers you have installed, such as Apache, MySQL, and Postfix, denoted by a check.

This gives you a snapshot of what services are currently running on your machine; however, it's not going to be very useful if you aren't watching the machine at the time something goes down. It would be better if the system could contact you – thankfully it can through the "Scheduled Monitoring" options. Click the "Scheduled Monitoring" button, and you will see a screen similar to Figure 7-22.

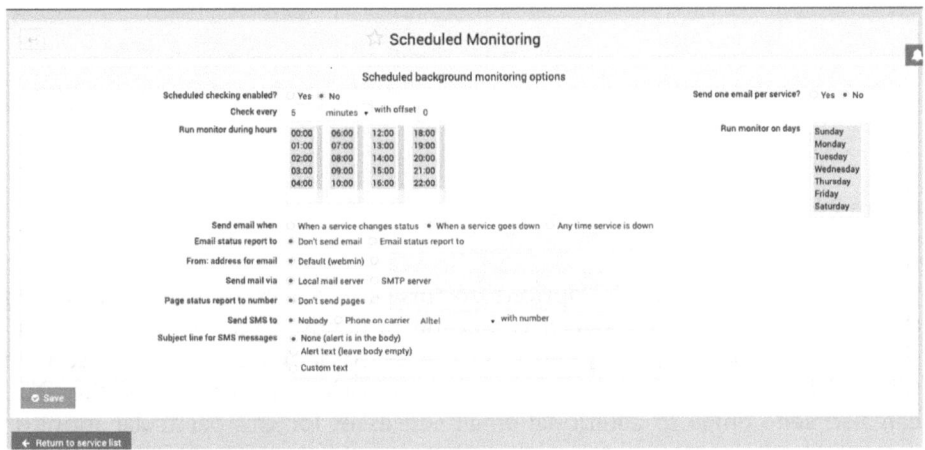

Figure 7-22. The Scheduled Monitoring options

To get your system to check regularly, you'll first want to change the "Scheduled checking enabled" to "Yes." A check interval of 5 minutes should be sufficient, and you can choose to only have it run during certain hours or days. This is useful if you know you're going to be rebooting the VPS regularly or if for some reason you plan on turning off certain services at certain times. You'll want to customize when it sends you an email and also where to send the email to. If you've set up Postfix to route through a smart host, you can leave the "Send mail via" option set to "Local mail server," and it will be routed through the smart host the same as any other mail. Otherwise, you can specify a specific SMTP mail server to route through. Likely though, you'll need to authenticate through that SMTP server, which means the smart host/ Postfix option is probably more reliable.

Once you've configured your scheduled checking, click the Save button.

Now that your scheduled checking is set up, let's look at some of the options we can tweak to make your monitor more useful. Click the "Apache Webserver" option, and you should see a screen similar to Figure 7-23.

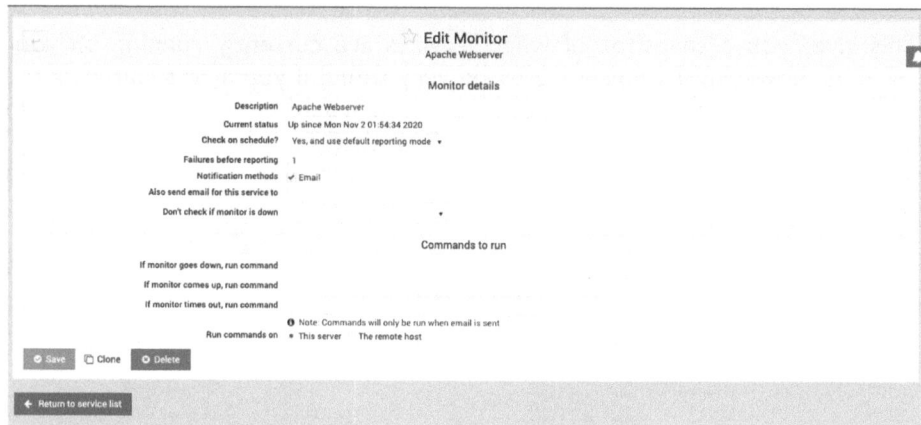

Figure 7-23. The Apache Webserver monitor

There are some very useful options on this screen. First, it tells us how long the service has been up, which can come in handy if you have a "flapping" service – one that frequently restarts itself for some reason. You can also turn this monitor on or off of the scheduled monitoring that you just set up. You can also send email to additional email addresses for this particular monitor (perhaps letting your web team know that the web server is down, in addition to yourself), and you can also tell Webmin not to check additional services if this service is down (e.g., the database server that only serves data through the website).

Finally, there are some options that allow you to try to "repair" the system itself. In the "If monitor goes down, run command" option, you could type systemctl restart apache2, which would start the web server. If there was some transitory issue that caused the server to crash (perhaps a sudden spike in traffic or some other phenomenon), a simple restart might be all that is needed. In this case, Webmin can run the command and perhaps fix the issue before you even have a chance to log in. In more complex cases, you might eventually write a "diagnostic" script that should be run if a monitor goes down, which could gather information for you allowing you to diagnose the problem quicker. Once you're done tweaking the monitor, choose "Save" and go back to the main service list.

Finally, let's talk about the different monitor types that you might find useful. In the dropdown box next to the "Add monitor of type" button, you'll see a number of options. Here are some of the more useful:

- Alive System – This checks to see if the current VPS is active and responding. You might wonder why you'd need this – after all, if the system is not responding, it can't really run Webmin to monitor things, can it? This is true. However, this monitor does allow you to view system uptime, and perhaps if the system is under severe stress, it could be able to trigger at least once before the system completely locks up. You might put in a command to shut down the most processor-intensive service if "Alive System" goes down, such as the web or database server, in an effort to keep the rest of the system up.

- Bootup Action: This can check to see if a service that is enabled to start on bootup actually does. Useful if you have a number of tasks that you need to monitor that you don't already have a monitor option for in Webmin.

- Check File or Directory: Useful to see if a certain file has been created or deleted, is larger or smaller than a given size, and so on. If you have a script that writes a file to a certain location each day, this would be one way to make sure it had been successfully done.

- Check Process: Useful to make sure something is running. I use this on servers that I have Duplicati installed on, to make sure the Duplicati process is always running.

- Disk Space: To keep an eye on available disk space before it runs low.

- Free Memory: To make sure that you aren't using too much RAM.

- Load Average: Your "load" in Linux is the amount of tasks your CPU is doing relative to its capacity. A load of 1 indicates perfect balance – your CPU can handle all of the tasks currently running in a timely manner within capacity. Loads above 1 indicate excessive load, or processes waiting to be executed. Loads above 5–10 will typically start to seriously impact system performance.

- Remote FTP/HTTP/Ping/SSH/TCP: Useful if you're keeping an eye on other servers, perhaps those that don't have Webmin installed.

- SSL Certificate: Useful to keep an eye on SSL certificates, to make sure they're properly installed on a web server and to notify you several days in advance of their expiration.

I'm sure as you build out your monitoring system, you'll also notice that many of the options allow you to run them either on "This server" or "The remote host" – this means that if you have multiple VPSs with Webmin installed in a cluster, you can actually create one unified dashboard on one machine to monitor all of the others as well. Think of it as your own central command.

Hopefully as this chapter draws to a close, you've got a few ideas of how to extend your VPS to be truly useful. In the next chapter, we'll apply all of this to a common open source software package, WordPress, and build our own personal blog or product homepage!

Installing an Open Source Software Product: WordPress

One of the most common uses for a VPS is to host a website, whether it be for your own personal blog or projects or for your company or service. Initially, when the Web was "young," web pages were fairly simple things. You had an HTML file filled with the text that would be on the page, with instructions on how to format it, and then perhaps a handful of image files that you would sprinkle throughout the page. Today, the landscape is much more complex, with the rise of the "CMS" or content management system.

© Jon Westfall 2021
J. Westfall, *Set Up and Manage Your Virtual Private Server*,
https://doi.org/10.1007/978-1-4842-6966-4_8

In this chapter, we're going to talk about downloading and installing one of the most popular CMSs, WordPress, and configuring it to be reliable and secure. We'll also talk about extending it with plugins to customize your site!

What Is a CMS and Do You Need It?

If all you want to do is have a simple homepage that has your name on it, your photo, and your resume, then do you really need a full-blown CMS? It's an interesting question and one that we can discuss from a few different angles. In the following table, I'm going to compare a "traditional" web page, which I created in Microsoft Word (see Figure 8-1 for the page in Word, Figure 8-2 for the files Word created when I chose "Save as..." and then "Web Page" as type, and Figure 8-3 for how it appears in a web browser), vs. using a CMS.

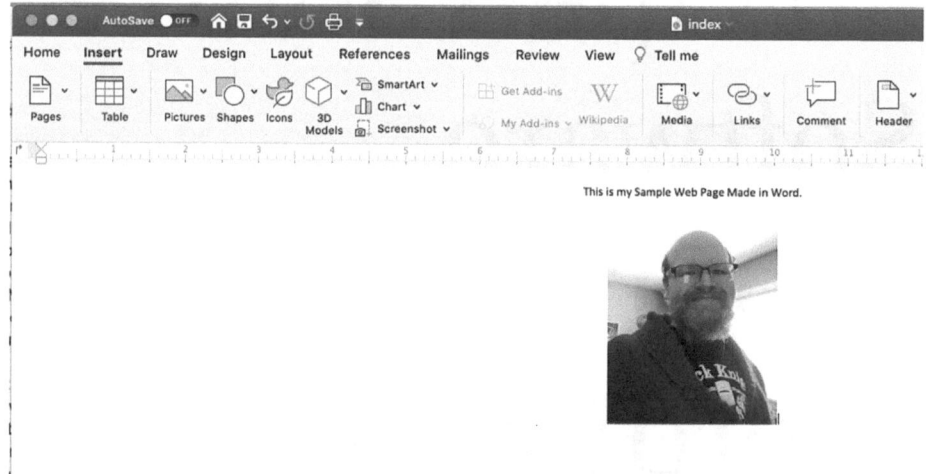

Figure 8-1. Creating a sample web page in Word

Figure 8-2. Files created by Word after using the Save as Web Page option

file:///Users/jon/OneDrive/Desktop/index.html

This is my Sample Web Page Made in Word.

Figure 8-3. The Word web page in a web browser

Dimension	Traditional Web Page	Page Generated by the Content Management System (CMS)
Ease of navigation and use	This fully depends on your time spent tinkering and designing in Word or a dedicated HTML editor. If you already know HTML, you can make very intuitive and useful pages; however, we have all probably seen web pages that really work poorly because someone thought certain colors looked good (when they didn't) or that buttons were obvious (that weren't) or that a picture needed to be a certain size (that was too large or too small for most screens). You'll be devoting substantial time to getting the page perfectly set up, tweaking it until it's just right.	Most CMSs are designed to have ease of use from the ground up. They ship with helpful navigation options such as menus that automatically change when you add a new page or layouts that are responsive to larger or smaller screens. Simply put, you can rapidly choose a design you like and be up and running after just adding your own content.
Ease of updating	Each update you make to a traditional web page will require you to either modify the files directly or generate a new set of files. Depending on the size of the update, this can take between 30 seconds and 3 hours.	Updates typically are made through a graphical user interface, allowing you to easily add or edit content. You'll need to log into the interface, and it may take a few moments to load; however, generally it will be faster and more intuitive.

(continued)

Dimension	Traditional Web Page	Page Generated by the Content Management System (CMS)
Ease of integrating other services	Each new service you want to integrate you'll need to investigate and fully configure. Adding something simple like a contact form may take 2–3 hours for a beginner.	Plugins in CMSs allow you to extend the capabilities easily. A contact form may only be two to three clicks away. Integrating with a shopping cart system may take an hour vs. a week if you were to build it from the ground up.
Visual appeal	You'll need an eye for design. If you have one, that's great — use it. But most of us aren't natural artists.	CMSs ship with templates that anyone can use, and there are hundreds of thousands more on the Internet, most available for free. This makes it easy to not only tweak your web page but also to update the look to keep it "fresh."
Ability to back up/restore	Traditional web pages have a solid win in this column — they typically are just a collection of files like Figure 8-2. So all one needs to do is back those up and save a copy, and you're done.	CMSs typically rely on database tables to store content, so you'll need to back up not only the files that the CMS uses but also the database. Restoring also adds an extra step of restoring the database.
Security	This is also one where traditional web pages have a slight advantage — they tend to be less complex, and so inherently, there are fewer ways they can be compromised. This doesn't mean they are completely safe from attack. In fact, if you're a new programmer who has decided to branch out into something more complex, say a database-driven web page, you might have issues with security given your relative inexperience.	A CMS is a complex system of moving parts, so security is dependent on keeping all of the parts up to date and following the best practices of security, which we'll discuss in the following. Properly updated, a CMS can be very secure. Leave it alone for a few months, though, and it will likely get compromised without regular updates.
Accessibility to humans/ search engines	Humans tend to like logical navigation, easy-to-find menus, and descriptive text that is easy to read. Search engines tend to look at the actual HTML tags used in the page to see if the page is relevant to a given search term. If you know a lot about Search Engine Optimization (SEO) and Human Factors Engineering/ Ergonomics, then you can build a very accessible traditional web page.	Most CMSs try to take the guess work out of Ergonomics and SEO by building helpful guides for humans and search engines alike. I give them the advantage in this category.

As you can see, there are good reasons to go with a CMS and bad reasons. I'd say that in my professional life, a CMS has been the way to go around 75% of the time; however, every so often when I just need a static web page that doesn't change much (and needs to be dead simple to update), I revert back to a traditional HTML page with some basic images and a simple layout. If you go beyond this point, I'm going to assume you're ready to take the plunge with a CMS!

Downloading and Installing WordPress

To get started installing WordPress, you'll first want to follow the instructions in Chapter 7 to install Apache 2, MySQL/MariaDB, and Postfix. Once you've done that, start with the following steps:

1. Log into your VPS and download the latest version of WordPress by using the command wget https://wordpress.org/latest.tar.gz.

2. Decompress and unpack the files by running tar xvzf latest.tar.gz.

3. You now have a directory of files named wordpress. It's time to decide if you want the files to be at the root of your website (e.g., http://stitch.jonwestfall.net) or a subdirectory (e.g., http://stitch.jonwestfall.net/blog). If you decide to go with the root directory, then use the command mv wordpress/* /var/www/html. If you want to go with a subdirectory, use the following commands, replacing blog with the name of the subdirectory: mv wordpress /var/www/html and mv /var/www/html/wordpress /var/www/html/blog.

4. On CentOS, install the PHP JSON library (yum install php-json) and restart Apache (systemctl restart httpd).

5. Now you can navigate to the WordPress Installer, by opening your web browser and going to the location you installed WordPress to (e.g., http://stitch.jonwestfall.net/ or http://lilo.jonwestfall.net/blog). You should see the WordPress Installer, as seen in Figure 8-4. If you do not, delete the file /var/www/index.html and try reloading again.

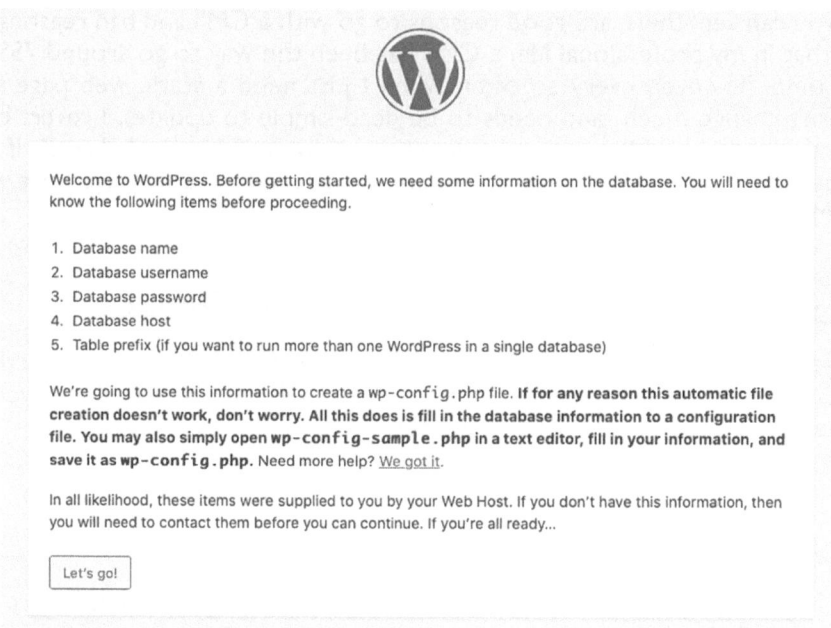

Welcome to WordPress. Before getting started, we need some information on the database. You will need to know the following items before proceeding.

1. Database name
2. Database username
3. Database password
4. Database host
5. Table prefix (if you want to run more than one WordPress in a single database)

We're going to use this information to create a wp-config.php file. **If for any reason this automatic file creation doesn't work, don't worry. All this does is fill in the database information to a configuration file. You may also simply open wp-config-sample.php in a text editor, fill in your information, and save it as wp-config.php.** Need more help? We got it.

In all likelihood, these items were supplied to you by your Web Host. If you don't have this information, then you will need to contact them before you can continue. If you're all ready...

Let's go!

Figure 8-4. The WordPress installation screen

If you do not see the installer and instead get a cryptic error message, there are a few files you'll want to check to see if there are errors. You can typically then search these errors on the Internet to find out what the fix may be. The files to look at on Debian would be /var/log/apache2/error.log and other files under /var/log/apache2. On CentOS, you'll want to check /var/log/php-fpm/www-error.log and /var/log/httpd/error_log. Assuming you see the installation screen, you can proceed by clicking "Let's go!"

1. Now you'll need to enter your database information. First, you'll want to create a database on your server. In my case, I've named my database "myblog" and used the command mysqladmin -u root -p create myblog to create it. It will prompt me for my MySQL root password, which is different than your normal root password (you set this password using the mysql_secure_installation command in Chapter 7).

2. Now you'll want to create a dedicated database user for your WordPress installation using the following code, replacing wordpress with the name of the database you created in step 1:

```
mysql -u root -p
CREATE   USER   'wpuser'@'localhost'   IDENTIFIED   BY
'alongandusefulpassword';
GRANT ALL ON wordpress.* to 'wpuser'@'localhost';
FLUSH PRIVILEGES;
quit;
```

3. Once you've created your database and user, fill in the details as seen in Figure 8-5. It is a good security practice to change the default database name, prefix, and username, as some hackers may try to modify MySQL database tables by knowing their names or their database names.

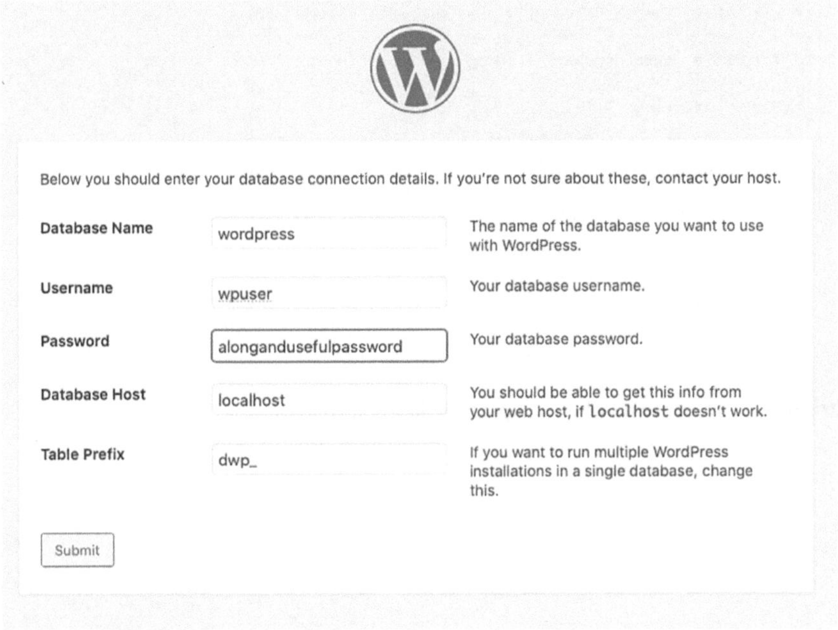

Figure 8-5. The database configuration screen

4. On the next screen, you'll get a large box of text that contains your wp-config.php file (see Figure 8-6). Copy the text from this file and create a new file with your WordPress installation named wp-config.php (e.g., with a command similar to nano /var/www/html/wp- config. php or nano /var/www/html/blog/wp-config.php depending on if you installed in the root directory or a subdirectory). Paste the text into that file, as seen in Figure 8-7, and then click "Run the installation."

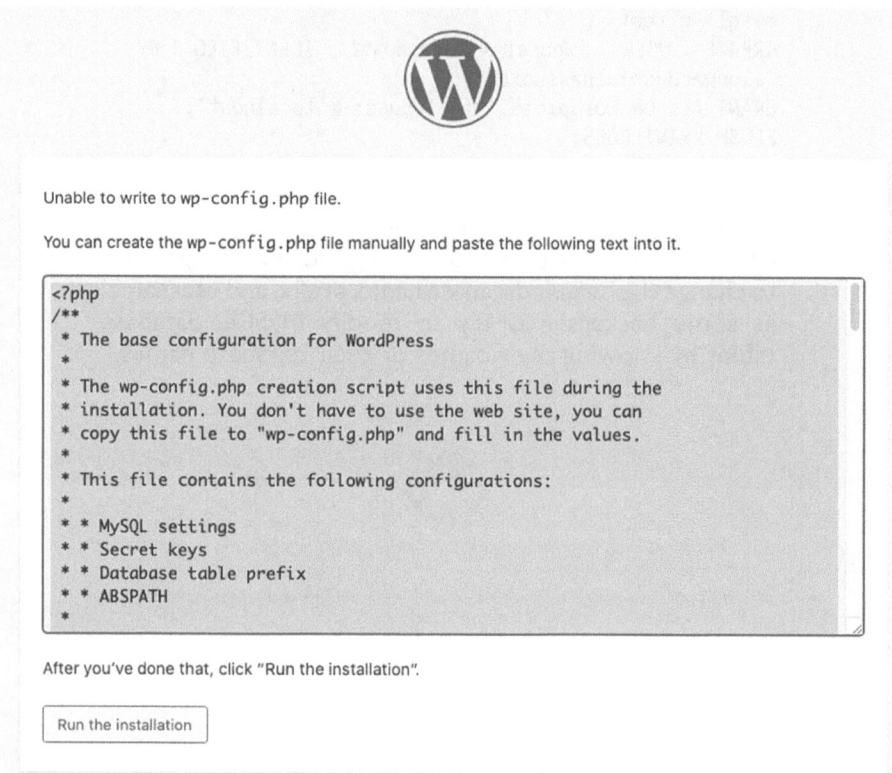

Figure 8-6. The contents of your wp-config file

```
  GNU nano 3.2                        /var/www/html/blog/wp-config.php                    Modified

 * WordPress Database Table prefix.
 *
 * You can have multiple installations in one database if you give each
 * a unique prefix. Only numbers, letters, and underscores please!
 */
$table_prefix = 'dwp_';

/**
 * For developers: WordPress debugging mode.
 *
 * Change this to true to enable the display of notices during development.
 * It is strongly recommended that plugin and theme developers use WP_DEBUG
 * in their development environments.
 *
 * For information on other constants that can be used for debugging,
 * visit the documentation.
 *
 * @link https://wordpress.org/support/article/debugging-in-wordpress/
 */
define( 'WP_DEBUG', false );

/* That's all, stop editing! Happy publishing. */

/** Absolute path to the WordPress directory. */
if ( ! defined( 'ABSPATH' ) ) {
        define( 'ABSPATH', __DIR__ . '/' );
}

/** Sets up WordPress vars and included files. */
require_once ABSPATH . 'wp-settings.php';




^G Get Help    ^O Write Out    ^W Where Is    ^K Cut Text     ^J Justify     ^C Cur Pos     M-U Undo
^X Exit        ^R Read File    ^\ Replace     ^U Uncut Text   ^T To Spell    ^_ Go To Line  M-E Redo
```

Figure 8-7. Pasting the wp-config contents into a file on your server

5. The next page will ask you to specify certain details for your WordPress installation. Your Site Title can always be changed at anytime, so don't stress over it if you're not sure what you want to call your website. Set a username that is *not* admin or preferably anything like admin. A good username might be 9cabeab2sdba, something no one is likely to guess.

6. After clicking "Install WordPress" (see Figure 8-8), you'll receive a confirmation screen (Figure 8-9) stating that the installation was successful.

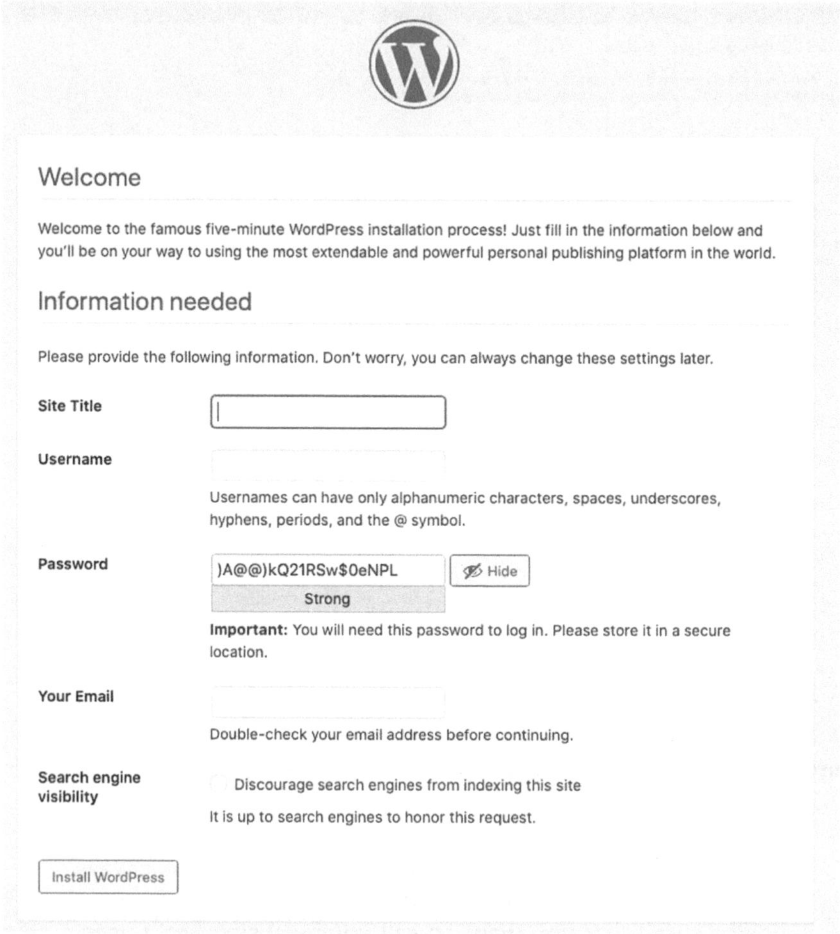

Welcome

Welcome to the famous five-minute WordPress installation process! Just fill in the information below and you'll be on your way to using the most extendable and powerful personal publishing platform in the world.

Information needed

Please provide the following information. Don't worry, you can always change these settings later.

Site Title

Username

Usernames can have only alphanumeric characters, spaces, underscores, hyphens, periods, and the @ symbol.

Password

)A@@)kQ21RSw$0eNPL   👁 Hide

Strong

Important: You will need this password to log in. Please store it in a secure location.

Your Email

Double-check your email address before continuing.

Search engine visibility   ☐ Discourage search engines from indexing this site

It is up to search engines to honor this request.

Install WordPress

Figure 8-8. The final installation screen

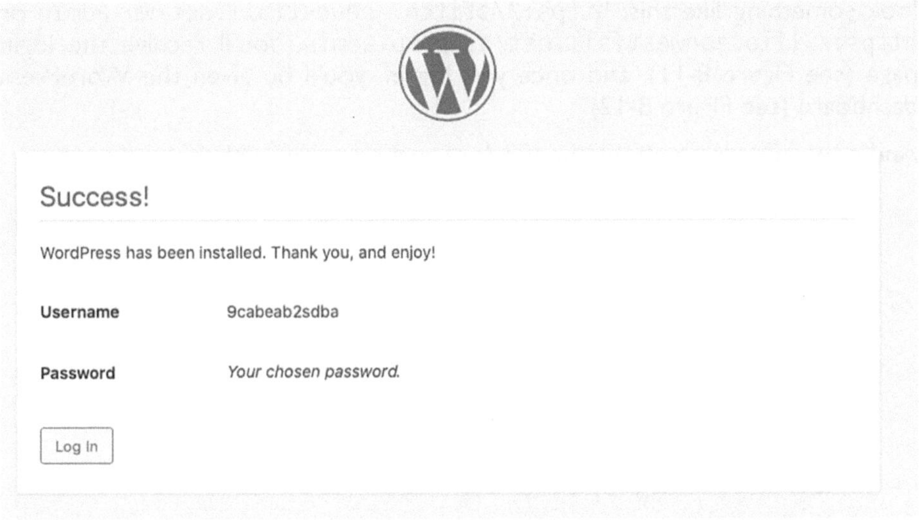

Figure 8-9. Confirmation installation was successful

To verify your installation worked, visit your blog's address again (e.g., `http://stitch.jonwestfall.net/` or `http://lilo.jonwestfall.net/blog`), and you should see a default page similar to Figure 8-10.

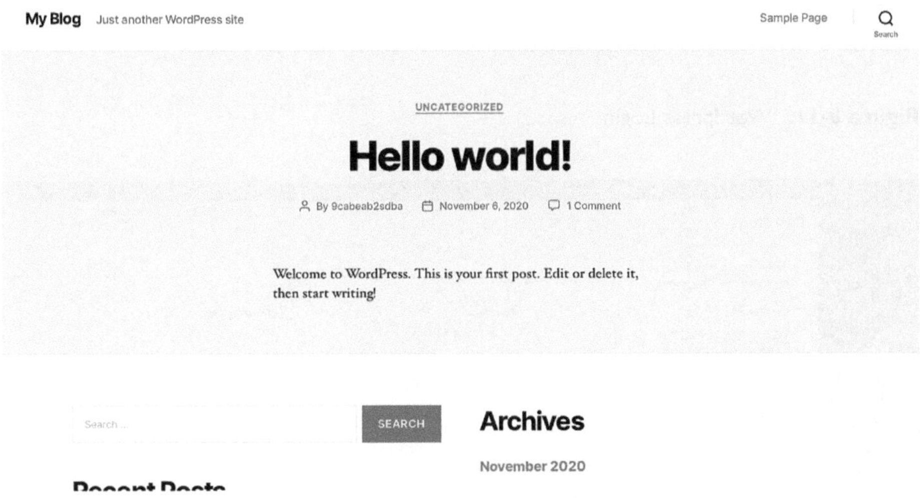

Figure 8-10. The default WordPress installation homepage

You can also now log into your WordPress installation to administer it by going to your *secure* web address (see section "Installing a Free SSL Certificate with Let's Encrypt" in Chapter 7) and adding `wp-admin` at the end. Your address will look something like this: `https://stitch.jonwestfall.net/wp-admin` or `https://lilo.jonwestfall.net/blog/wp-admin`. You'll receive the login page (see Figure 8-11), and once you log in, you'll be given the WordPress dashboard (see Figure 8-12).

And now you can go about the work of securing your website!

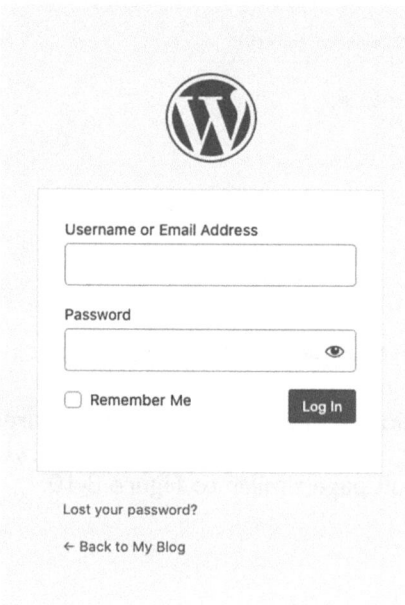

Figure 8-11. Wordpress Login

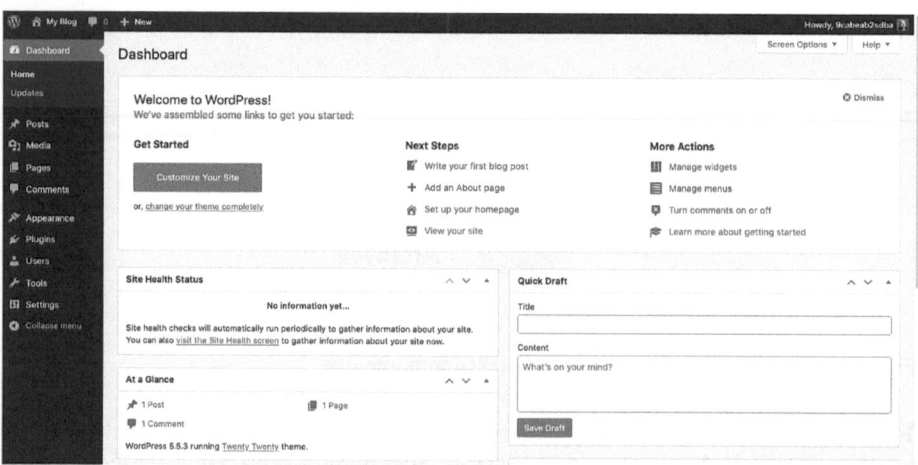

Figure 8-12. Wordpress Dashboard

Configuring WordPress to Be Secure

WordPress is one of the most popular CMSs available today, which also means it's one of the most frequent targets for hackers to exploit. Most of the time this isn't to steal data, but to inject your website with code that will redirect users to advertisements or other malware. Thus, it's vital that you secure your WordPress website as best as possible.

You've actually already done that in a few ways, and WordPress did it for you in another. So far we've

- Changed the default database username, password, database name, and table prefix
- Set a default admin username that is *not* admin or wordpress (very easy to guess)
- Set a superstrong password
- And seen that we cannot log in using the regular http address – we must use https to encrypt our communication

However, there are still a number of things you can do to make sure your WordPress site is secure. In this section, we'll go through a number of them.

Configuring File and Directory Permissions

By default, WordPress cannot write files to your web server. This is a good thing in that no script can automatically change your theme or add files to your VPS. If you try to install a plugin or theme, you'll likely get a dialog box similar to the one in Figure 8-13, asking for your FTP information to upload the file.

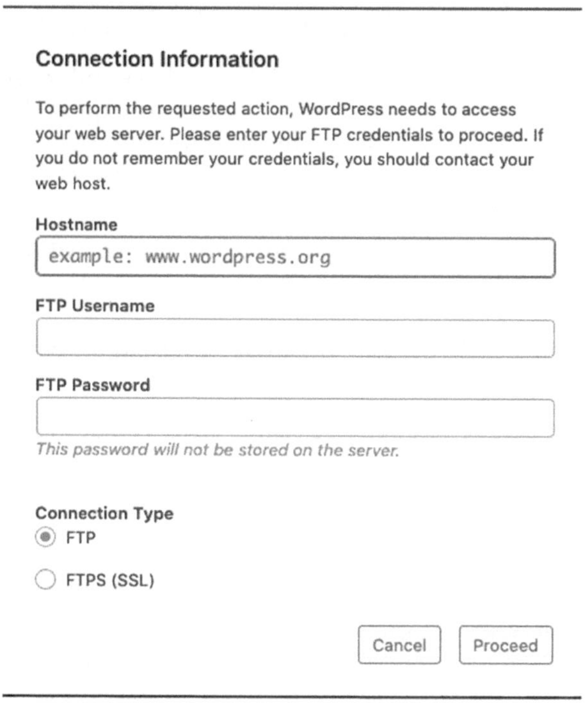

Connection Information

To perform the requested action, WordPress needs to access
your web server. Please enter your FTP credentials to proceed. If
you do not remember your credentials, you should contact your
web host.

Hostname

    example: www.wordpress.org

FTP Username

FTP Password

This password will not be stored on the server.

Connection Type

⦿ FTP

○ FTPS (SSL)

    Cancel   Proceed

Figure 8-13. Upload information

While this is secure, it's likely going to become problematic when you'd like
to install updates to your plugins, themes, and WordPress itself. Therefore, I'd
suggest making the following tweaks. While they do allow the web server to
write new files and thus do compromise security in a small way, they also
make it much easier for you to be diligent about updating your files. I'd argue
that an outdated plugin is more vulnerable than allowing WordPress to update
important files on a regular basis:

1. Open your wp-config.php file and add the line define('FS_
   METHOD', 'direct');.

2. Change the owner and group of your wp-content
   directory:

   On Debian: chown www-data:www-data -R /var/www/
   html

   On CentOS: chown apache:apache -R /var/www/html

WordPress can now automatically update itself and its files. You will still want
to lock down the wp- config file, however, so I'd suggest changing its ownership
back to root (e.g., chown root:root /var/www/html/wp-config.php).

General WordPress Hardening Tips

WordPress itself publishes a page on "hardening," or the process of making your WordPress website more secure. You can find it at `https://wordpress.org/support/article/hardening-wordpress/`. It is a comprehensive article that will likely take you some time to work through and can be a bit more technical than you might be ready for. Therefore, I'd put it on your list to review over time, tweaking and monitoring your website as you go.

In addition to the security precautions the article specifies, there are also a number of WordPress plugins that can be used to secure your website. We'll talk more about plugins later, but a few common plugins you might be interested are listed in the following. All of them have a free and paid tier; however, I don't suspect you'll need the paid level of monitoring unless you have a very high-traffic website:

- Wordfence Security – Firewall & Malware Scan

- All in One WP Security & Firewall

- iThemes Security

In addition to these plugins, you can also do the following to help keep your website secure:

- As mentioned, be sure to regularly check for updates. We'll cover this in Chapter 9 as we talk about a weekly administrator's checklist.

- Create a new user for yourself in WordPress that will be your "blogger" or editor user. Give it the "Editor" level of permissions so that all it can do is add new content or modify existing content. That way, if someone were to compromise that account, they wouldn't have full access to change everything the way your admin account has.

- Only install themes, plugins, and tweaks from trusted sources. WordPress's dashboard contains links to the WordPress Theme directory and Plugin directory – only install from there. Never install a WordPress theme or plugin that you find on the Internet as a ZIP file unless you are certain it is safe.

- Regularly remove unused plugins and themes, or at least deactivate them. This way if they do become compromised, you aren't as likely to suffer consequences.

- Regularly back up your WordPress site, which we'll talk about in the next section.

- Utilize some form of Two-Factor Authentication. Several plugins exist that can add support for Google Authenticator, Authy, Duo, and other Two-Factor or Multifactor Authentication options.

Above all else, you must remain vigilant to remain secure. WordPress can be set to automatically update plugins and themes; however, I actually recommend against this – keep it a manual process that you do regularly, perhaps once per week. This way you know what files are being updated (in case there is an issue with the update), and it forces you to remember that your blog (which you may not have updated in months!) still exists and thus still needs to be monitored. Sometimes automation is great (e.g., backups), but sometimes it can cause you to forget to be diligent!

Speaking of backups, let's talk about how to do that with WordPress!

Backing Up WordPress

After taking the time and effort to set up WordPress, you'll probably want a way to back it up. Thankfully, the process can be very straightforward:

1. Make a copy of the files under /var/www/html.

2. Make a copy of the database that you created; in my following example, it's simply named wordpress.

To do this, we can use a simple shell script. To create it

1. Create a new file named wordpressbackup.sh.

2. Paste the following contents into that file (note that there are two lines, one using the mysqldump command and the other using the tar command), replacing the username and password if you used something other than my preceding defaults:

```
mysqldump --user=wpuser --password=alongandusefulpassw
ord wordpress > backup.s tar -cvpzf wordpress.tar.gz
./backup.sql /var/www
```

1. Make the file executable by running chmod   +x ./wordpressbackup.sh.

2. Run the file by typing ./wordpressbackup.sh.

You'll notice that you now have a file named wordpress.tar.gz that contains your entire WordPress installation – the database backed up in a file named backup.sql and the files under the /var/www/html directory. You can now move this file somewhere else for safekeeping, such as another VPS or a computer at home.

Restoring Your Backup

Of course backups are only useful if they can be restored in an emergency. To do so, you simply reverse the process:

1. Extract the files back out by running tar xvf wordpress. tar.gz.

2. You now have a directory named var inside your home directory. You'll want to move the files under your backup var back to wherever they go under /var/www/html. You can do this by using the mv or cp command. The command will look something like this: mv –r ./var/ www/* /var/www.

3. You now need to restore the database. To do this, use the following commands to log into the database server, drop the old database, and add in your backup, replacing wordpress with your database name:

```
mysql -u root -p
drop database wordpress;
create database wordpress;
\. backup.sql
quit;
```

And just like that, your backup is restored. I'd recommend taking backups of your website weekly or, if you have a lot of activity, perhaps even nightly. Nothing is worse than publishing a long blog entry or updating your website with new products only to have an issue at the end of that week and have a backup that is "stale" with old content to restore and then reupdate. You can also take a backup at any time that you want a "snapshot" of your site.

And now that we have backups and security set, we'll finish up by talking about the plugins that you can use to extend WordPress, to make it more useful to you.

Extending WordPress with Plugins and Themes

Part of the power of WordPress is the ability to extend it into several different directions. The following are a list of plugins that I think really showcase the ability of the platform and give you some ideas of what you can do beyond simply using WordPress as a static website for your company or a blog for your own personal publishing. All of these can be found in the WordPress Plugin directory (see Figure 8-14), found by going to the Plugins menu in the dashboard and choosing "Add New."

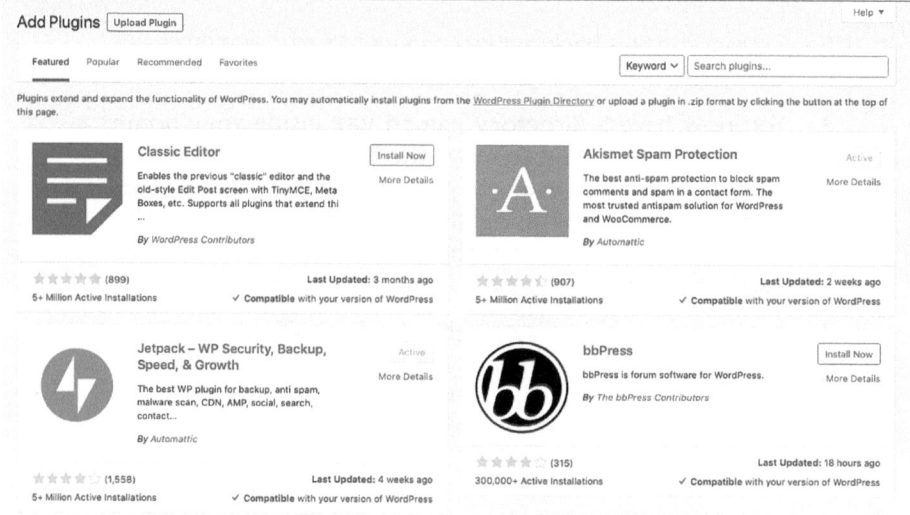

Figure 8-14. The WordPress Plugin directory

- Google Analytics for WordPress by MonsterInsights – Connect your website to Google's free Analytics platform (http://google.com/analytics) to analyze your traffic and see information about your visitors!

- Jetpack by wordpress.com – A mega plugin created by the commercial wordpress.com team that allows you to enable several useful features, both from a security standpoint and to connect your site to other content. Definitely worth the time to investigate and install.

- Post Snippets – Do you found yourself saying the same thing over and over again? Post Snippets lets you create short snippets of text that you can reuse in multiple posts or pages. Great for an author bio or a disclaimer that you use across your website. Then whenever you need to change the text, you simply update it in Post Snippets and not on every single page.

- Simple Tags – If you like the idea of tagging your posts, but don't like to have to think about it, Simple Tags will help you by suggesting tags, helping you mass edit your tags and auto link terms that you frequently use.

- Contact Form 7 – This plugin allows you to easily create contact forms or forms for really any purpose on your website. You can easily create your form, and the plugin gives you a tag that you can place on the pages or posts you want it to be accessible from.

- Yoast SEO – A plugin that allows you to tweak your pages to be better indexed and accessed by search engines, such as Google or Bing.

- WooCommerce – An open source ecommerce platform that allows you to run your own store from your WordPress site.

- Redirection – A plugin that lets you keep track of file not found (404) errors as well as set up temporary and permanent redirects. Great for when you have a page that you've had to update or delete and want the old link to go to the new content!

There are literally thousands more plugins that you can also explore, customizing your site as you like. Once you've got the features you want, you'll also want to think about the look. For that, you can install and customize your site with themes. Clicking the Appearance menu and then Customize will let you modify your existing theme. Clicking the Appearance menu, then Themes, and then "Add New" takes you to the Theme directory (see Figure 8-15). Like plugins, there are thousands of freely available themes that you can browse through, installing and tweaking them as you like.

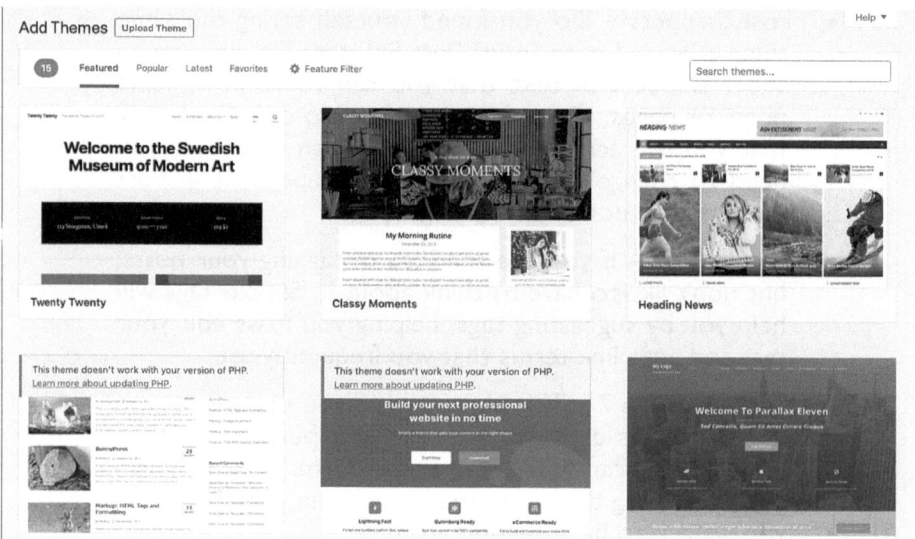

Figure 8-15. Theme directory

Entire books have been written about WordPress, so this chapter really just taps the surface – there is a lot for you to explore as you set up your own page. Hopefully it's inspired you and given you a good weekend's worth of fun as you write your pages, create posts, tweak your theme, and add items to your active plugins. My best advice is simply to click all of the menu items in WordPress and read through what each one does. You'll find it insanely customizable and useful.

And with that, you likely now have something on your VPS that is worth protecting and keeping running. After all, you learned how to use the VPS in Chapters 3 and 4, how to secure it in Chapter 5, how to back it up in Chapter 6, how to install commonly used servers in Chapter 7, and how to install WordPress in this chapter. In Chapter 9, we're going to focus on keeping everything running smoothly, with your weekly checklist of items!

Administrator's Weekly Checklist

Perhaps no subject in server administration is as tedious and annoying as "preventive maintenance." After all, you aren't actually doing anything "cool" when you do this. You aren't creating a new service that will make your life better, and you certainly aren't going to be recognized for all of your hard work since the whole point of the exercise is to avoid anything that would be noticed later – namely, your system going down in a metaphorical puff of smoke. So it's probably not surprising that I sat and stared at my screen for a few moments before getting the motivation up to write these opening words. After all, how can I make this sound exciting when it isn't? Well, perhaps by sharing stories throughout the way of times when I've been burned profoundly by my lack of routine maintenance. For each of the following steps, I'll try to give you my best horror story, so that you're motivated to break out your calendar, schedule your maintenance windows, and set those recurring to-dos to alarm if you don't check "server maintenance" off your list on a regular basis. Grab some time for comfort, because it's going to get scary.

© Jon Westfall 2021
J. Westfall, *Set Up and Manage Your Virtual Private Server*,
https://doi.org/10.1007/978-1-4842-6966-4_9

First Off, the List!

The following is my weekly server administration checklist. I suggest running through each week, and I'll explain each step in the following sections. However, I've placed it in "quick reference/checklist" format here, such that you can copy it or easily add it to your own notes.

Action	Interval	Description	Check When Complete
Update software packages	Weekly	Update to latest available packages in Debian or CentOS repositories.	____
Verify backups ran	Weekly	Verify that backups were correctly run and files properly sent.	____
Review log files	Weekly	Perform a cursory glance at common logs for irregularities.	____
Check disk usage	Weekly	Verify enough disk space is present for common operations.	____
Check memory utilization and your VPS provider dashboard	Weekly	Verify that your VPS isn't going over limits specified by your provider.	____
Take and check baselines of load	Weekly	Check server load; record in a file.	____
Test restore backups	First week of the month	Do a test restore of a backup.	____
Follow mailing lists/visit vendor websites	Second and fourth weeks of the month	Review software mailing lists for notices, and check websites of frequently used software for updates or previews.	____
Check user behavior/ provide "professional development"	Third week of the month	Check on what your users are doing, and provide resources to help them thrive.	____

And now let's walk through each step, with more detail and the promised horror stories.

Updating Software Packages

Software is never finished being written – instead, it is updated continuously, meaning that the day you install your VPS, your software is likely already out of date. Thankfully, updating is pretty simple – the following commands will do nicely each week:

Debian: `apt-get update && time apt-get dist-upgrade`

CentOS: `time yum update`

Both of these commands will update all of the available packages you have on your system to the latest published versions in the Debian or CentOS repository, respectively. Figures 9-1 and 9-2 show you how they appear if you have no updates available. I've added the `time` command because it can be useful to get a sense of how long updates take over time, so that if you have a particularly busy machine, you plan enough downtime to do your upgrades before people begin to need resources on the box.

```
root@lilo:~# apt-get update && time apt-get dist-upgrade
Get:1 http://security.debian.org buster/updates InRelease [65.4 kB]
Hit:2 http://ftp.debian.org/debian buster InRelease
Get:3 http://ftp.debian.org/debian buster-updates InRelease [51.9 kB]
Get:4 http://security.debian.org buster/updates/main amd64 Packages [245 kB]
Get:5 http://security.debian.org buster/updates/main Translation-en [134 kB]
Fetched 496 kB in 1s (456 kB/s)
Reading package lists... Done
Reading package lists... Done
Building dependency tree
Reading state information... Done
Calculating upgrade... Done
0 upgraded, 0 newly installed, 0 to remove and 0 not upgraded.

real    0m0.410s
user    0m0.374s
sys     0m0.033s
root@lilo:~# ▮
```

Figure 9-1. Updates on Debian Linux – nothing to be done

```
[root@stitch ~]# time yum update
Last metadata expiration check: 0:20:46 ago on Wed Nov 11 17:18:57 2020.
Dependencies resolved.
Nothing to do.
Complete!

real    0m4.321s
user    0m0.897s
sys     0m1.096s
[root@stitch ~]# ▮
```

Figure 9-2. Updates on CentOS, showing the system up to date

An important note with CentOS is the difference between yum update and yum upgrade – CentOS by default will not remove obsolete packages if you use update, but will remove them if you use upgrade. While more secure, this also can cause problems if you have newer software that depends on the older less secure software. You'll want to be careful if you take the hard-line upgrade approach.

Eventually, you'll also run into the situation where your operating system switches to a new major version. As of this writing, the current version of Debian is 10 and CentOS is 8. In software speak, we care about the EOL, or End of Lifespan. Typically, for Debian, EOL is approximately every 3–5 years, or the 1 year after the last stable release at minimum (see Figure 9-3). CentOS 8 will receive full updates until May 2024 (see Figure 9-4). Once you hit EOL, though, you'll need to do a distribution upgrade to keep receiving updates. This process varies by distribution, but it generally does take some time and planning. Both Debian and CentOS publish guides on transitioning from major version to major version, so you'll want to keep an eye on their official mailing lists and web pages so that you're aware when EOL is approaching for your distribution.

Production Releases

Version	Code name	Release date	End of life date	EOL LTS	EOL ELTS
13	Trixie				
12	Bookworm				
11	Bullseye				
10	Buster	2019-07-06	~2022		
9	Stretch	2017-06-17	2020-07-06	~2022	
8	Jessie	2015-04-25	2018-06-17	~2020-06-30	~2022-06-30
7	Wheezy	2013-05-04	2016-04-25	2018-05-31	~2019-12-31
6.0	Squeeze	2011-02-06	2014-05-31	2016-02-29	
5.0	Lenny	2009-02-14	2012-02-06		
4.0	Etch	2007-04-08	2010-02-15		
3.1	Sarge	2005-06-06	2008-03-31		
3.0	Woody	2002-07-19	2006-06-30		
2.2	Potato	2000-08-15	2003-06-30		
2.1	Slink	1999-03-09	2000-09-30	2000-10-30	
2.0	Hamm	1998-07-24	-		
1.3	Bo	1997-07-02	-		
1.2	Rex	1996-12-12	-		
1.1	Buzz	1996-06-17	-		
0.93R6		1995-10-26	-		
0.93R5		~1995-03-01	-		
0.91		~1994-01-01	-		

Figure 9-3. Debian release and EOL dates

About / Product
Last updated at 2020-10-24 08:40:14

CentOS Product Specifications

This page contains an overview on the capabilities and limits of CentOS.

End of Lifetime (EOL) Dates			
	CentOS-6	CentOS-7	CentOS-8
Full Updates[1]	May 10th, 2017	Q4 2020	May 2024
Maintenance Updates[2]	November 30th, 2020	June 30th, 2024	May 31st, 2029

Figure 9-4. CentOS EOL dates

You may also wonder, what would happen if I forgot to update my machines? I mean, if it's not broken, why fix it? Because as the next story will tell, it can be broken without you realizing it. I think of this most vividly with the Windows Remote Procedure Call (RPC) exploits of the early 2000s.

To make a long story short, a vulnerability was discovered in Windows 2000 that allowed a hacker to launch a denial-of-service attack, essentially taking a server offline by putting it into near-perpetual reboots. If you were at the computer at the time and the computer's RPC port was open (e.g., the firewall wasn't blocking it), you'd get a message telling you that RPC had crashed. The default behavior for Windows then was to reboot the machine in order to get RPC to come back up again.

Back at that time, I was doing web hosting work with a company that didn't have a lot of resources or rigorous network isolation. This meant that for a very short period of time after you clicked the network cable into the machine, the machine was on the "open" Internet. In hindsight, that was our biggest mistake – ever having such a policy, despite the fact that it was typically for less than 30 seconds. However, in those 30 seconds, nine out of ten times, the RPC exploit would happen and I'd have to rush to stop the system shutdown. It reminded me just how frequently attacks on vulnerable software are happening on the Internet. This server hadn't even existed 3 minutes earlier, and already an automated attack had targeted it. Once Microsoft uploaded a patch for the RPC vulnerability, it was always installed on a new server via USB stick, before we'd ever connect the server to the network and run the rest of the required updates!

Thus, you can have issues without knowing them, or they'll manifest in strange ways. Without knowing the RPC exploit existed, I wouldn't have known why my machine was rebooting every few minutes. Keeping your system software up to date is absolutely vital, not because it's broken now, but because it might break – and you won't necessarily see the bullet that hits it coming at you or know exactly where the bullet hit!

Verifying Backups

Having up-to-date software is the first step in securing your machine, but it is not the only vital piece – having a reliable and regularly checked backup system (as discussed in Chapter 6) is also important. Backups, though, have a bad tendency to fail.

Another horror story time: Years ago I had a series of servers that all backed up to their own dedicated external hard drive. On Windows, to accomplish our backup, we had a script run nightly that would synchronize directories from the active hard drives to the external. We didn't have anything for version control, but didn't necessarily need it. If a client lost data, they typically didn't want something from several weeks ago; they wanted data from the night before – the most up to date we had. Periodically we'd log into the server and make sure there were files written on the external hard drive. This seemed fine.

Until we realized that when the script failed, the files still appeared to have been written. But they were old versions. It was at that point we also realized that the script didn't send up any error message when it failed – it simply didn't run. Other than an obscure entry in the system log saying the task had failed, we had no easily visible way to tell that the files hadn't been written. This was all fixed after the first time that we found 3-week-old stale backups and lost a client over it.

Verifying your backups is a two-step process. The weekly step is easier – making sure that the backup job ran and that files were written and updated on the destination machine. If you're using Duplicati, as discussed in Chapter 6, you can simply log into the administrative interface and see when the last successful runtime was. Then log into the destination machine, and look at the last time files were written. Using the command `ls -lArt | tail -n 1` on a Linux machine will show you the most recent file written to that directory, and in this case, I can see (Figure 9-5) that my backup file was last written within the last 24 hours (as I'm writing this later in the day on November 11). Exactly as it should be.

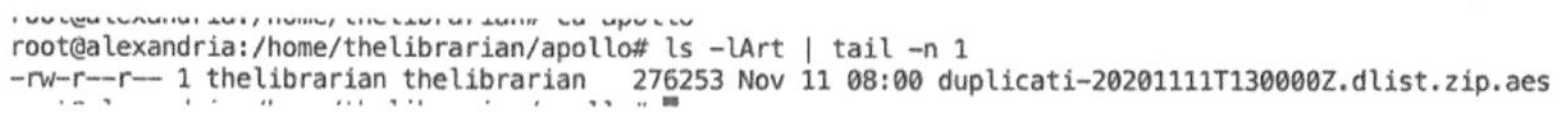

```
root@alexandria:/home/thelibrarian/apollo# ls -lArt | tail -n 1
-rw-r--r-- 1 thelibrarian thelibrarian   276253 Nov 11 08:00 duplicati-20201111T130000Z.dlist.zip.aes
```

Figure 9-5. Showing that the backup file was written within the last 24 hours

For a weekly quick check, this should be sufficient. However, at least once a month, you'll want to try to restore a file. I'll talk about that more in the following section.

Reviewing Log Files

For the horror story in this section, I don't really have to do much other than log into my Stitch VPS. I last logged in at 5 PM yesterday, and it is now 9 AM. In that time, CentOS informs me (see Figure 9-6) that there were 582 failed login attempts, with the most recent being about 8 minutes ago. In other words, automated bots on the Internet are flooding my VPS with attempts to log in. It's an ever-present reminder of how vital this step and the next few are, in terms of monitoring your overall VPS health.

```
Last failed login: Wed Nov 11 15:54:51 CET 2020 from 175.24.16.61 on ssh:notty
There were 582 failed login attempts since the last successful login.
Last login: Tue Nov 10 16:59:48 2020 from 209.147.242.247
[root@stitch ~]# []
```

Figure 9-6. *The number of failed logins*

I briefly discussed log files in Chapter 5, and in this section, I'd like to revisit a few as well as provide some commands that are useful in parsing them. Using Webmin (Chapter 4), we can also view our logs in a graphical environment that allows us to search, but this can just as easily be done from the command line. Let's start with the log file that tracks login actions, successful or unsuccessful. On CentOS, that file is /var/log/secure and on Debian /var/log/auth.log. In the following commands, I'll be using CentOS, so if you're on Debian, just change secure to auth.log.

First, I want to see what the last few ten lines of the log are – I can do this with the tail command.

tail /var/log/secure will provide something similar to Figure 9-7. You'll notice that each time a user failed the password check, I have several lines for them – "jay" failed password authentication at 16:02, and the system disconnected him a second later and then received confirmation that he was disconnected. Three lines that essentially tell me that "jay" tried to get in. Let's filter these down a bit by piping the tail command to grep – a utility that will search it for just what I want, lines that include "Failed password" (see Figure 9-8).

```
[root@stitch log]# tail secure
Nov 11 16:02:10 stitch sshd[73957]: Failed password for invalid user jay from 175.24.16.61 port 44098 ssh2
Nov 11 16:02:11 stitch sshd[73957]: Received disconnect from 175.24.16.61 port 44098:11: Bye Bye [preauth]
Nov 11 16:02:11 stitch sshd[73957]: Disconnected from invalid user jay 175.24.16.61 port 44098 [preauth]
Nov 11 16:02:52 stitch sshd[73959]: Invalid user admin from 163.172.37.72 port 36548
Nov 11 16:02:52 stitch sshd[73959]: pam_unix(sshd:auth): check pass; user unknown
Nov 11 16:02:52 stitch sshd[73959]: pam_unix(sshd:auth): authentication failure; logname= uid=0 euid=0 tty=ssh ruser=
rhost=163.172.37.72
Nov 11 16:02:53 stitch systemd[73961]: pam_unix(systemd-user:session): session opened for user root by (uid=0)
Nov 11 16:02:53 stitch sshd[73959]: Failed password for invalid user admin from 163.172.37.72 port 36548 ssh2
Nov 11 16:02:54 stitch sshd[73959]: Received disconnect from 163.172.37.72 port 36548:11: Bye Bye [preauth]
Nov 11 16:02:54 stitch sshd[73959]: Disconnected from invalid user admin 163.172.37.72 port 36548 [preauth]
[root@stitch log]# []
```

Figure 9-7. *The tail output*

```
[root@stitch log]# tail secure | grep "Failed password"
Nov 11 16:05:40 stitch sshd[74022]: Failed password for invalid user router from 165.232.107.168 port 59752 ssh2
Nov 11 16:07:13 stitch sshd[74042]: Failed password for invalid user ftpuser from 175.24.16.61 port 41396 ssh2
[root@stitch log]#
```

Figure 9-8. Just the Failed password lines

tail /var/log/secure | grep "Failed password" will provide something similar to Figure 9-8. Now I see that I have two new "candidates" for usernames, "router" and "ftpuser." This is useful, but remember that tail only gives me the last ten lines, and I further filtered out eight of those with grep. I'll add the following to the command to tell tail to go back 100 lines, to give me a better picture of the situation.

tail -n 100 /var/log/secure | grep "Failed password" shows me a lot more information, as you can see in Figure 9-9.

```
[root@stitch log]# tail -n 100 /var/log/secure | grep "Failed password"
Nov 11 15:55:20 stitch sshd[73820]: Failed password for invalid user readonly from 163.172.37.72 port 41446 ssh2
Nov 11 15:56:38 stitch sshd[73831]: Failed password for invalid user username from 163.172.37.72 port 54318 ssh2
Nov 11 15:57:16 stitch sshd[73842]: Failed password for invalid user musicyxy from 175.24.16.61 port 46806 ssh2
Nov 11 15:57:53 stitch sshd[73844]: Failed password for invalid user ftpserver from 163.172.37.72 port 38946 ssh2
Nov 11 15:58:22 stitch sshd[73857]: Failed password for invalid user guest from 165.232.107.168 port 54092 ssh2
Nov 11 15:59:09 stitch sshd[73897]: Failed password for root from 163.172.37.72 port 51818 ssh2
Nov 11 15:59:43 stitch sshd[73899]: Failed password for invalid user jobs from 175.24.16.61 port 45454 ssh2
Nov 11 16:02:03 stitch sshd[73946]: Failed password for invalid user tony from 165.232.107.168 port 56912 ssh2
Nov 11 16:02:10 stitch sshd[73957]: Failed password for invalid user jay from 175.24.16.61 port 44098 ssh2
Nov 11 16:02:53 stitch sshd[73959]: Failed password for invalid user admin from 163.172.37.72 port 36548 ssh2
Nov 11 16:04:14 stitch sshd[73989]: Failed password for root from 163.172.37.72 port 49416 ssh2
Nov 11 16:04:50 stitch sshd[73991]: Failed password for root from 175.24.16.61 port 42748 ssh2
Nov 11 16:05:40 stitch sshd[74022]: Failed password for invalid user router from 165.232.107.168 port 59752 ssh2
Nov 11 16:07:13 stitch sshd[74042]: Failed password for invalid user ftpuser from 175.24.16.61 port 41396 ssh2
Nov 11 16:07:59 stitch sshd[74048]: Failed password for root from 163.172.37.72 port 34118 ssh2
Nov 11 16:09:28 stitch sshd[74069]: Failed password for invalid user appadmin from 165.232.107.168 port 34364 ssh2
Nov 11 16:09:40 stitch sshd[74071]: Failed password for invalid user ftptest from 175.24.16.61 port 40044 ssh2
```

Figure 9-9. All of the failed logins in the past 100 lines

At this point, I can see a few interesting things:

- The IP address 163.172.37.72 is continually trying a lot of different logins. I might want to block that IP address permanently using a command like firewall-cmd --permanent --add-rich-rule="rule family='ipv4' source address='163.172.37.72' reject", or I could use a free product like fail2ban to actively monitor my logs and add these rules automatically after a certain number of failed logins.

- Further, there are certain usernames that are pretty common – "ftptest," "ftpuser," "admin," "guest," and so on. If I do have any of those as valid usernames on my system, I'm going to want to make sure that they use very strong passwords.

- I also see that the root account is also being tried, so I may wish to disable root login through SSH or switch all SSH logins to keyfile only as discussed in Chapter 5.

Aside from the secure or auth.log, other logs you'll want to keep an eye on include

- firewalld, which logs errors encountered when configuring, starting, or stopping the firewall.

- cron on CentOS or cat /var/log/syslog | grep "cron" on Debian to monitor the Cron scheduler, letting you see what has been executed automatically and if there are any errors associated with it.

- The Apache log files, found under the /var/log/ httpd directory on CentOS and /var/www/apache2 directory on Debian. These are also your first line of troubleshooting if a website starts acting up and doesn't display a meaningful error message.

Generally, whenever you install new software, you'll want to see where it stores its log files and then make a note to check those regularly. It's also useful, at times, to see what files are being modified in the log file directory. You can do this by issuing the command ls -lt /var/log – it will sort all of the files in that directory by those last written to. This should help you see what software is actively logging information, especially if the system is having issues with resources or load. This brings us to our next sections!

Check Disk Usage

Disk space is one of those things you don't worry about until you don't have it anymore. I can recall several times in my career where a computer was acting strangely – abnormally slow, weird error messages, files not opening, and other odd glitches, all traced back to the fact that the hard drive was full. I still don't know why the computer didn't just tell me that; it would have saved so much time troubleshooting all of the other symptoms!

In Linux, you can easily find out how much free disk space you have by using the command df -h, which will give you something similar to Figure 9-10. The command shows all mounted file systems (which you can also view by simply issuing the mount command) and tells you how much available space is on them. The line you are most interested in, generally, is whatever is mounted on /, or the root of the file system. In my case, I have 18 gigabytes available, so I'm doing fine. But what if I'm getting close to my limit or I'm at 0% – how do I find the files taking things up?

```
root@lilo:/var/log# df -h
Filesystem         Size  Used Avail Use% Mounted on
/dev/ploop17428p1   20G  1.2G   18G   7% /
none               384M     0  384M   0% /sys/fs/cgroup
none               384M     0  384M   0% /dev
tmpfs              384M     0  384M   0% /dev/shm
tmpfs              384M   39M  346M  11% /run
tmpfs              5.0M     0  5.0M   0% /run/lock
none               384M     0  384M   0% /run/shm
tmpfs               77M     0   77M   0% /run/user/0
```

Figure 9-10. The df command output

First, I can do a quick glance at the entire VPS's file sizes by doing the following:

```
cd /
du -h --max-depth=1
```

This should give me something similar to Figure 9-11. I can see that I am using 70 GB total and that most of my files are under the directory vlab- data at 64 GB. If I run the same preceding commands, but replace cd / with cd / vlab-data, I can now dig into that directory and so forth until I find my "big" directories.

```
jon@vlab:/$ sudo du -h --max-depth=1
11M     ./etc
81M     ./run
2.9G    ./usr
4.0K    ./opt
1.9G    ./var
16K     ./lost+found
4.0K    ./lib64
15M     ./home-old
du: cannot access './proc/31886/task/31886/fd/4': No such file or directory
du: cannot access './proc/31886/task/31886/fdinfo/4': No such file or directory
du: cannot access './proc/31886/fd/3': No such file or directory
du: cannot access './proc/31886/fdinfo/3': No such file or directory
0       ./proc
801M    ./lib
531M    ./root
4.0K    ./mnt
4.0K    ./srv
64G     ./vlab-data
8.1M    ./bin
109M    ./boot
4.0K    ./media
0       ./sys
4.0K    ./dev
96K     ./tmp
11M     ./sbin
70G     .
```

Figure 9-11. Using the du command to find large directories

Once I'm in a directory that's quite large, I can use a different command, du -ah ./ | sort -n -r | head -n 20, which will list all of the files in the current directory, sort them by size, and then show me the top 20. Output looks similar to Figure 9-12. In my case, I can see that I have a few Python packages that are taking up the most space in my home directory.

```
jon@vlab:~$ du -ah ./ | sort -n -r | head -n 20
1016K   ./test/lib/python3.7/site-packages/django/contrib/postgres/locale
1004K   ./test/lib/python3.7/site-packages/django/contrib/admin/static/admin/js/vendor
988K    ./packages/php5-5.2.6.dfsg.1-1+lenny3/main
988K    ./packages/php5-5.2.6.dfsg.1-1+lenny3/apache2filter-build/ext/hash/.libs
988K    ./packages/php5-5.2.6.dfsg.1-1+lenny3/apache2-build/ext/hash/.libs
948K    ./packages/php5-5.2.6.dfsg.1-1+lenny3/ext/pcre/pcrelib/testdata
944K    ./test/lib/python3.7/site-packages/pkg_resources
928K    ./sql-from-vlab2/svoslider
928K    ./packages/php5-5.2.6.dfsg.1-1+lenny3/ext/oci8/tests
924K    ./test/lib/python3.7/site-packages/pip/_vendor/chardet
912K    ./packages/php5-5.2.6.dfsg.1-1+lenny3/Zend/zend_vm_execute.h
912K    ./packages/php5-5.2.6.dfsg.1-1+lenny3/.pc/gentoo/019_new-memory-corruption.patch/Zend/zend_vm_execute.h
912K    ./packages/php5-5.2.6.dfsg.1-1+lenny3/debian/php5-dev/usr/include/php5/Zend/zend_vm_execute.h
904K    ./.mozilla/firefox/6sh3en2z.default/XUL.mfasl
888K    ./packages/php5-5.2.6.dfsg.1-1+lenny3/test-results.txt
880K    ./packages/php5-5.2.6.dfsg.1-1+lenny3/apache2-build/ext/interbase
868K    ./packages/php5-5.2.6.dfsg.1-1+lenny3/apache2filter-build/main/streams
868K    ./packages/php5-5.2.6.dfsg.1-1+lenny3/apache2-build/main/streams
864K    ./packages/php5-5.2.6.dfsg.1-1+lenny3/cli-build/main/streams
864K    ./packages/php5-5.2.6.dfsg.1-1+lenny3/cgi-build/main/streams
```

Figure 9-12. Using the du command to find the largest files in the directory

By using these commands, you can not only see your overall disk usage, you can also hunt down the large files that you didn't realize had "ballooned" up so large. If those happen to be log files, you might investigate tweaking your logrotate settings to rotate them out more frequently or, at the very least, compress them. Now that we have the disk space sorted out, let's look at memory and other important limits.

Check Memory Utilization and Your VPS Provider's Dashboard

We're used to understanding that more free memory, or RAM, is a good thing. How do I check that on my VPS? Well, simply with the free command. Running free -h will give you an output similar to Figure 9-13. From that, it looks like all is well – I have around 543 megabytes out of 768 free.

```
root@lilo:/var/log# free -h
              total       used        free      shared  buff/cache   available
Mem:          768Mi      120Mi       543Mi        18Mi       103Mi        628Mi
Swap:         768Mi       39Mi       728Mi
```

Figure 9-13. The free command output

Memory on a VPS can be a tricky thing though – because of the way your provider might allow virtual machines to share resources of the physical machine. If one particular VPS starts using more resources, it can sometimes affect others. It's your provider's job to make sure that this doesn't start unfairly impacting you. Most providers give you a dashboard of some sort that lets you see pertinent information about your VPS. We can see this for my lilo machine in Figure 9-14. My provider gives me information about the machine, including the physical server that it lives on (a server named "CLT01-V207"), how much bandwidth I've used and an estimate for the month (nice to know, so I don't have an issue with too much traffic), the uptime on my box (how long since it was last rebooted), and my load averages (which I'll talk about more in the following). Finally, I get the disk utilization and memory utilization that I saw with the df and free commands. If these hadn't matched up, I would likely contact my provider to see what the discrepancy is.

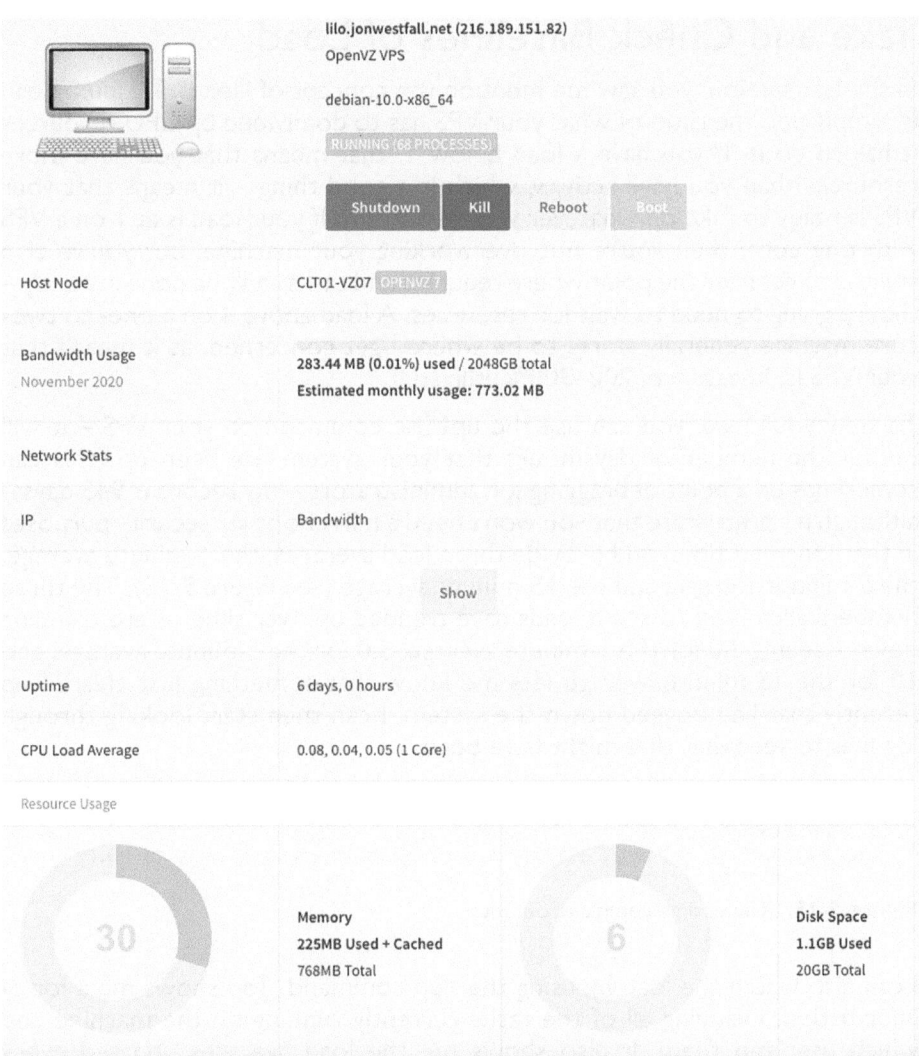

lilo.jonwestfall.net (216.189.151.82)

OpenVZ VPS

debian-10.0-x86_64

RUNNING (68 PROCESSES)

| Shutdown | Kill | Reboot | Boot |

| Host Node | CLT01-VZ07 OPENVZ 7 |

| Bandwidth Usage | 283.44 MB (0.01%) used / 2048GB total |
| November 2020 | Estimated monthly usage: 773.02 MB |

Network Stats

| IP | Bandwidth |

Show

| Uptime | 6 days, 0 hours |

| CPU Load Average | 0.08, 0.04, 0.05 (1 Core) |

Resource Usage

| 30 | Memory
225MB Used + Cached
768MB Total | 6 | Disk Space
1.1GB Used
20GB Total |

Figure 9-14. *The dashboard provided by my hosting provider*

In general, as a VPS owner, it's good to know what you can do easiest through your provider's web interface or through your own command-line or GUI tools. In my case, my provider gives pretty minimal control through their interface, although some providers have more enhanced control panels that may actually take a lot of the work out of your life – they may even have something as full featured as Webmin through a product such as cPanel, a popular commercial GUI management tool. It's in your best interest to check out all of their features before spending time reinventing the wheel.

Take and Check Baselines of Load

In the last section, you saw me mention the concept of "load" in Linux. Load is, simply put, the ratio of what your VPS has to do divided by CPU resources it has to do it. If you have a load below 1, that means that you have more resources than you have activity, which is a good thing – it means that your VPS is ready to take on whatever you throw at it. If your load is at 1 on a VPS with one core, then you're not overworking your machine, but you've also started to get near the point where requests and tasks can't be done instantly – they're going to need to wait for resources. A load above 4 on a one- to two-core machine generally starts to be where I get concerned, as it means that your VPS is, in essence, 200–300% utilized.

To view your load, you can use the uptime command on your VPS – it will output the number of days/hours that your system has been up (this can sometimes be a point of bragging for administrators – my record is 945 days – although it's pretty rare that you won't need a full reboot for security purposes in that long of a time) and provide three load averages, the 1-minute average, the 5-minute average, and the 15-minute average (see Figure 9-15). The three numbers allow you to see if loads have trended up over time or are trending down – seeing 2.0 for the 1-minute average, 5.0 for the 5-minute average, and 10 for the 15-minute average lets me know that something just cleared up recently that had bogged down the system. I can then start looking through log files to see what that might have been.

```
jon@vlab:~$ uptime
 10:47:18 up_512 days,  1:35,  1 user,  load average: 0.00, 0.01, 0.00
```

Figure 9-15. The uptime command output

I can also watch the load by using the top command. Top shows me a lot of information, including all of the tasks currently running on the machine and which user ran them. It also shows me the load averages updated every second. Hitting the "q" key will quit top.

As you work with your machine, you're going to want to start looking at loads regularly, to get a sense of what the normal load is for you. If your loads are normally 1–2 on a regular day, then you know on days that spike to 3–4 that something might be up or that a load of 0–0.25 might show that something is wrong (e.g., software isn't running properly). Every server is going to be different. Getting a feel for it now will help you later when you're unsure if what you're seeing is within a "normal" range or "abnormal."

Test Restore Backup

This step is pretty straightforward, although you can get more complex with it if you like. In the simplest form, restoring a backup consists of downloading the backup file to another computer, even your personal computer will work, unzipping it, and verifying that the files are all physically present. This can be done by comparing the files to the files on your VPS or by even doing a mock "rebuild" of your VPS within a virtual machine or another VPS. In doing these tests, you get to establish the following:

- Knowledge of how to do the restore, which will come in handy when you have to do it while your blood pressure and pulse go through the roof. The feeling of adrenaline when you realize your entire server is dead in the water can be paralyzing. Having experience restoring files when it's not a crisis can be vitally important.

- Knowledge of any information you may have forgotten you needed. This is especially important if you had set up encryption keys or passphrases when you created your backups. If you had set those 3 years ago and then forgotten which one you used (or, horribly, forgotten all of them), you don't want to find out about that during a crisis. Better to know you don't know the password when you still have time to change it and then invest in a password management tool.

- Knowledge of any quirks of the process. Are there files that aren't restored in exactly the same place they were backed up from? Are there files that need to be further processed, decompressed, or unencrypted? All of that comes with practice runs of the restore.

- Ideas about streamlining the process – you may find that as you restore files and check them, you see opportunities to tweak your backup policy or schedule, or you find directories that need backing up that you hadn't noticed before.

So in general, this step is vital to your health, safety, and wellbeing during an emergency. Better to have a dry run so that when a user comes to you in a panic saying "I've lost the file!" you can calmly reply, "Give me a few minutes. I'll get it back." No better feeling than that (trust me!).

Follow Mailing Lists/Vendor Websites

We've now gotten into two topics that aren't as much one action as they are good policy for you to stay continually aware of. In this section, I'll talk about how to get news and updates that you'll need to know for your VPS. In the next, I'll talk about how to support your users.

In the world of commercial software, it's pretty easy to know when a new version comes out – principally because your sales representative calls you to extol all of the wonderful benefits of shelling out a lot of money for an upgrade. Conversely, the world of open source software tends to be dominated by a culture of somewhat ornery old men (yes, sadly men, although thankfully women are becoming more common!). This culture tends to value stability, reliability, and the known over change and growth. Not a bad thing, but it also means that when a new version of the Apache Web Server comes out, no one is going to be banging down your door telling you to upgrade. In fact, you'll likely get guidance in the opposite direction: don't upgrade until you've thought through all of the ramifications (unless it's purely a security fix).

So how do you know what's going on? The first way is through mailing lists for the various software products you use. The CentOS-announced mailing list and Debian-announced mailing list both provide general interest announcements to their respective communities. While email might not be popular with the youth of today, mailing lists are still the number one way to be informed of changes to your favorite software products. Thankfully for your inbox, you don't necessarily have to get them all at one time – you can usually choose either a digest option (which will group messages together and send you one message, once a day or once a week) or just bookmark the list's archives and regularly scan the subject lines to see if there is anything of note.

Second to mailing lists, you can also bookmark the news and announcements web pages of the software products you use. You may also find active user forums or communities that you can follow that will not only tell you what's going on but also give you a place to post questions. You will likely want to get to know these communities *before* you have a problem. Why? Because you'll want to know what the community standards are – if you notice that each new post is continually asked questions like "what version are you using" or "post your configuration file" or "we need more details," then you can ask your question with that information already available and skip the snarky replies of your peers who can sometimes come off as more adversarial than helpful if they sense you haven't already learned the ways of the community. Remember, people are likely eager to help, so give them everything they need from the start.

Finally, let's talk about how we can help our users, both by watching out for them and giving them information they need.

Check User Behavior/Provide Professional Development

About 10 years ago, I was administering a machine that had about 25 active users. The predecessor server, which I inherited, had been hacked several times (which also meant that I decommissioned that server pretty quickly). Each time it had been hacked, it was because someone guessed a password. So I started doing regular password audits using a tool named "John the Ripper" – basically this tool would run through a wordlist and check to see if any of the passwords on my machine matched it. The process would take 2–3 days, running in the background, and at the end of it, I'd write emails to people that literally said, "Ya know, mydogdora is not a great password – change it!" People got the message, especially since they knew that I couldn't look up their password, so the only way I knew it was by hacking it myself.

In retrospect, this was probably using a bit more of the stick approach than the carrot – I could have probably been a little more friendly in my solving of the password problem. And there were ways I did this – one of the first policy changes I made with that group was to outlaw "shared" passwords. I used Usermin, discussed in Chapter 4, to build a common "single sign-on" hub for our users, which let them access all of the resources they needed through their own username and password, in a format that was logged and controlled and easy for them to use. In this way, I provided a service to my users that made their lives easier and made my server more secure. A win- win.

Your users are not likely going to spend time doing what we talked about in the last section – jumping on mailing lists and hanging around forums learning about the software that runs on the VPS. You'll need to do that for them in some way. Here are my tips for what a good administrator can do to keep their users happy, safe, and well informed:

- First, regularly check logs and audit passwords, to check to see if people are doing things that aren't safe. Remember that sudo and Webmin provide logging to see which users with administrative rights are logging in and what they're doing. You can also lock down those tools to prevent bad behavior. So if people are using sudo just to launch a root shell (such as sudo bash) instead of putting sudo in front of all of the their commands, you can disallow this by modifying the sudo configuration.

- Second, talk to your users. Ask them what they find most unfriendly about your setup or what they do to get around common problems. If they tell you something that is "scary," such as "Yeah, my password is really hard to remember, so I just write it on a sticky note next to my computer" or "Yeah, Bob's account can do that, so I just use his password," you'll want to avoid freaking out and make a note to adjust your policies to prevent such things. Talking to your users is also the best way to find out what sort of resources they need or may be interested in seeing.

- Set up some sort of "status" page for your users. Somewhere they can go and see if there is something currently wrong with the VPS or if you have taken the VPS down for maintenance. This will avoid phone calls and emails. It can be as easy as saying "Check my Twitter feed" or "Check this free blog – I'll post there anytime we have an issue."

- If there is a free online event that you think may be of interest (say regarding a new version of software you regularly use), perhaps organize a viewing party, or at least send the information to your users.

- And finally, set up a way to solicit suggestions for changes. Nothing is more frustrating to a user than an administrator who isn't open to any change. If you don't work with your users, they'll find ways around you that you probably won't like.

Conclusions

Being an administrator can be tough work. And sometimes we're tempted to think that the work is done once we have the VPS up and running. But in reality, it's at that point that we need to be more vigilant than ever. After all, you don't want all of your hard work going up in a cloud of virtual smoke. By following the guidelines in this chapter, you should be on your way to keeping your system up and running without worry!

Open Source Application Possibilities

We've been on a long journey together in this book – from learning what a VPS is to how to manage one to setting up a full web application and WordPress and thinking about routine maintenance. For this last chapter, I want to give you some ideas regarding the possibilities of use for your VPS, principally by introducing you to a variety of open source applications that you can install on your VPS and use. Along the way, I'll provide tips and tricks for each application that you might be able to employ, as well as suggestions on the best ways to set them up and use them with others. And if there are competing applications, commercial or open source, I'll mention those to give you an idea of the overall landscape. I won't be giving extensive installation instructions for each of these; however, you can learn how to install them by visiting their respective homepages. Most installations will follow a similar pattern as we saw with WordPress:

1. Download the software onto your VPS.

2. Unpack it.

© Jon Westfall 2021
J. Westfall, *Set Up and Manage Your Virtual Private Server*,
https://doi.org/10.1007/978-1-4842-6966-4_10

3. Create a database and database user.

4. Install the software either through a web interface or by modifying a configuration file.

5. Navigate to the software in your web browser and begin using/customizing.

It's also very helpful that most of the web pages listed in the following walk you through the installation process, often with the exact commands you'll need.

Since this chapter is a bit less heavy on narrative, more on content (think a series of short articles), the following table may be useful in helping you find what section you're looking for. While you can certainly read this chapter start to finish, it may be easier to use this table as a quick reference, in case you have a specific task you want to accomplish.

You'll also notice that the last column mentions a website, Open Source CMS (`https://opensourcecms.com`). This site contains demos of over 350 content management system (CMS) packages. It's a great resource that one can use to "try out" most of the following products before installing them on your VPS. If you like what you see there, you can then install the software on your own system and start using it. It's also useful when learning about new software – as it contains user reviews as well as "last updated" information (nothing worse than installing a piece of open source software that has been abandoned by its development group!).

Software Product	Use	On Open Source CMS?
Moodle	A Learning Management System (LMS) that allows you to teach online courses or conduct online trainings.	Yes
osTicket	A help desk/issue tracking/trouble ticket system that allows you to handle customer or client service requests and track their progress.	Yes
YoURLS	A URL shortener package that allows you to create your own short, easy-to-remember, web addresses.	No
OpenVPN	Software to create a Virtual Private Network connection, allowing you to route all traffic from your computer through your VPS.	No
Odoo	Customer Relationship Management (CRM) software that you can use for your business.	No
LimeSurvey	A survey suite that allows you to launch questionnaires, collect data, and analyze it.	No

(continued)

Software Product	Use	On Open Source CMS?
GNU Mailman	Mailing list software, useful in setting up an email listserv and archive.	No
osCommerce	An online shopping cart and ecommerce package.	Yes
MediaWiki	The Wiki package that powers Wikipedia, which you can use to run your own wiki.	Yes

That's nine packages that you might be interested in – let's dig into each one of them and learn about what it can do for you for free!

Moodle

When not writing books or being a giant computer geek, my daily life sees me mostly teaching classes as a psychology professor. Having taught for nearly 20 years, I've seen the rise (and sometimes fall) of several Learning Management Systems (LMSs). In 2000, it was more common for a professor to have a simple website that they would link course materials off of than it was for them to use an LMS. Today personal websites are nearly nonexistent, and professors receive more and more training on the LMS of choice from their institution. The most popular commercial LMSs, such as Blackboard or Canvas, cost a college, university, or K–12 school system thousands of dollars per year. Lower-cost options, such as Google Classroom, require other resources and have limited customizability. And for an educator who isn't affiliated with a large institution (or an educator who is but their institution doesn't have substantial resources), an LMS might not even be an option. Unless one considers Moodle (`http://moodle.org`, Figure 10-1), the premier open source LMS.

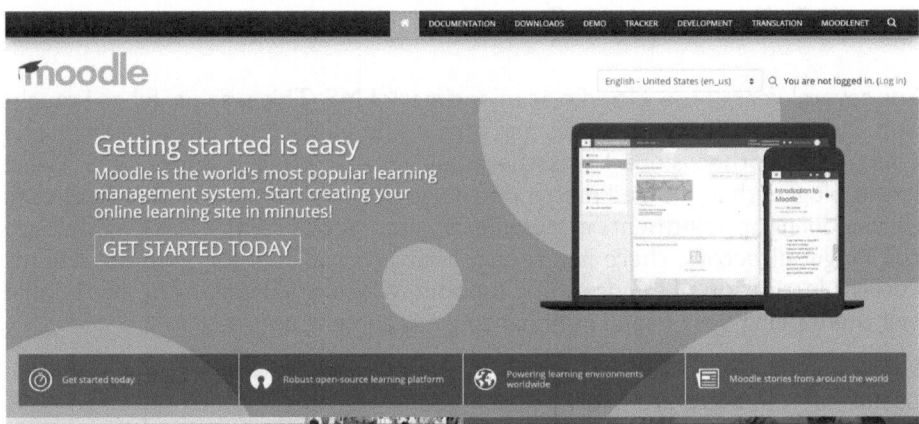

Figure 10-1. Moodle.org homepage

Created by Martin Dougiamas and first released in 2002, Moodle boasts over 50% market share in Europe and Latin America and nearly 20% market share in the United States. You may have actually used it already without realizing it, since it supports extensive customization and can be named virtually whatever you want (vs. Blackboard and Canvas that are usually branded by their respective companies). Moodle also benefits from an extensive library of plugins that users can use to extend the software in several different ways, from different assignment types, quiz question types, and connections to other platforms.

Trying Moodle out is a fairly simple affair – you can use the demo on Moodle. org (Figure 10-2) or on OpenSourceCMS.com, and installer packages exist for macOS and Windows in case you'd like to run it for a bit on an old computer you have before you install it on your VPS. Installers are downloadable in Gzipped tar format (*.tgz) similar to WordPress, at `https://download. moodle.org/releases/latest/`.

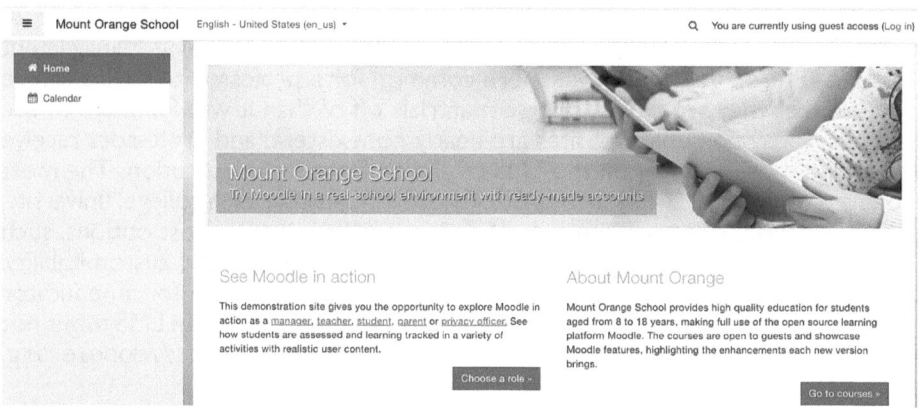

Figure 10-2. Moodle.org's Mount Orange demo

For several years I ran Moodle as my primary LMS. This was useful as I taught at a variety of different schools and also could easily copy content from one course to another, since I was the administrator for the entire LMS. I also found plugins that allowed me to do things that my current LMS lacked, such as scheduling appointments or running an anonymous survey. Looking through the Plugin directory, there are several that are available for Moodle that my current institution's LMS does not support, which is frustrating in that I could see them being very useful in enhancing my current courses.

If you aren't a professor or teacher, you may wonder why Moodle would be useful for you. Here are a few possibilities:

- Your business sells a product that requires some level of training to use. You could create your own training course to offer your customers, allowing them to complete their training virtually instead of having to schedule with you.

- Your organization requires new employees to complete several trainings, and you'd like to run them in-house rather than pay someone else to do them.

- Your children are struggling in school, and you'd like a safe and supervised place for them to complete basic tutoring assignments that you can customize and view.

Thinking along these lines, anytime you want to try to inform someone of something, an LMS like Moodle may be an option for you!

osTicket

If you recall, way back in Chapter 1, I opened with a story of setting up a help desk ticket system. The software I used to do this was osTicket. Viewing their website at `https://osticket.com` (Figure 10-3), one sees three different versions: open source, cloud hosted, and enterprise. The only difference is that the cloud hosted and enterprise come with technical support, walk-through sessions, backups, and upgrades. The actual software you get and features are exactly the same whether you run them yourself on your own VPS or pay them.

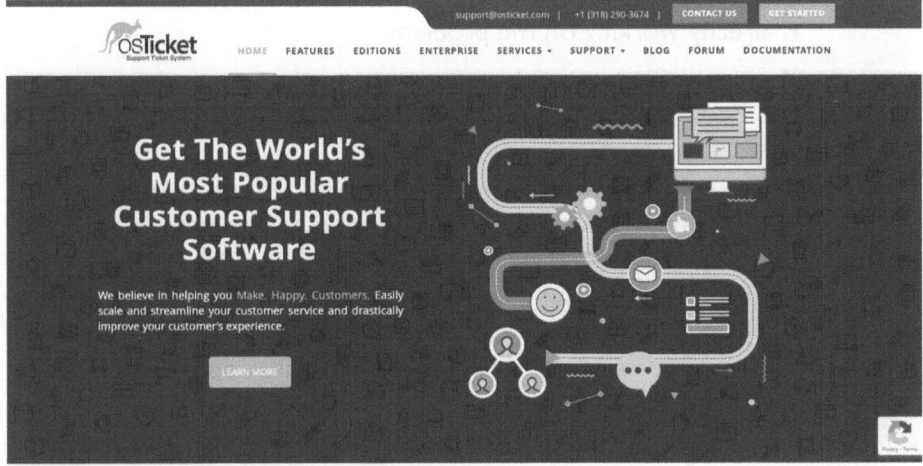

Figure 10-3. osTicket homepage

Most of us have used systems like osTicket as an end user, so we know the drill. You send an email or make a phone call to a company, and they send you back an email with a ticket ID number at the top and perhaps information about your case. When you reply back, you likely assume that the ticket ID is used to match your email, going to a generic email address such as support@ whatever.com to your case, and it does. What you don't realize is how useful this is to the company. Here's a list of reasons why you may find something like osTicket much more useful to you than the "old-fashioned" way of email:

1. You can easily track all of the support requests for a given customer, client, or person.

2. You can easily track how long it takes to resolve an issue.

3. Working with multiple colleagues becomes much easier – if the person requesting action sends in a ticket, the person on your team (called an "agent") who's most qualified can answer it, rather than whoever happens to get the email.

4. In a team of support agents, you can keep track of how well they do their jobs by easily seeing how many tickets they have taken care of.

5. You can customize the software to record information you need – whether that be technical in nature or situational.

6. You can "lock" tickets, so that you don't have an issue where two people try to fix the same problem and get in each other's way – the second agent knows that someone is already working on the problem.

7. You can easily move tickets from one person to another, so if one of your staff is out sick, someone else can take over.

8. You can easily create a customer portal that lets your users submit requests and view FAQ documents, perhaps even helping themselves before they need to email you.

9. Finally, you can create an internal to-do list for each agent on your staff, so that when they're not working on tickets, they can be working on other things you need them to do.

At first when I suggest using a ticket system, I'm often told by people that it "seems like overkill." After a few weeks of using it, even small teams wonder what they did without it. It simply stops people from having to spend time figuring out the next step – everything is in one place.

You may have noticed earlier that I also mentioned that you can email directly to the ticket board. Knowing what you do about technology after reading this book, you might wonder how that happens. It's actually pretty easy. The osTicket document includes instructions that allow you to set up a "pipe" from your incoming email (through the Postfix mail server) to the osTicket web application, so that as soon as a new email comes in, Postfix hands it off to the web server to process. In a rudimentary way, it creates a sort of webmail system within osTicket, which is capable of accepting file attachments as well. This way if your user sends in a screenshot or a document, it's attached to the ticket.

osTicket also allows for a number of customizations, everything from the email templates used to the fields and columns in reports. Perhaps even better, you can run multiple ticket boards off of the same installation. So once you install it for your company, you could also offer it to the civic organization you volunteer with or to your friend who runs a different company. User access control allows everything to stay private unless you have access.

Finally, installation is fairly simple. You can download the community open source edition at `https://osticket.com/download/`, and a detailed installation guide can be found at `https://docs.osticket.com/en/latest/` (Figure 10-4).

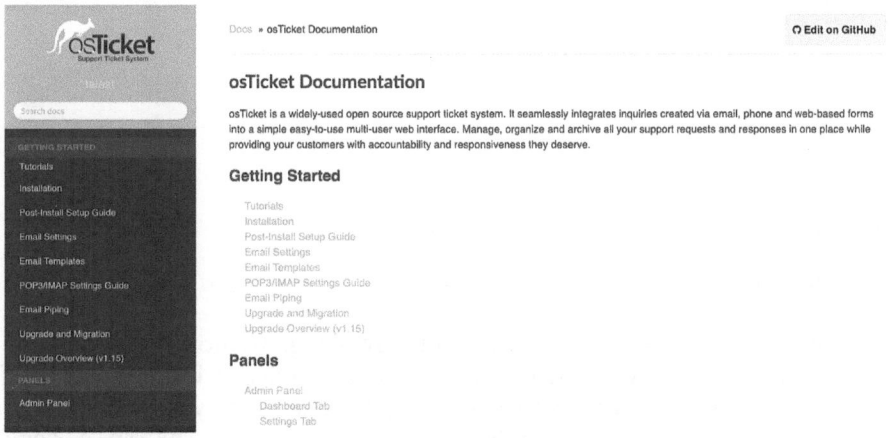

Figure 10-4. osTicket Documentation

YoURLS

Few things match the pain and frustration of telling someone a web address. Sure, over text in an email or text message, a web address is easy to relate. But verbally telling someone can be challenging. In fact, the website Slashdot was named after the difficulty it would be in telling someone the address (h-t-t-p-colon-slash-slash-slash-dot-dot-com)! And some addresses are just too long to tell – the address for a Google form, for example, might be extremely long and require proper casing in order to be usable. Even the shortened URL might be a bit frustrating.

Enter the world of URL shortening services. Many are familiar with the most common, such as TinyURL and Bitly; however, your options for customization with these two platforms can be rather limited. Perhaps you can adjust the last few letters of your URL, but you likely can't do more than that. And if your URL ever changes, you'll need a new short URL – which can be frustrating. Wouldn't it be nice to run your own URL shortening? YoURLS (Figure 10-5, yourls.org) allows you to do just that!

Figure 10-5. YoURLS homepage

To be clear, you can already do some of these things without YoURLS. The Apache Web Server will allow you to create redirect URLs so that if someone were to visit your website, example.com, and type in example.com/homepage, it could be configured to take them to example.com/longerwebsiteaddress/evenmoreinformation/whyisthissolong/index.htm All you would need to do is modify the configuration files as you added or removed "short" URLs.

But YoURLS allows a lot more than just the redirection. Sporting a web user interface that allows you to easily see all of the URLs that you've created and add or edit them, you can also see in Figure 10-6 that it keeps track of statistics for each address you've created.

exit	Exit Ticket https://docs.google.com/forms/d/e/1FAIpQLSfbtUnie2ou_4d[...]	Sep 16, 2019 16:14	209.147.242.29	494
entry	General Psychology Entry Ticket https://docs.google.com/forms/d/e/1FAIpQLSespnewdPVzPDL[...]	Sep 16, 2019 16:11	209.147.242.29	550
eas	General Psychology EAS Temperament Survey https://secureresearchservices.com/i43/index.php/827816[...]	Sep 07, 2019 23:19	67.61.224.118	56

Figure 10-6. YoURLS listing of addresses

Digging into one of the entries, the entry item (which my students use at the start of in-person classes to do a pre-class survey), we can see in Figure 10-7 the basic statistics on traffic to the short URL, and I could also drill down by location and source. Trust me, as soon as this pandemic ends, this URL will be much more active!

General Psychology Entry Ticket

Short URL: ⊕ http://dontgetfried.com/entry

Long URL: G https://docs.google.com/forms/d/e/1FAIpQLSespnewdPVzPDL[...]

| **Traffic statistics** | **Traffic location** | **Traffic sources** | **Share** |

| Last 24 hours | Last 7 days | Last 30 days | All time |

Number of hits : All time

Historical click count

Short URL created on September 16, 2019 @ 4:11 pm (about 435 days ago)

Last 24 hours	1 hit	0.04 per hour
Last 7 days	1 hit	0.14 per day
Last 30 days	1 hit	0.03 per day
All time	551 hits	1.27 per day

Best day

35 hits on September 18, 2019. Click for more details

| 18, 2019 | Feb 02, 2020 | Jun 21, 2020 | Nov 08, 20 |

Figure 10-7. Statistics on the entry entry

And finally, in addition to the basic functionality, YoURLS allows you to use a series of plugins (Figure 10-8) to enhance its feature set. You can create time-limited links with expirations, QR codes for your links, and password-protected links.

Plugins

You currently have **15 plugins** installed, and **7** activated ▤

Plugin Name	Version	Description	Author	Action
Allow Hyphens in Short URLs	1.0	Allow hyphens in short URLs (like http://sho.rt/hello-world)	Ozh	
Expiry	1.5.1	Will set expiration conditions on your links (or not)	Josh Panter	
Fallback URL	1.0	This plugin allows you to define a fallback URL in case there isn't a match for your short URL, so you can specify something different than $YOURLS_HOME.	Diego Peinador	
IQRCodes	1.5.1	Integrated QR Codes	Josh Panter	
Mass Remove Links	1.0	Remove several (or all) links.	Ozh	
Merge query string	2.1	Merge query string of request and target URL. *License*: Creative Commons Attribution 3.0 Unported: https://creativecommons.org/licenses/by/3.0/	fnkr	
Preview URL with QR Code and Thumbnail image	1.1	Preview URLs before you're redirected there with QR code and Thumbnail image	progit	
Random Backgrounds	1.0	Pretty random background patterns	Ozh	
Sample Admin Page	1.0	A example of a plugin administration page to save user defined option	Ozh	
Sample Plugin	0.1	Sample plugin to illustrate how actions and filters work. Read its source. Refer to the Plugin API documentation for more details.	Ozh	
Time limited Links with Fallback	1.0	Transmit a Link with Fallback link and set a global valid time limited in minutes	Stefan Mies	
Upload & Shorten	1.3.1/stable	Upload a file and create a short-YOURL for it in one step.	Fredl	
YOURLS Toolbar	1.0	Add a social toolbar to your redirected short URLs. Fork this plugin if you want to make your own toolbar. *Disclaimer*: Toolbars ruin the user experience. Be warned.	Ozh	
YOURLSs Password Protection	1.2	This plugin enables the feature of password protecting your short URLs!	Matthew	
detect-mobile-device	1.0.2	A simple plugin for converting query string by device type	guessi	

Figure 10-8. *Plugins installed on my YoURLS server*

As you can see, YoURLS can be a very useful tool for communicating web links in speech instead of text and even for marketing. If you're going to go to the trouble of buying a domain name for yourself, you might as well use it as much as possible. Here are some of the uses I have for YoURLS beyond just shortening obnoxiously long addresses:

- I use an appointment booking service, but know that if they change their pricing or don't have certain features, I may go to another in the future. So I give my students and colleagues my custom YoURLS link, and if I ever change booking services, that link can just be updated to the new service.

- I have several resources that I want to be able to give out in a "somewhat" secure manner – so I password protect the YoURLS link. It's possible for people to bookmark the page they are taken to after using the link, thus bypassing the password, but for a way to keep prying eyes out who overhear me giving the link, it's useful.

- On promotional material, my YoURLS links look much nicer than a commercial URL shortener, such as tinyurl.com.

- Finally, if students or colleagues need a link to information online (such as a blog post or another resource), I can always shorten that URL with my YoURLS installation, enabling me to give that out as a way to quickly direct them to the website, no matter how long or confusing the actual address is.

YoURLS allows a lot of flexibility in how you use it, and once you do, you'll never want to use a commercial service again. Even better, if you use your own domain, you don't have to worry about a commercial service changing their policies or going out of business, thus killing all of your links in the process!

OpenVPN

You may have seen advertisements for VPN, or Virtual Private Network, services as you watch YouTube videos or heard them on your favorite podcasts. And if you're not that tech savvy, you may not have any idea what they're talking about. Or you know of a VPN because your job requires you to connect to one before you can access your company's applications or services, like email, but you're still unsure as to why they're also being advertised on YouTube. So let's break down what it is and then how you can use OpenVPN to turn your VPS into one.

Fundamentally, the Internet is made up of millions of devices that all connect to each other by routing their traffic through various established routes. You can think of it as an extremely complex pipe system. Anytime you want to connect to something, you move through a series of pipes. Most of the time this is fine; however, there are two situations in which it might not be optimal.

First, sometimes you don't want people to get to your server, or series of servers, through all of the possible routes. You'd rather they all come to you via one particular pipe, which you can control. You can open and close it at will and place restrictions on it so that only certain people can use it. In this case, the pipe is a Virtual Private Network – a "virtual" pipe that companies can use to restrict access.

In a second case, you might not like the fact that in order to get somewhere, you had to go through a series of pipes. Some of those pipes might be slow, or some might not be very direct. Wouldn't it be great if you had a teleporter that moved you somewhere else on the Internet, so that you'd be closer to your destination? Well, you could also build a virtual pipe there, with the added benefit that no one knew exactly where you came from once you exited it, since it doesn't really exist. That's the second use for a VPN – a "virtual" pipe that teleports you somewhere else on the Internet, to either speed up your access, hide your original destination, or help keep your traffic private, thanks to the same access controls and encryption that a company might use in the first scenario.

Thus, VPNs are discussed both in corporate worlds, to secure resources, and on podcasts and YouTube, to entice people to buy a subscription to a VPN service that will let them route their traffic in a more secure, anonymous, and spoofed location sense.

Common uses for a VPN include the following:

- Encrypting all of your traffic so that computers that might see it between you and your destination aren't able to read it or modify it. An example: You might not want your ISP (Internet service provider) to know what sites you view, since they might use that information to target advertisements to you.

- Making it appear that your traffic is coming from another region or country. An example: You want to watch a video that's only available in the United States, and you're in England (or vice versa)!

- Connecting to a wider network that normally wouldn't be available to you, such as your home network while traveling or your work network while working from home. Example: You want to print a file to the office printer, but need to be on the office network to do so.

Now that you know what a VPN is, we can discuss a product that allows you to use your VPS as a VPN, OpenVPN (Figure 10-9). Initially released in 2001, OpenVPN is one of the most common open source Virtual Private Network servers available today. With broad support from various companies, it can provide all of the same ability to encrypt all of your traffic and make it appear that your traffic is coming from another region or country, namely, by routing all of your incoming and outgoing traffic through your VPS. In a simple sense, installing OpenVPN on your VPS located in Chicago, Illinois, will make it appear, to your favorite Internet websites and services, that you are in Chicago, Illinois, when you connect to them through your VPN.

Figure 10-9. OpenVPN homepage

So should you install OpenVPN Community Edition (https://openvpn.net/community-downloads-2/) on your VPS? There are a number of pros and cons to consider, as outlined in the following table:

Item	Pro	Con
It can be challenging to set up	The time invested will help you really learn how networking happens on the Internet and also help you understand how to keep yourself safe.	It is one of the more challenging software packages to configure, especially if you want to do anything beyond a basic setup.
It will route all of your traffic through your VPS	Your ISP will not know what you are visiting or doing on the Internet, which can be nice at home but also essential while traveling. Complimentary Wi-Fi at hotels, restaurants, and other locations might not always be secure.	If you have a rather small bandwidth limit on your VPS, you may use up a lot of your bandwidth on your own VPN traffic than on traffic to your website.
It creates a direct connection to your VPS	If you're running services such as Duplicati, you can configure them to only be available through the VPN. This way you don't have to open extra ports on your VPS, keeping it more secure.	Additional VPS resources will be used to keep an active VPN connection open, which could slow down other tasks you've given your VPS, such as serving web pages.

OpenVPN is one of the most useful applications that you can run on your VPS, but also one that you would only want to use if you have a specific need for it. When you do, the price of free plus the nearly 20 years of program history helps you to know that OpenVPN is a viable option for you.

Odoo

One of the primary uses of a VPS is for someone to run a small business. Small businesses require a lot of things and can grow fast. Thankfully, software exists that can manage your accounting, projects, sales leads and customer interaction, Human Resources functions, inventory, website, and more. And if you're willing to set it up on your own VPS, you can do it for free using Odoo (Figure 10-10).

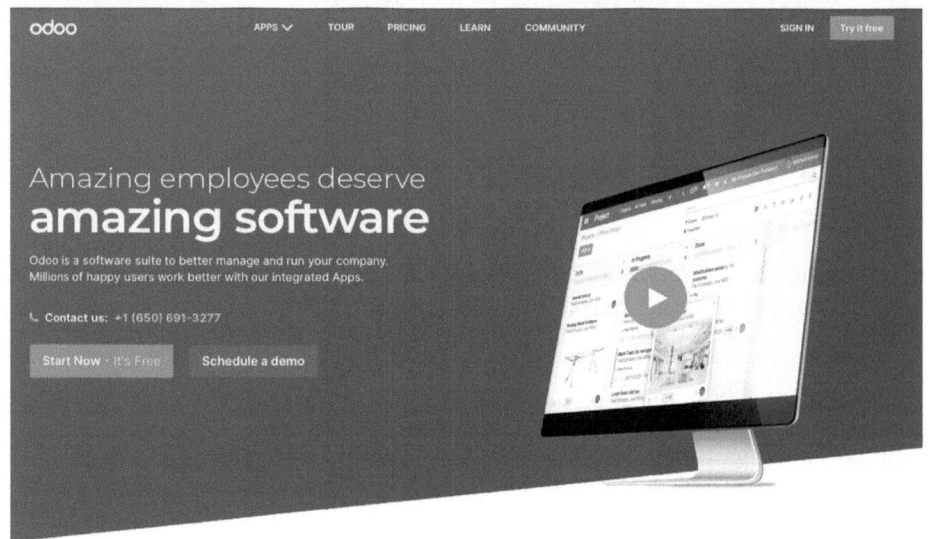

Figure 10-10. Odoo homepage

Like many open source products, Odoo has been around for a while (first released in 2005) and has grown to be a huge suite of business management software. Sporting a community edition that is free and open source and making money to support development through an enterprise edition that has extra features you may need down the line (www.odoo.com/page/editions provides a nice comparison), if you're running a new small business, Odoo should have you covered for several months or years before you'd need to start paying for the advanced features. Modularly based, you can also elect to only use certain portions if you like, meaning that if you don't need everything, you can simply focus on the essentials.

Most of the time I pitch a product like Odoo to someone, they tell me it's "overkill" for their small business. But as I alluded to earlier, small businesses tend to have a way of growing very quickly if you pour smart effort into them. The kind of person who starts a small business tends to also be the one who thinks more time and effort will equal growth and profitability, missing the point that as you grow, you need to change to become more efficient – not just throw more resources in.

Here's a quick example: You run a small mail order business. Each time someone sends you an order, your website takes the information and sends it to you via email. You open the email, check your inventory, verify you can fulfill the order, process the payment, create an invoice in Microsoft Excel, email that to the person, and then pack up the order and send it out. After a while, the whole process takes just under 20 minutes. Sounds reasonable.

But then your business grows. You need to put in more blocks of "20 minutes" as the orders pile up. Maybe you hire staff to help you, but now you're paying them which cuts into your profit. What you need isn't more people to put in "20-minute" blocks of time, you need something that cuts the 20 minutes down to 5. That's where software like Odoo is essential. Starting out with it and growing your business as you gradually learn the software and enable more features also means that you won't have that moment a year into your business where you need to devote a whole weekend or week to learning new software, while the orders still pile up.

Thus, if you think you're going to need software like Odoo to help with all of the things (or any of the things) it works with, don't wait, and give it a try while you're small!

LimeSurvey

Sooner or later, you may find yourself curious about what other people think. Whether it's sitting in your chair at home puzzling over world events or administering a civic organization debating its next volunteer project, you're likely to wonder what others are thinking so you know how to proceed. For simple questions, perhaps only two to three, then a Google form will likely be sufficient. However, what if you want something a bit more capable? Maybe you only want to show certain questions based on the answers to previous ones, or perhaps you want to calculate information based on what someone tells you and then show them the result. And finally, what if you want to survey the same group of people at different times and have a way to tie their answers together? You'll quickly find you need an actual survey solution.

Now you could go with a commercial option, such as Qualtrics or SurveyMonkey. However, an open source product exists with all of the same abilities, named LimeSurvey (Figure 10-11, `https://limesurvey.org`).

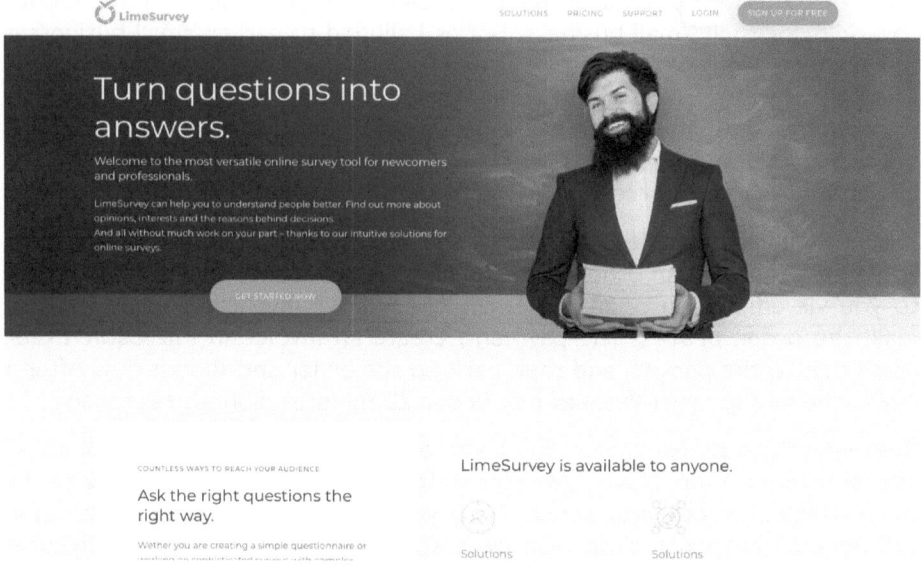

Figure 10-11. LimeSurvey homepage

LimeSurvey boasts an impressive suite of abilities, and like other products we've covered, the community edition is open source – they make their money off of hosting LimeSurvey for others, which is something you don't need if you own your own VPS.

I've personally used LimeSurvey for over a decade, dating back to when it was named PHPSurveyor. I've seen the user interface get progressively easier to use and the feature set grow from basic survey questions to more advanced responses as well as support for dynamic survey design. Here are just a few uses for LimeSurvey:

- A basic opinion survey, with multiple pages and conditional branching (e.g., only show the "How many packs of cigarettes a day do you smoke?" question if the person answers "Yes" to the "Do you smoke?" question).

- A more advanced survey that takes multiple answers, computes a result, and then shows that result to the person taking the survey, asking them if they agree with the result or not.

- A quiz that automatically scores and, optionally, tells the person their score at the end.

- A secure voting platform – each voter gets a special access token that they enter at the start, which can only be used once and can also be deactivated after the election.

- An experimental survey design that randomizes various elements, to test different designs.

LimeSurvey is such a versatile tool that I actually cover it more extensively in my previous book, *Practical R 4*, devoting an entire chapter to LimeSurvey and analyzing a survey in the R programming language (which is also free). However, you don't need any special tool to analyze your data – LimeSurvey can export your results to a variety of formats, from common such as Word, Excel, and CSV to more specialized such as R and SPSS.

In general, you'll find that if you need to understand what others are thinking, to the extent they know themselves, LimeSurvey will help you get the information you seek!

GNU Mailman

Whenever you visit a software product to find that its official web address is just a common word, you realize it's probably pretty well established. GNU (pronounced "new") Mailman, with its official website being `list.org` (Figure 10-12), is definitely one of those well-established products. It's been the de facto mailing list software for much of its 21-year history, after replacing the original best-known mailing list manager, Majordomo.

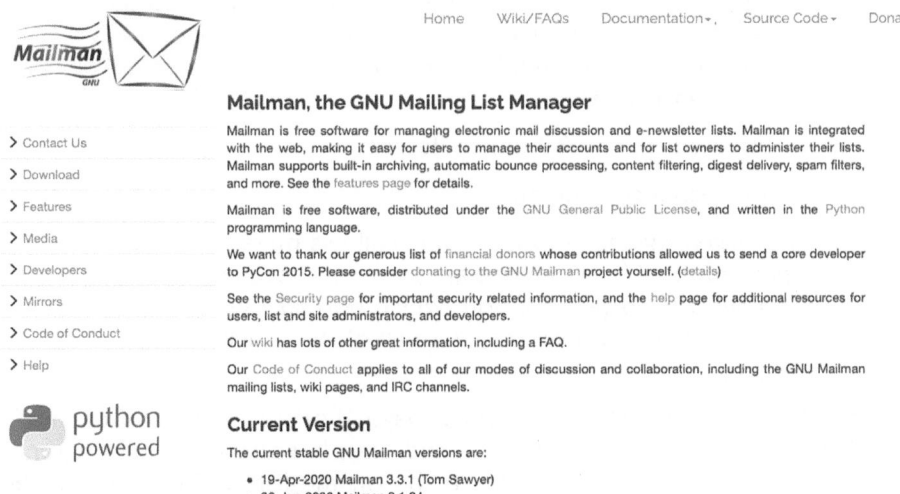

Figure 10-12. GNU Mailman homepage

It's really hard to make a mailing list manager seem exciting, but I'll do my best. The honest truth is GNU Mailman does largely one job – it manages email distribution lists that allow users to discuss various topics, separated into their own threads. However, if you've ever been in an active and useful mailing list, you know the power that this can bring. It never ceases to amaze me how tapping into the thousands of people who subscribe to a specialized mailing list (such as one revolving around technology or a particular academic discipline) can provide such immediate and rewarding interactions. Some may look at it as antiquated, but I prefer to think of it as the simplest way to engage with others. And with the ubiquity of email – thousands of ways to access, read, and respond to your email, including from your wrist through a smartwatch – it's very easy to interact with the group through a mailing list.

And beyond simple distribution lists (where one person sends to many) and discussion lists (where all read and respond), GNU Mailman also supports a plethora of features that make interacting with others easy and enjoyable, including the following:

- A web page for each mailing list and a web administrative interface. This allows administrators to add and remove members and moderate lists. Regular users can use the web interface to view the archive of older posts.

- A variety of "modes," including closed subscriptions (where an administrator needs to add each person), private archives, private membership rosters, and the ability for certain senders to have (or bypass) rules dictating their use.

- Integrated spam and bounce detection.

- Auto-response controls.

- An urgent header support, which allows messages to be pushed to all users immediately even if those users have chosen the "digest" option, which normally would only provide one email per day with all of the activity on the list.

Where GNU Mailman will excel, perhaps beyond other software discussed in this chapter, is the ease of use for the end user. In some cases, all they may have to do is click one link to agree to be on the list, and from there the messages will flow without interruption. As a small business or organization, a mailing list can be the most effective way to get your word out (as evidenced by my inbox today – I'm writing this on one of the biggest shopping days in North America, the Friday after Thanksgiving!).

A last benefit of GNU Mailman is that, while it is complex in operation, it's pretty easy to install, with many distributions having it built into the official repositories. On Debian, the Aptitude package `mailman3-full` is all you need to get up and running. On CentOS, the package is simply `mailman`.

osCommerce

If you're not just announcing something that people can discuss — perhaps you're launching a product — you might also want people to be able to buy that item. And thus you may want an ecommerce platform such as osCommerce (Figure 10-13), an open source ecommerce package that was originally launched in 2000.

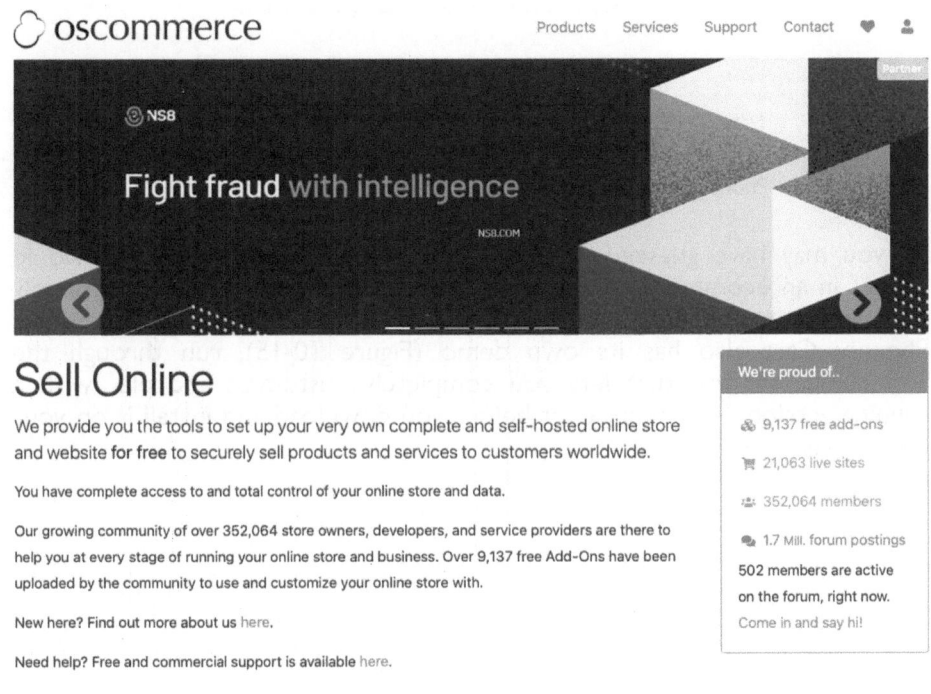

Figure 10-13. OsCommerce homepage, oscommerce.com

If you're new to osCommerce, you might find their naming a little confusing. In mid-2019, a new version of their community edition, named CE Phoenix, was released. This branch of the osCommerce code is the latest free version of osCommerce plus improvements. CE Phoenix has a homepage of its own at `phoenixcart.org` (see Figure 10-14). This is the version I'd recommend downloading and installing on your own VPS.

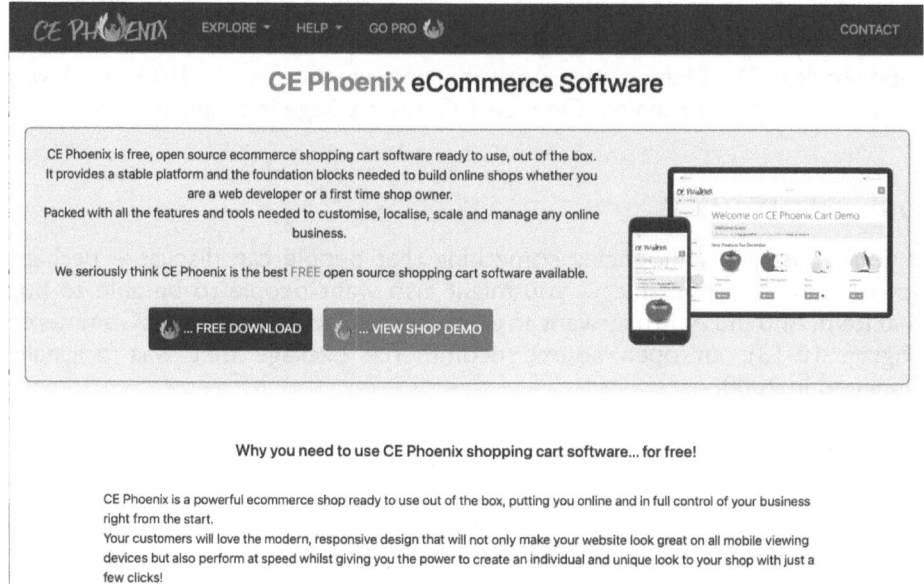

Figure 10-14. Phoenix Cart, based upon osCommerce

As you may have guessed, Phoenix Cart supports everything you would expect in an ecommerce platform, from customization to a mobile-friendly framework to various different payment processors and shipping integrations. Phoenix Cart also has its own demo (Figure 10-15), run through the Softaculous service, that lets you completely customize and play with a running version of Phoenix Cart before you download and install it on your own server.

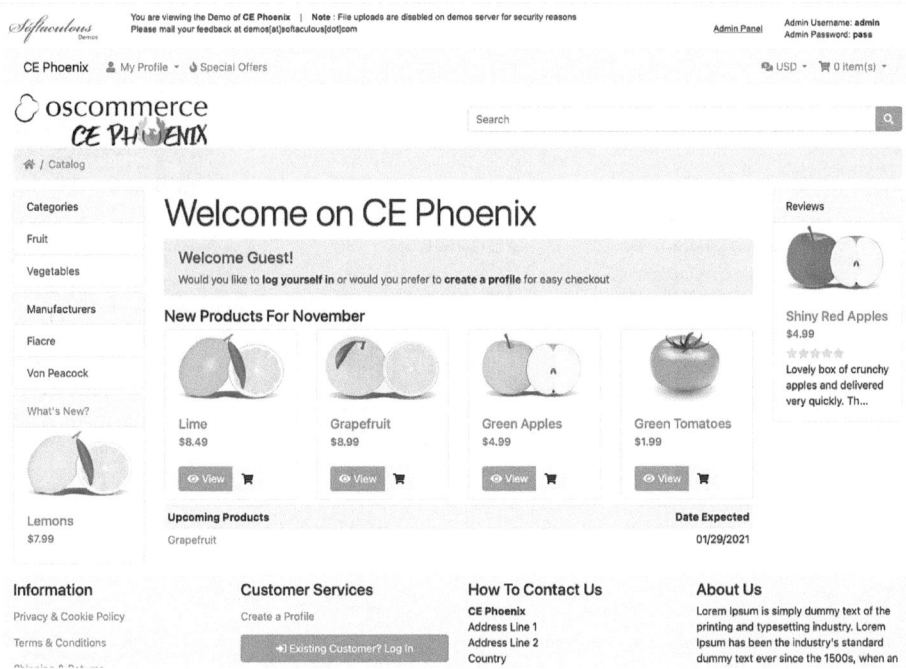

Figure 10-15. The Phoenix Cart demo

As I mentioned in the discussion of Odoo earlier, for many, they may avoid setting up their own ecommerce interface, especially if they do only a small amount of selling through their website. However, it will not take long before you find that third-party marketplaces that you can sell through may not always benefit you when it comes to fees and commissions. Of course, they may help you when it comes to security and liability. Running an ecommerce store of your own means you really will not want to skip weekly administrative tasks, checking mailing lists and web pages for updates that may affect security, and patching security holes as soon as they are known. After all, your ecommerce site typically has access to a lot of connections that can cost you money (e.g., direct debit information for your credit accounts, banking information, customer's saved shipping information, etc.). You'll want to be very sure that you're secure before launching your own shopping cart!

MediaWiki

If you've ever wanted to run your own Wikipedia, you'll be happy to know that you totally can, using the exact same software that Wikipedia uses – MediaWiki (Figure 10-16).

Figure 10-16. MediaWiki.org

But what exactly is a wiki? And how can it benefit you? Let's start with the what and then the purposes.

Named after the Wiki Wiki Shuttle at Honolulu International Airport, by Ward Cunningham in 1994, a wiki is an editable web page. It's designed to allow quick edits with version tracking so that a group of people can all collaboratively create a page or a repository of knowledge. That shuttle was a quick way to get around the airport and thus embodied the idea that a wiki should be fast. Recall from earlier chapters that in 1994, web pages were more time consuming to create and edit, since modern conveniences like content management systems didn't exist. Apparently the idea caught on, because less than 10 years after the idea took root, the largest wiki to date, Wikipedia, had been launched. Today it's likely people are more familiar with that particular wiki than the idea of a wiki in general.

However, wikis can be extremely useful outside of trying to create an all-knowing encyclopedia of human knowledge. You might find a wiki helpful for the following:

- Small group collaboration, where each member is responsible for researching various pieces of a project and combining them together.

- Group editing, with an ability to see what previous individuals have added or deleted using the version tracking features.

- A regularly updated homepage that preserves previous information rather than simply overwriting it. Imagine a group that puts on an annual conference that keeps the same page for the conference each year – you could easily see what was on the page the previous year(s) by simply looking back at the history.

- A Frequently Asked Questions document that anyone in a group or organization can update. For example, a new employee orientation module that contains a wiki page of FAQs that other new employees have found useful – it would help a new employee who wasn't sure what to ask.

Basically any time you need to collaborate on something that can be displayed on a web page, you can use a wiki. MediaWiki's homepage even provides a sandbox (see Figure 10-17) that allows you to practice your wiki editing skills to see how easy it can be to make and edit a page.

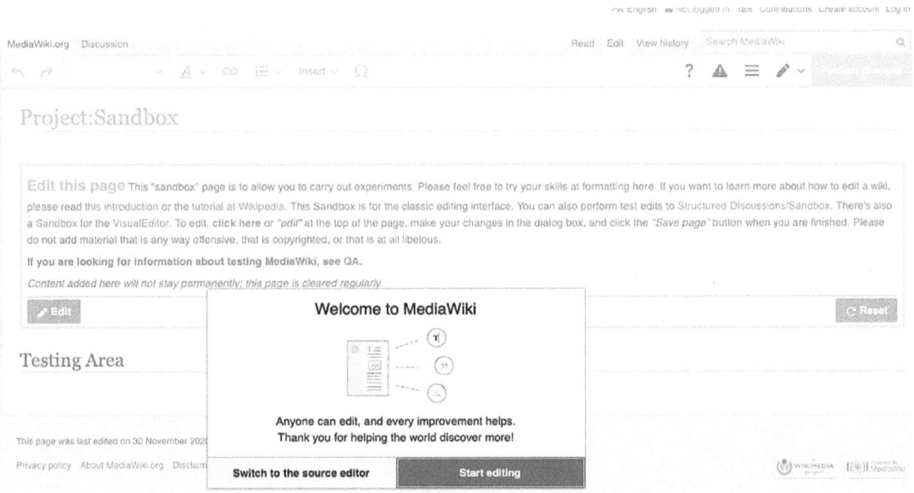

Figure 10-17. MediaWiki's sandbox

When it comes to wikis, you'll also find the functionality built into many other open source platforms, with wiki modules existing for Moodle and Odoo, for example. You may also want to consider a wiki when you need a tool that is broadly focused, as the software is designed to be customizable for a variety of collaborative purposes.

Conclusion

This chapter has covered a lot of ground, as has the entire book. When we started, I gave you the basics of what a VPS was and how it could benefit you. Now that we've reached the end, I hope that this chapter has inspired you to consider all of the various tools, features, and usage scenarios your VPS can fill in your professional life. And perhaps, best of all, you hopefully now feel empowered to take on these tasks without fear, as you have a guide along the way. I sincerely hope that this book has opened new doors for you and invite you to share your successes and struggles with me via Twitter (@jonwestfall).

Best,

Jon Westfall, December 2020

Index

© Jon Westfall 2021
J. Westfall, *Set Up and Manage Your Virtual Private Server*,
https://doi.org/10.1007/978-1-4842-6966-4